DATE DUE			

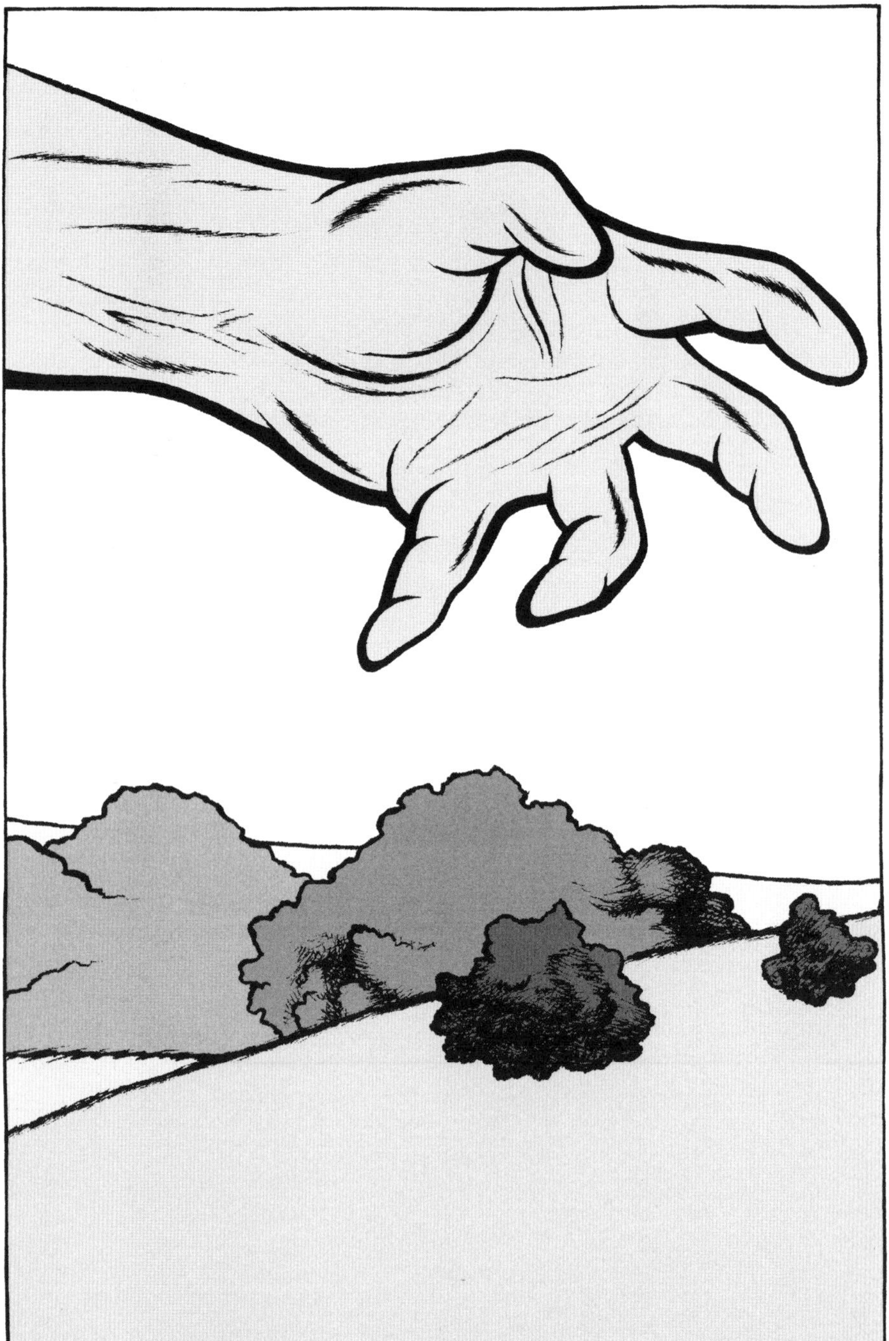

COMPULSIVE COMICS

by **ERIC HAVEN**

COMPULSIVE COMICS

COPYRIGHT © 2018 ERIC HAVEN. THIS EDITION IS COPYRIGHT © 2018 FANTAGRAPHICS BOOKS INC.
PERMISSION TO REPRODUCE CONTENT MUST BE OBTAINED FROM THE AUTHOR OR PUBLISHER.

FANTAGRAPHICS BOOKS INC. 7563 LAKE CITY WAY NE SEATTLE, WA 98115

EDITOR AND ASSOCIATE PUBLISHER: ERIC REYNOLDS
BOOK DESIGN: ERIC HAVEN
COVER DESIGN : JACOB COVEY
PRODUCTION: PAUL BARESH
PUBLISHER: GARY GROTH

LIBRARY OF CONGRESS CONTROL NUMBER: 2017950375
ISBN 978-1-68396-085-0

FIRST PRINTING: FEBRUARY 2018
PRINTED IN CHINA

STRANGE VARIATIONS IN THE EARTH'S ORBIT...

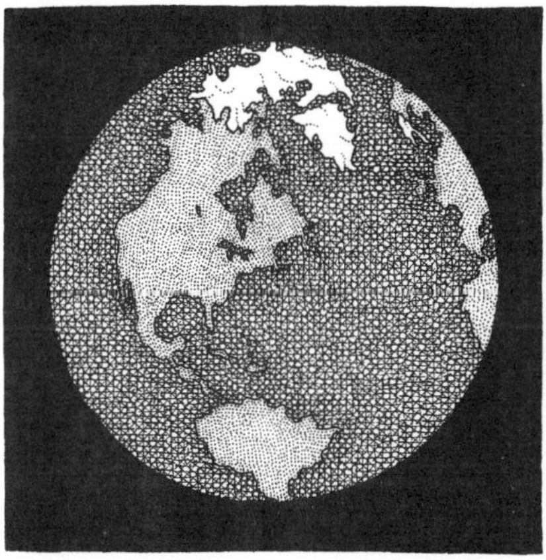

...HAVE RESULTED IN PERIODIC GLACIAL EPOCHS.

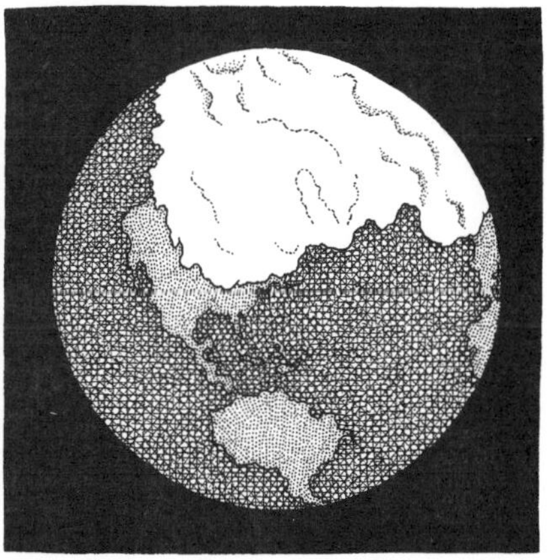

ONLY 20,000 YEARS AGO, MUCH OF NORTH AMERICA WAS BURIED BENEATH A SHEET OF ICE MORE THAN A MILE THICK.

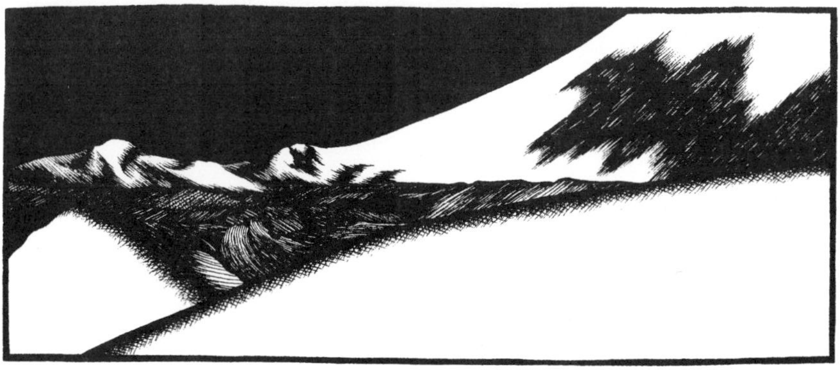

HUMAN CIVILIZATION SPRUNG UP AFTER THE LAST GLACIATION. WILL IT SURVIVE THE NEXT?

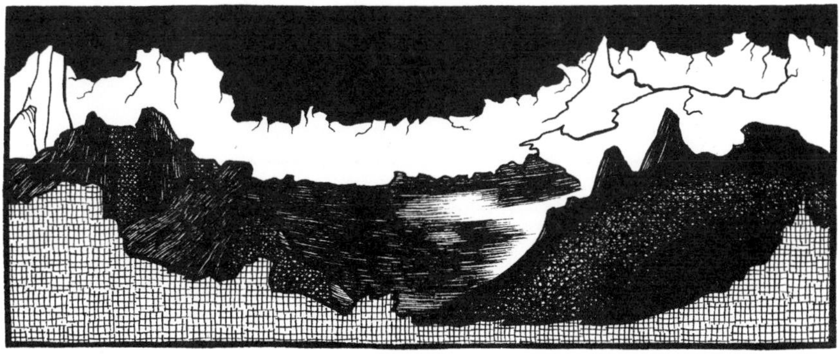

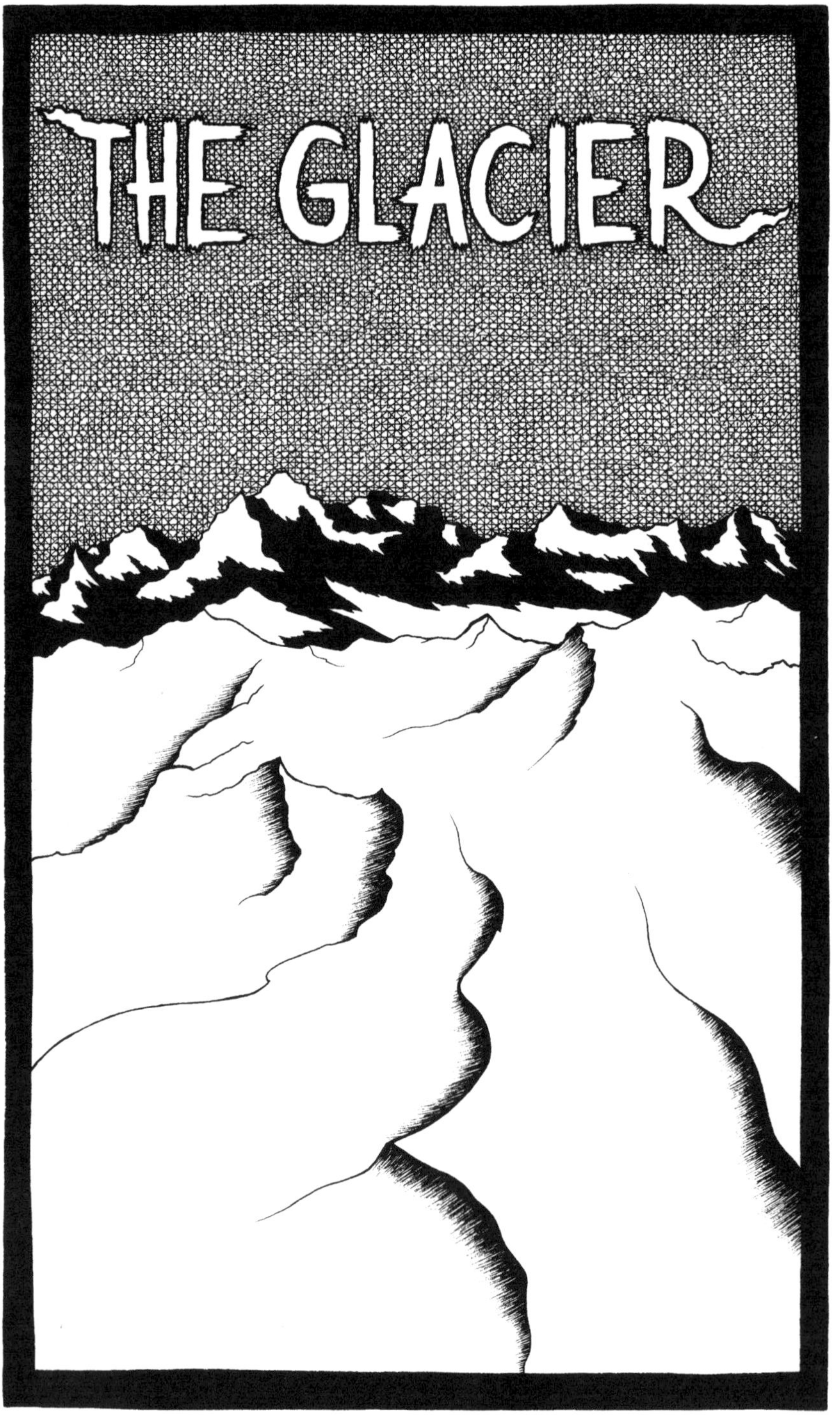
THE GLACIER

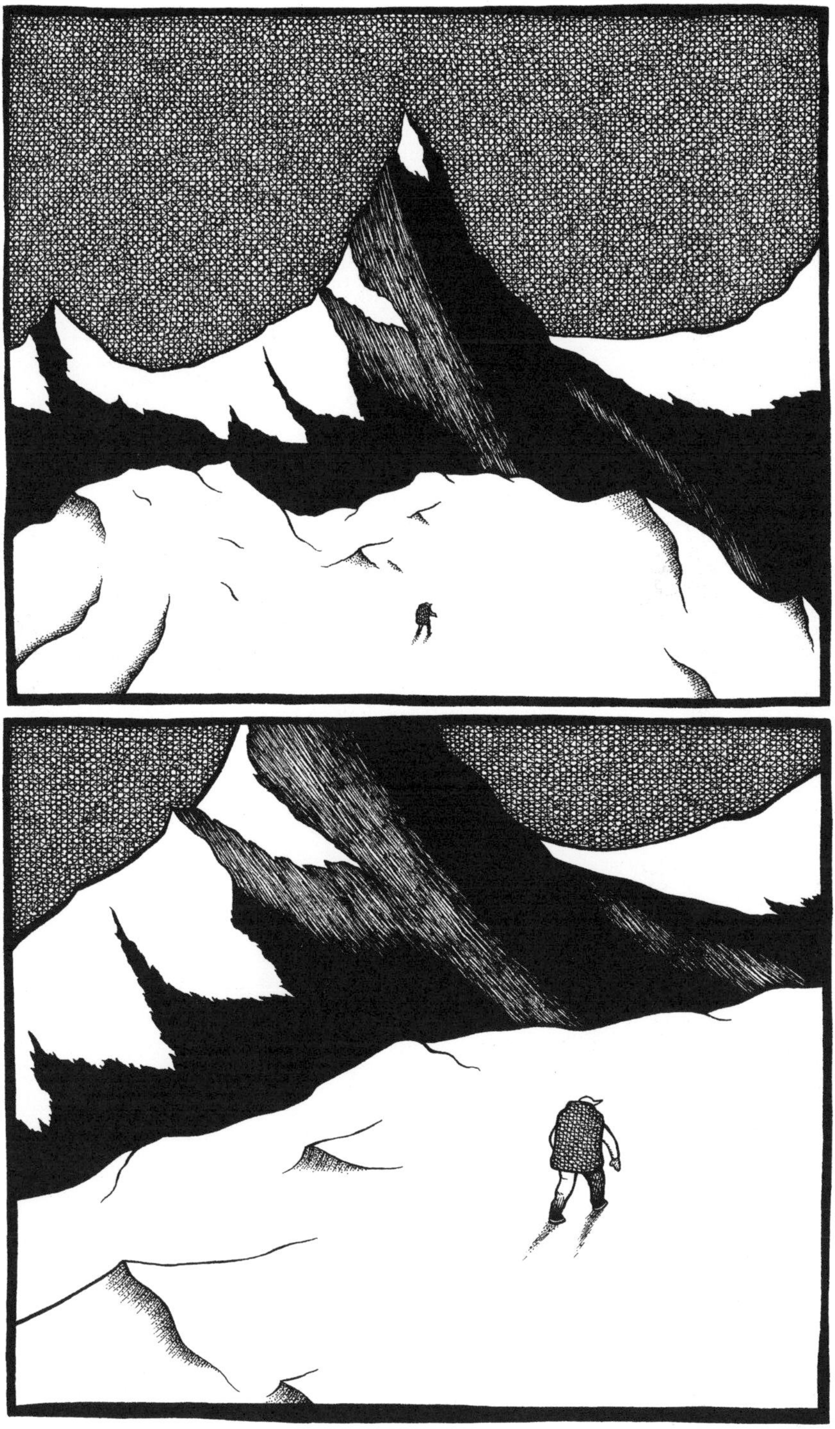

I'M A GLACIOLOGIST. IT'S MY JOB TO STUDY GLACIERS--
THEIR PHYSICAL PROPERTIES, THEIR DIRECTION OF
MOVEMENT, THEIR HISTORY, AND THEIR FUTURE.

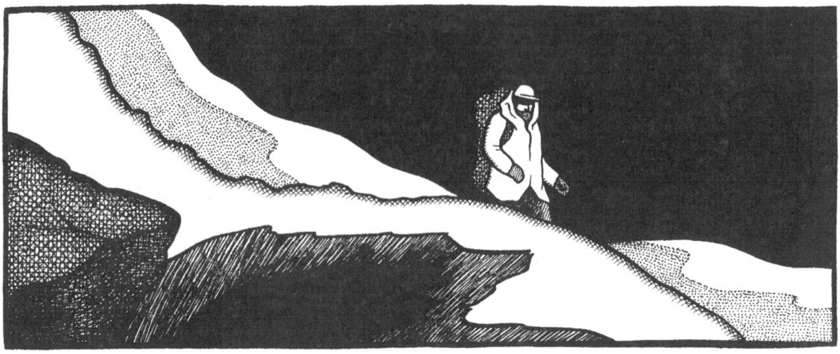

THAT'S WHY I'M HERE IN THE FREEZING COLD, ALONE, AT
THE TOP OF THE WORLD.

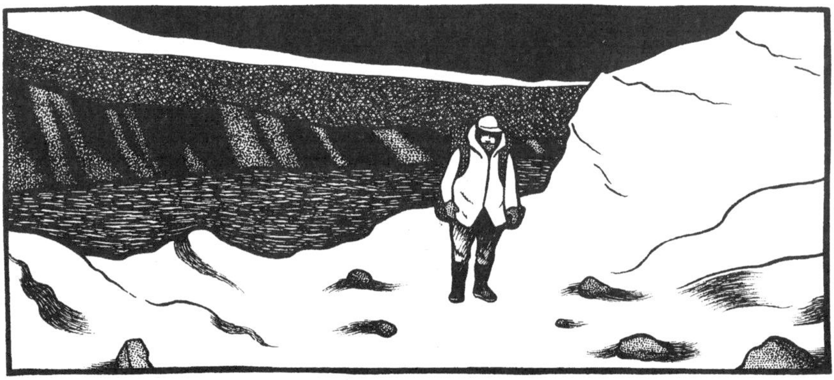

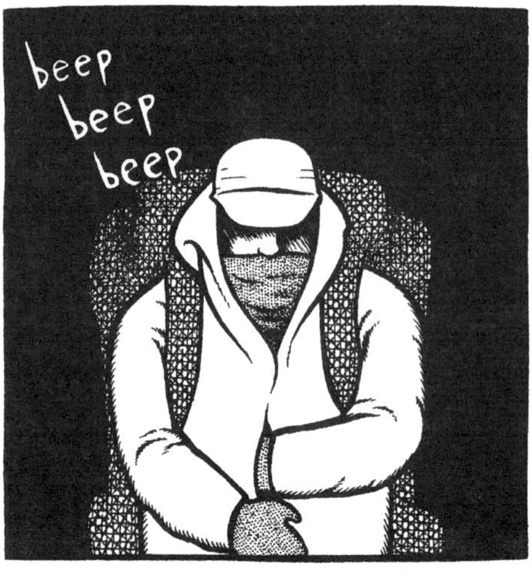
beep
beep
beep

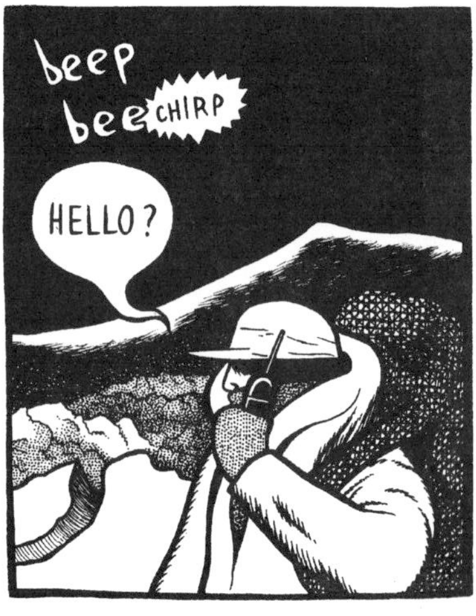
beep
bee CHIRP
HELLO?

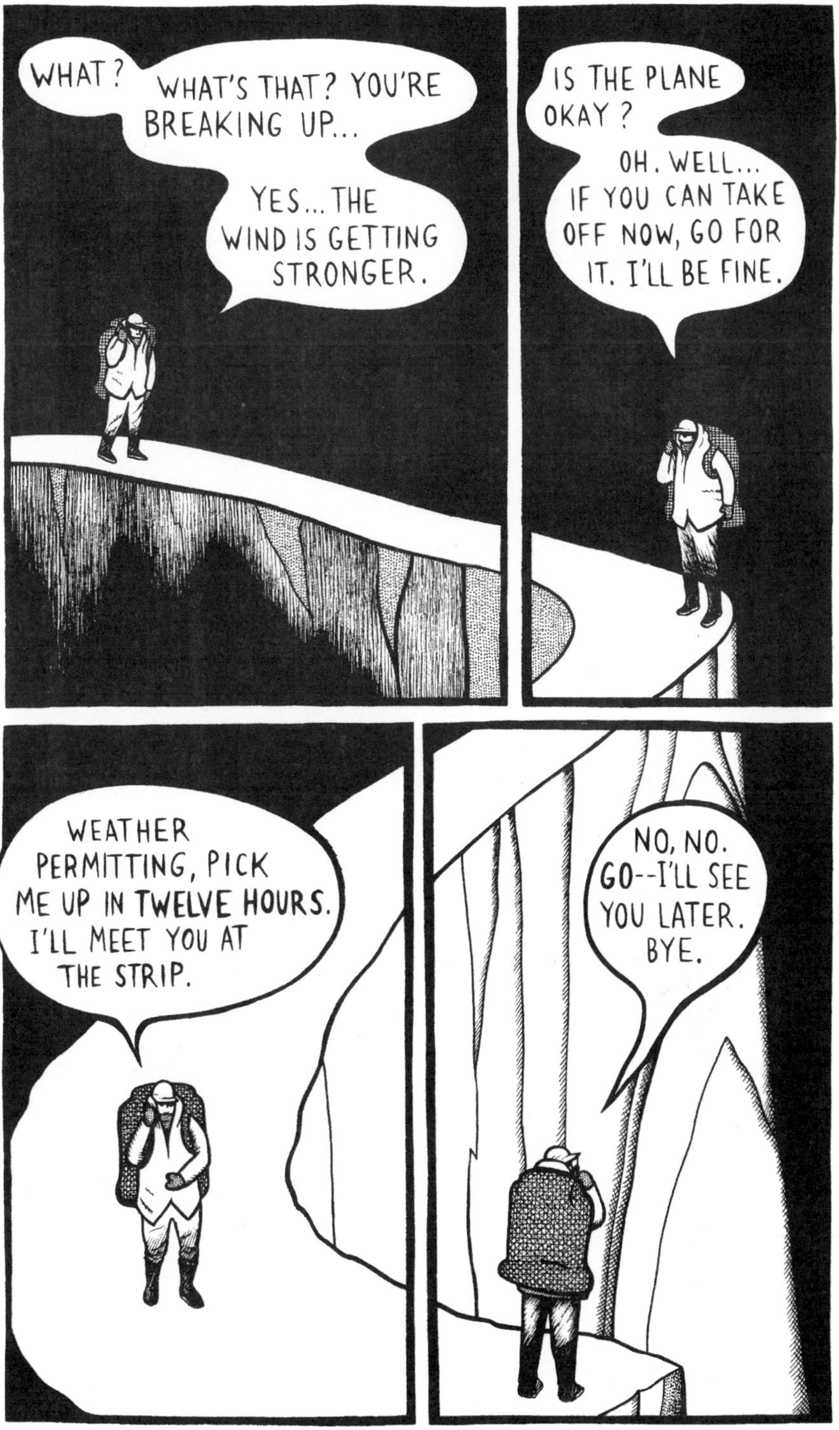
WHAT?
WHAT'S THAT? YOU'RE BREAKING UP...
YES... THE WIND IS GETTING STRONGER.
IS THE PLANE OKAY?
OH. WELL... IF YOU CAN TAKE OFF NOW, GO FOR IT. I'LL BE FINE.
WEATHER PERMITTING, PICK ME UP IN **TWELVE HOURS**. I'LL MEET YOU AT THE STRIP.
NO, NO. **GO**--I'LL SEE YOU LATER. BYE.

MY CONTACT WITH THE OUTSIDE WORLD IS SEVERED WHEN THE PLANE LEAVES. NOW IT'S UP TO ME TO STAY ALIVE LONG ENOUGH TO COLLECT ANOTHER DATA SET.

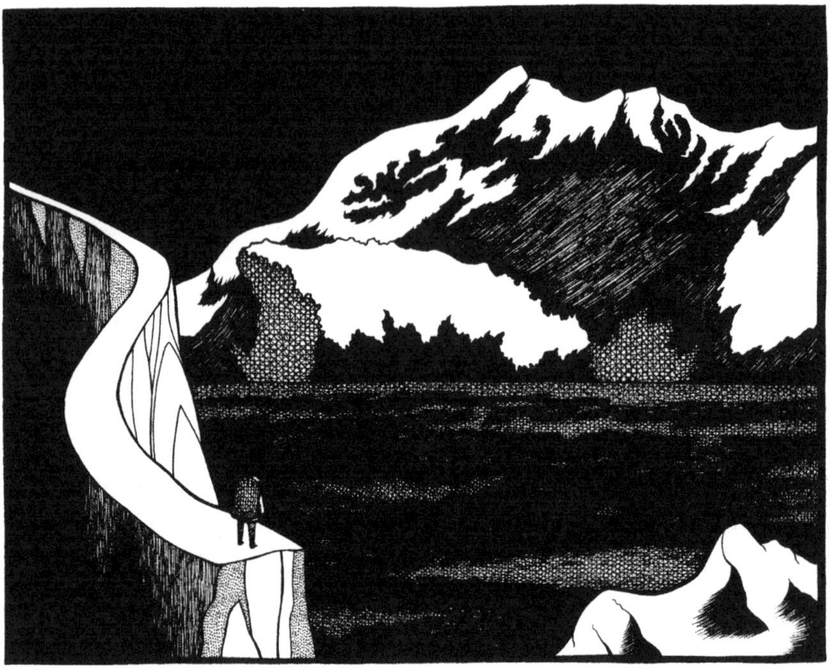

USING SATELLITE IMAGERY, I'VE BEEN ABLE TO PINPOINT THE MOST LIKELY COORDINATES FOR GLACIAL CALVING.

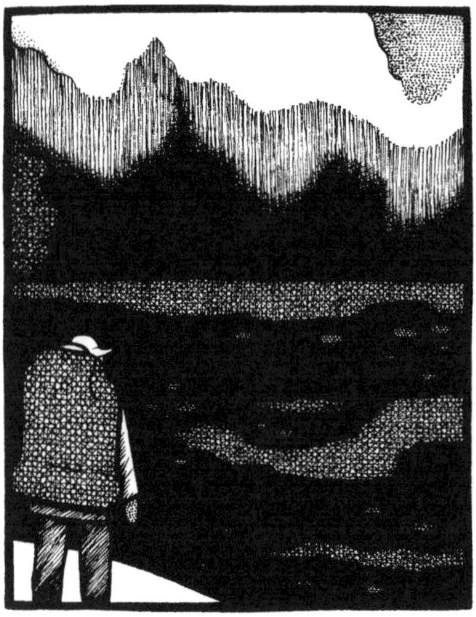

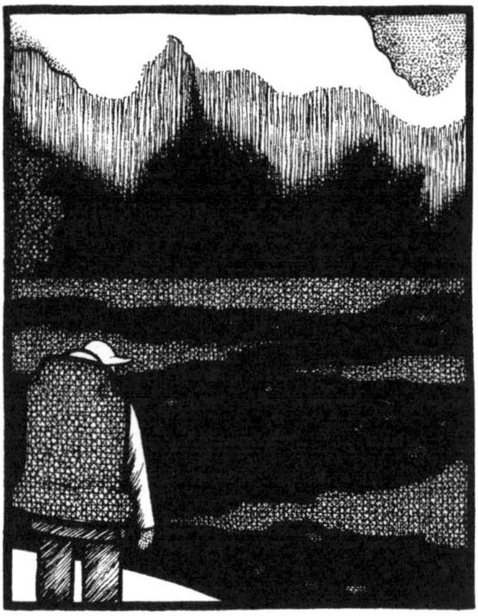

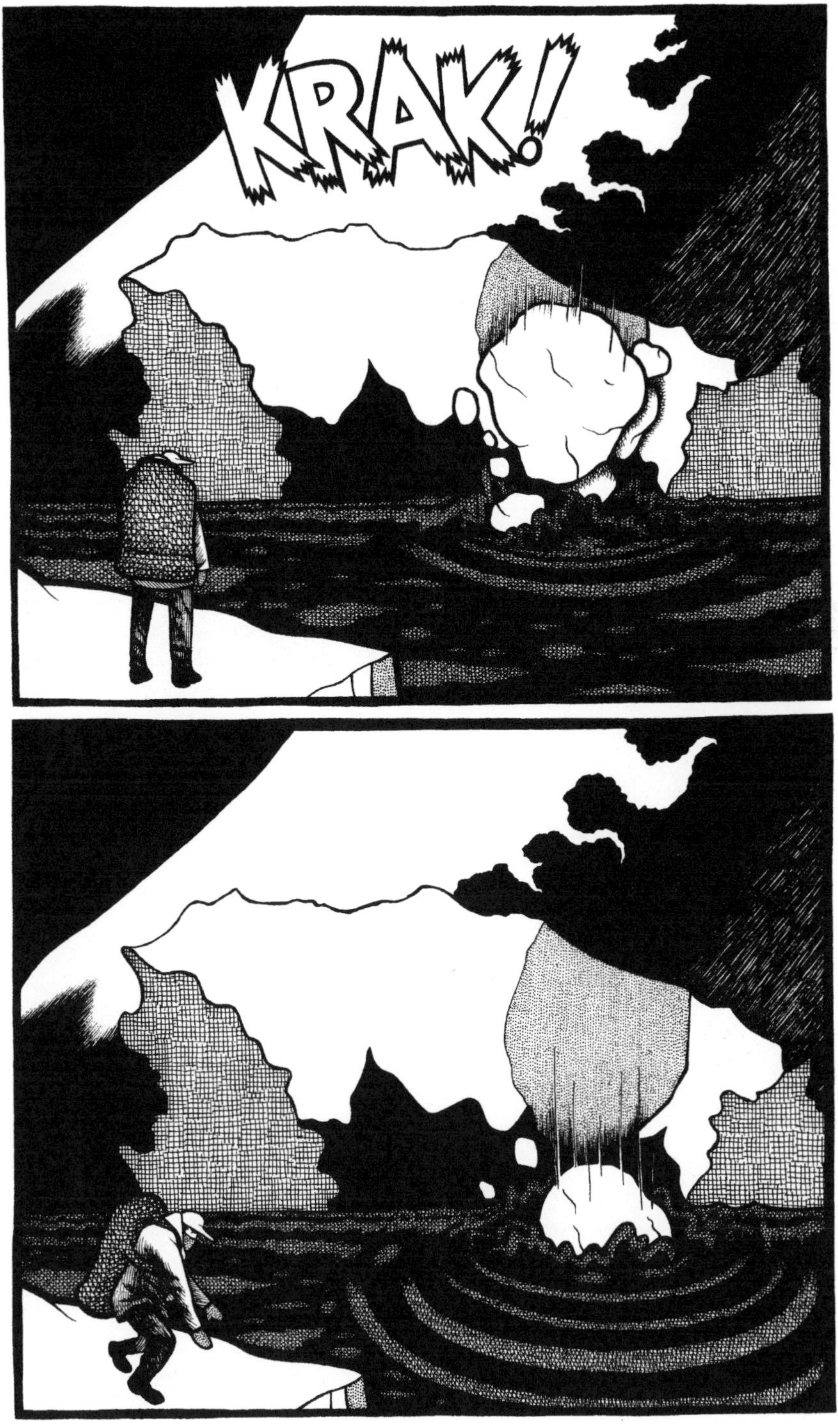
KRAK!

THERE'S BEEN FREQUENT CALVING IN THIS AREA. FOR
REASONS UNKNOWN, IT HAPPENS MOSTLY AT NIGHT--

AND NIGHT AT THIS LATITUDE LASTS FROM NOVEMBER
18TH THROUGH JANUARY 24TH.

THE AURORA BOREALIS SUDDENLY ILLUMINATES THE SKY,
BUT IT FAILS TO HOLD MY INTEREST.

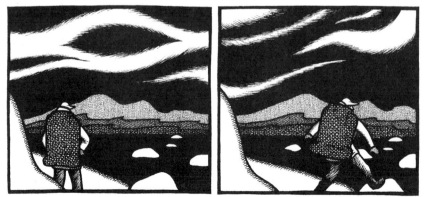

I HAVE TO FOCUS
ON MY JOB.

WHEN THE GLACIER CALVES, ITS HISTORY
IS EXPOSED ON THE SHEAR FACE.

AFTER EXAMINING THE CLUES, I'VE POSTULATED THAT
A CONVECTION FORCE EXISTS INSIDE THE ICE.

DEBRIS GETS CAUGHT AND GROUND
UP BY THE ADVANCING MASS...

...AND CIRCULATED WITHIN
THE GLACIER OVER EONS.

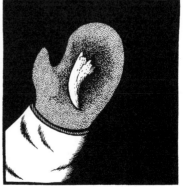

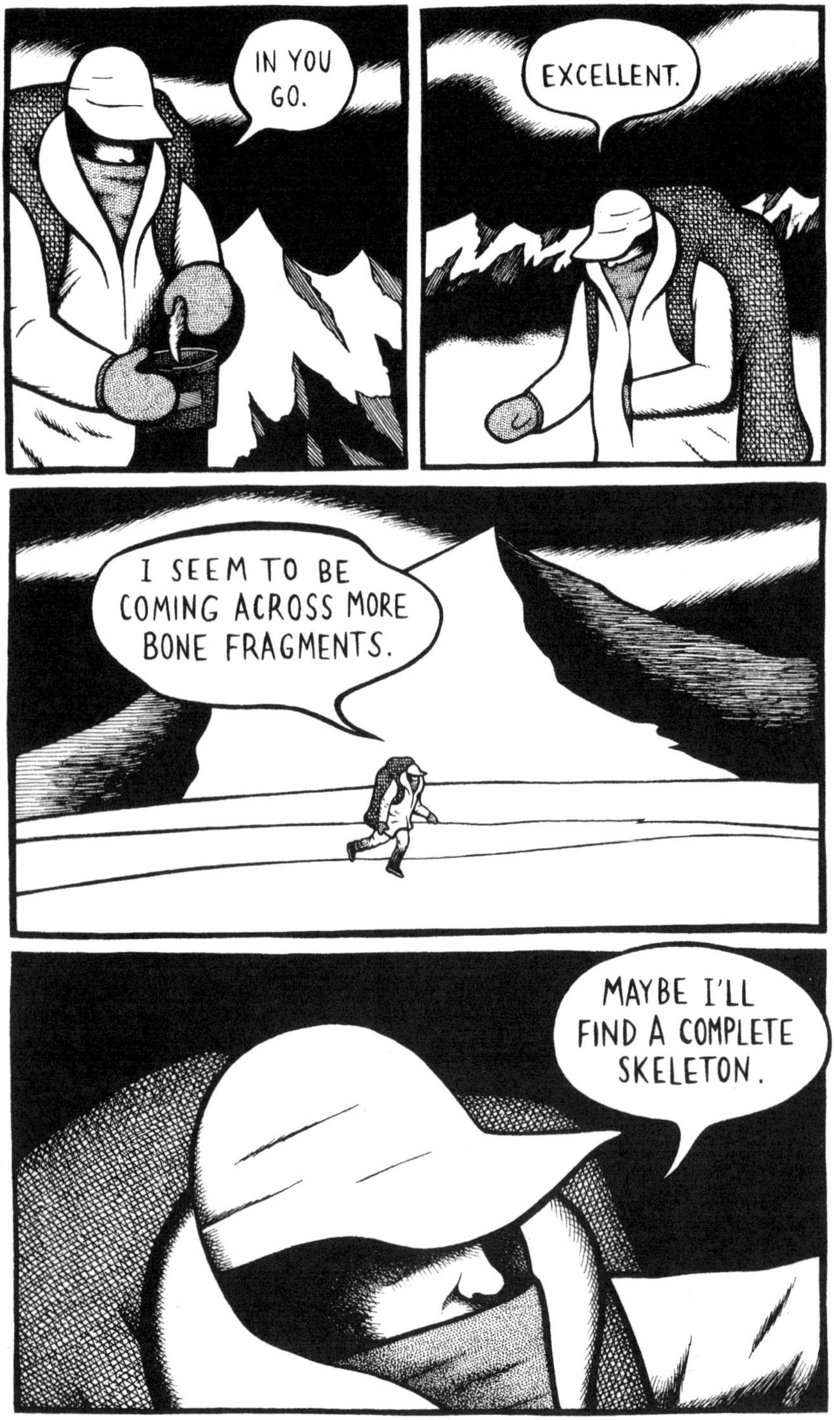
IN YOU GO.
EXCELLENT.
I SEEM TO BE COMING ACROSS MORE BONE FRAGMENTS.
MAYBE I'LL FIND A COMPLETE SKELETON.

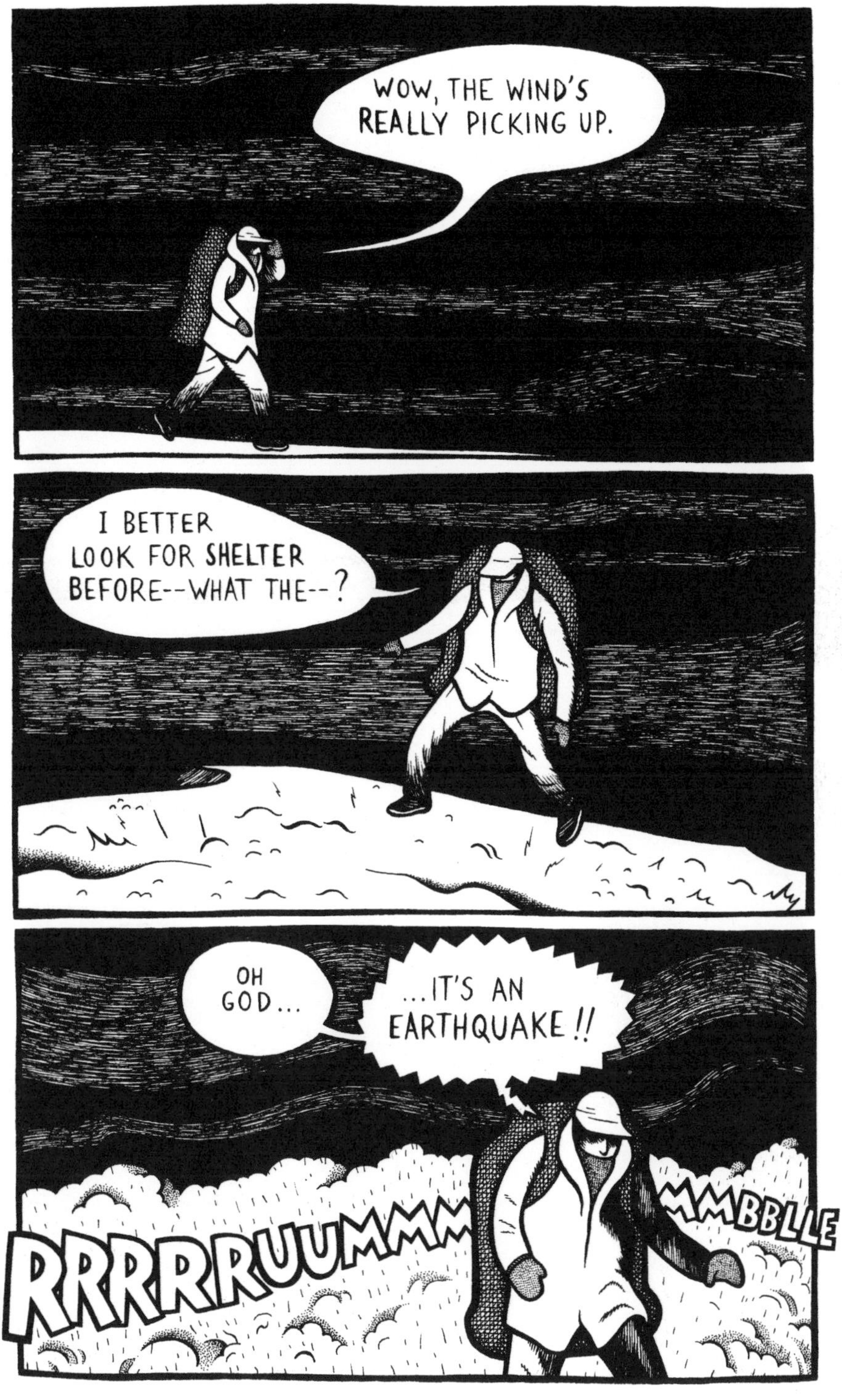
WOW, THE WIND'S REALLY PICKING UP.
I BETTER LOOK FOR SHELTER BEFORE--WHAT THE--?
OH GOD...
...IT'S AN EARTHQUAKE!!
RRRRRUUMMMMMMBBLLE

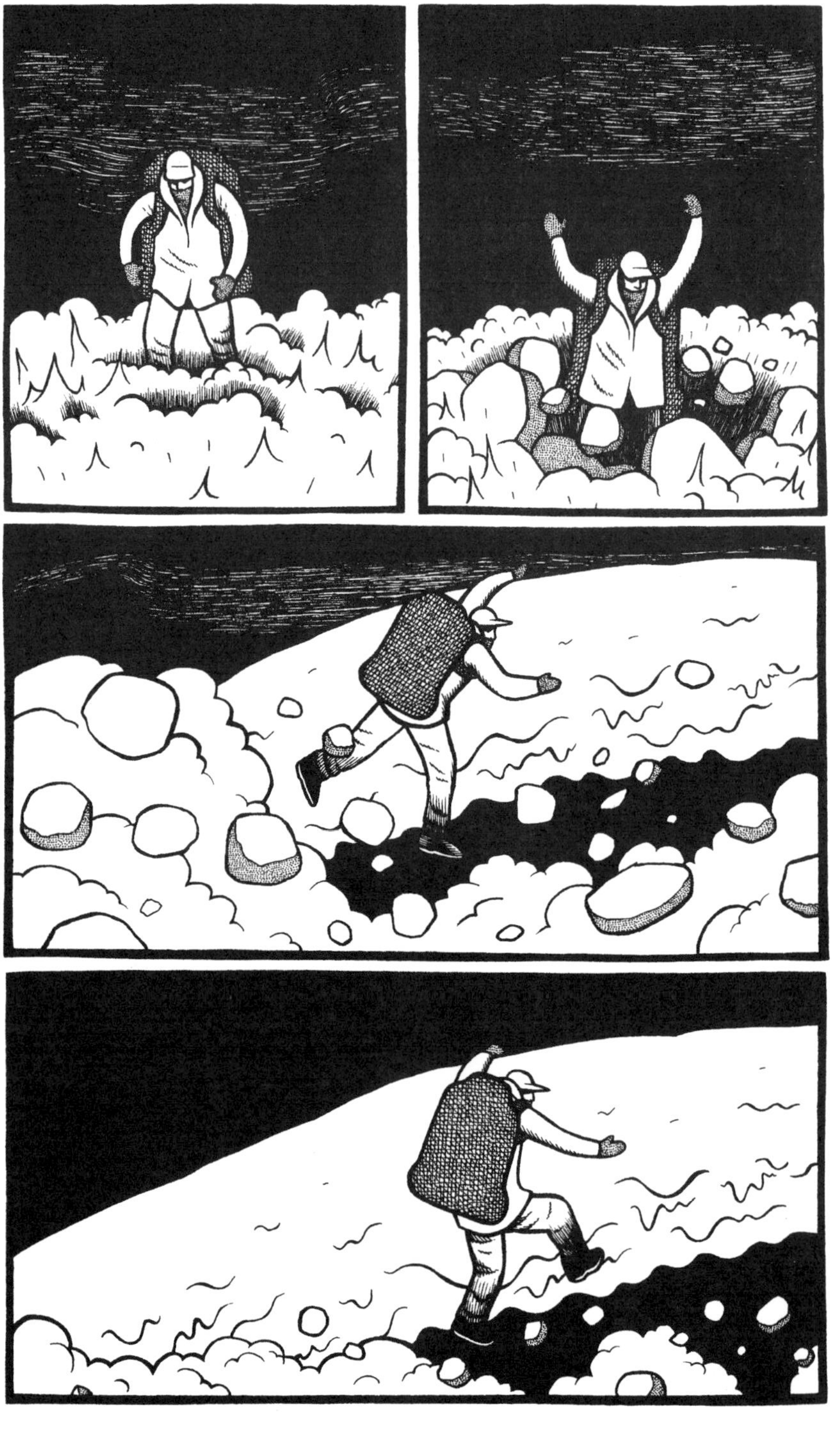

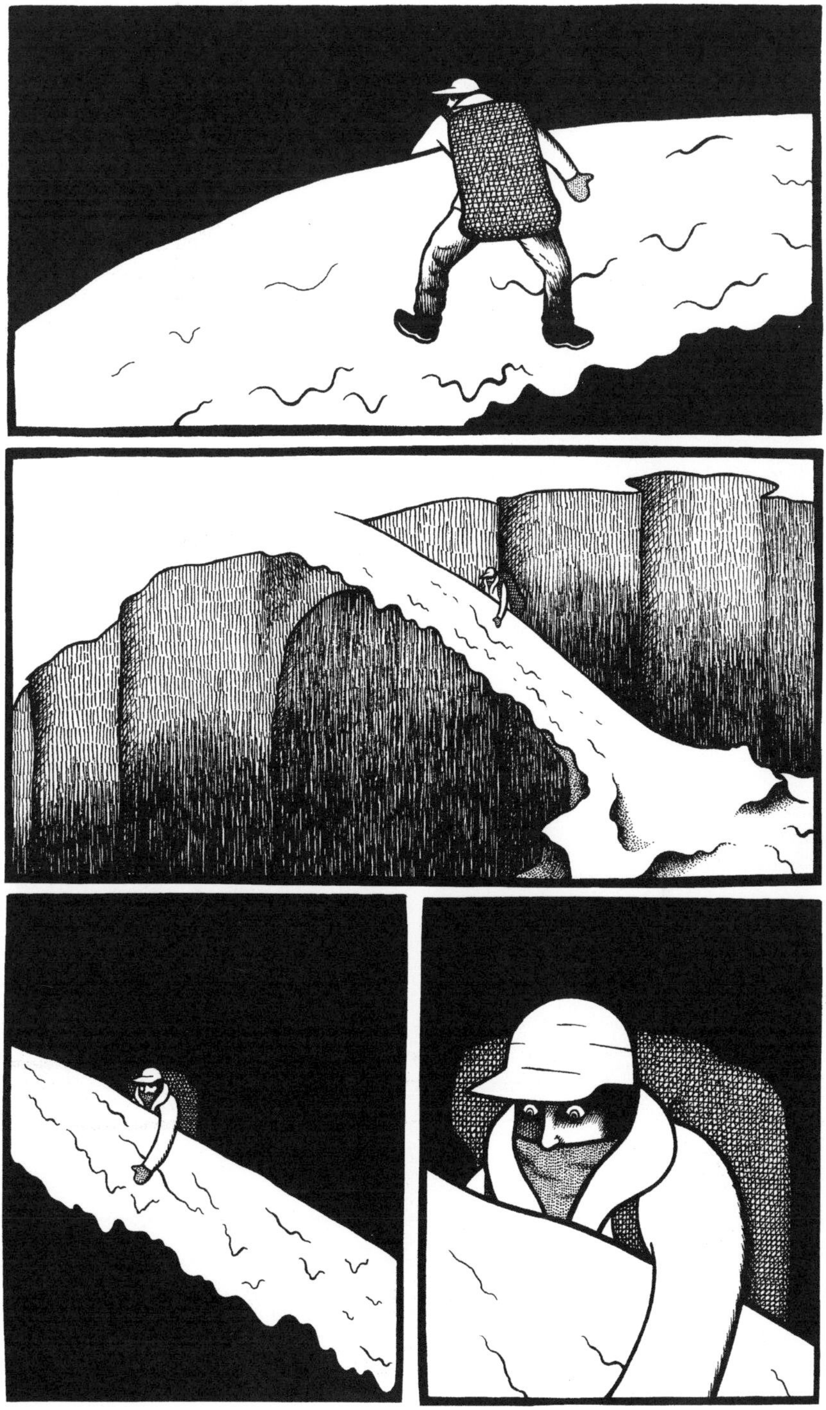

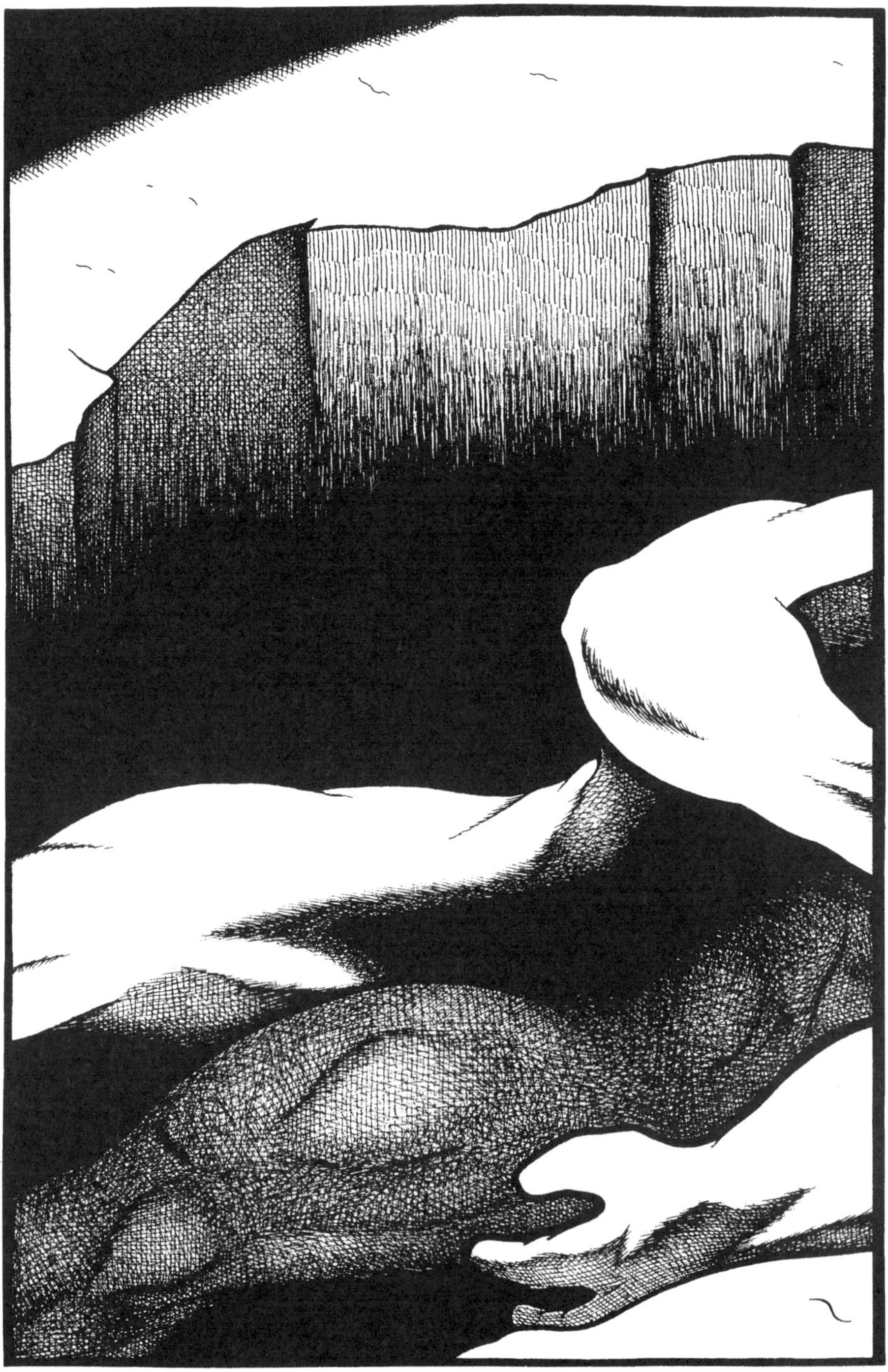

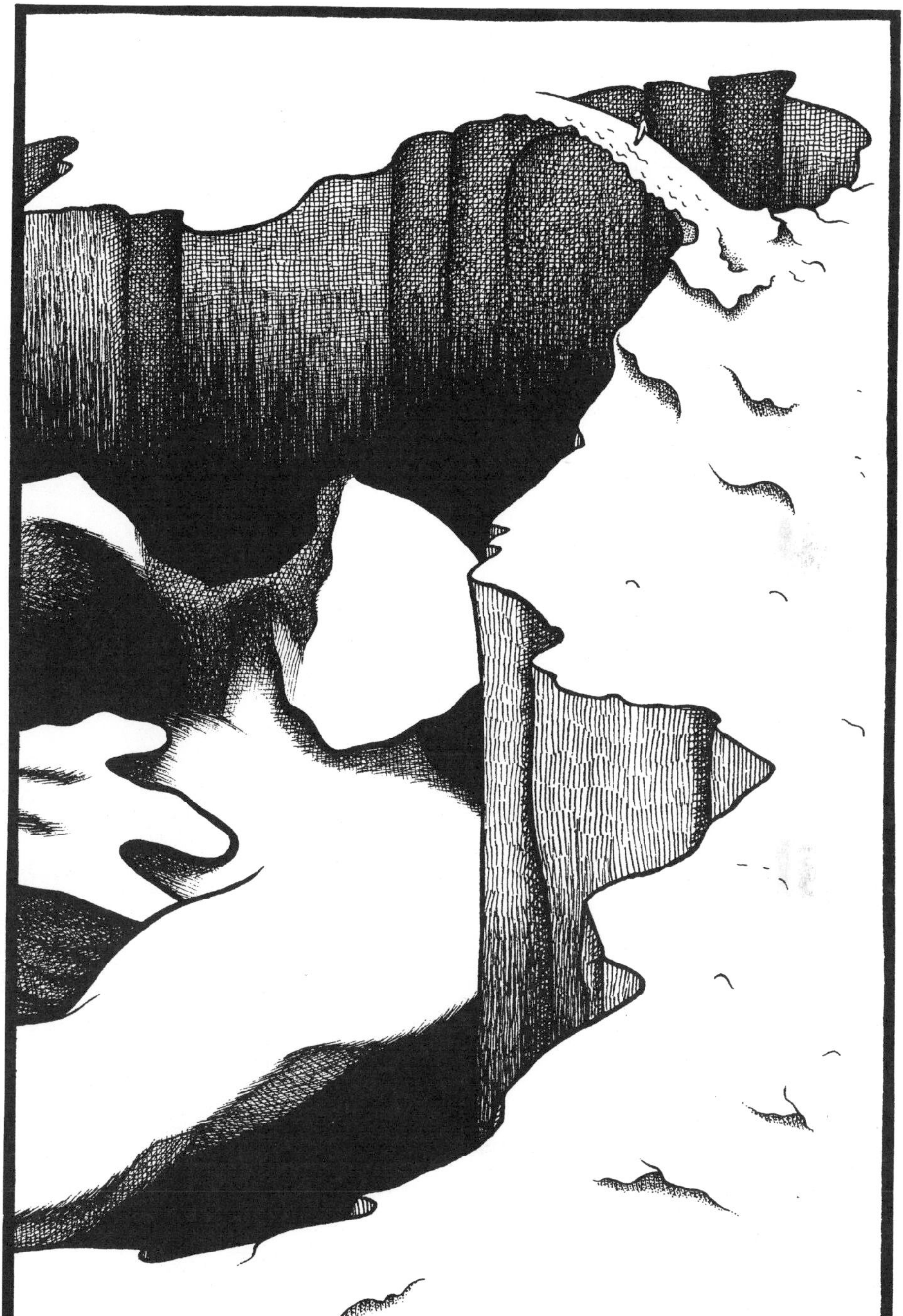

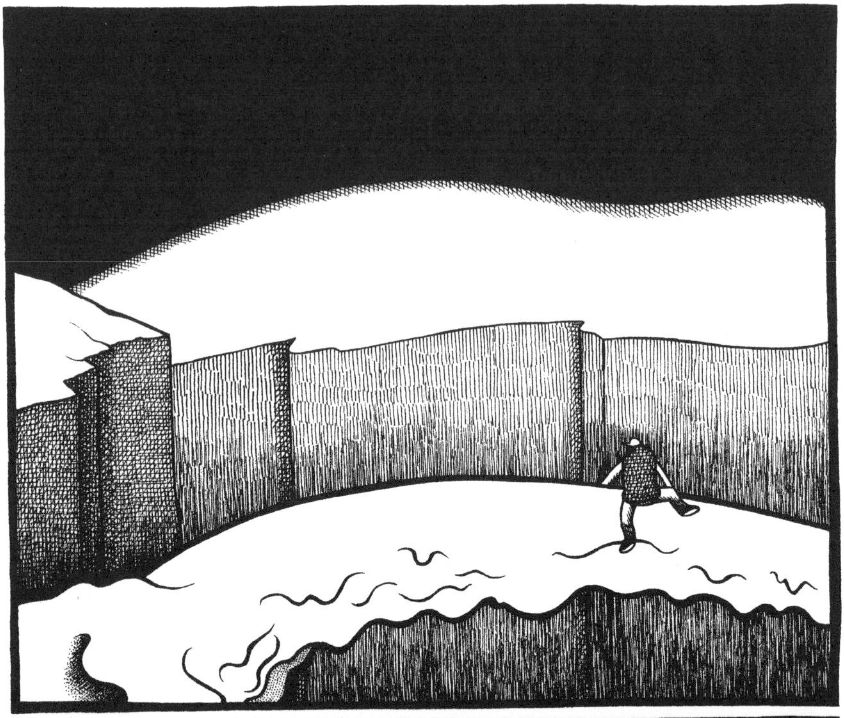

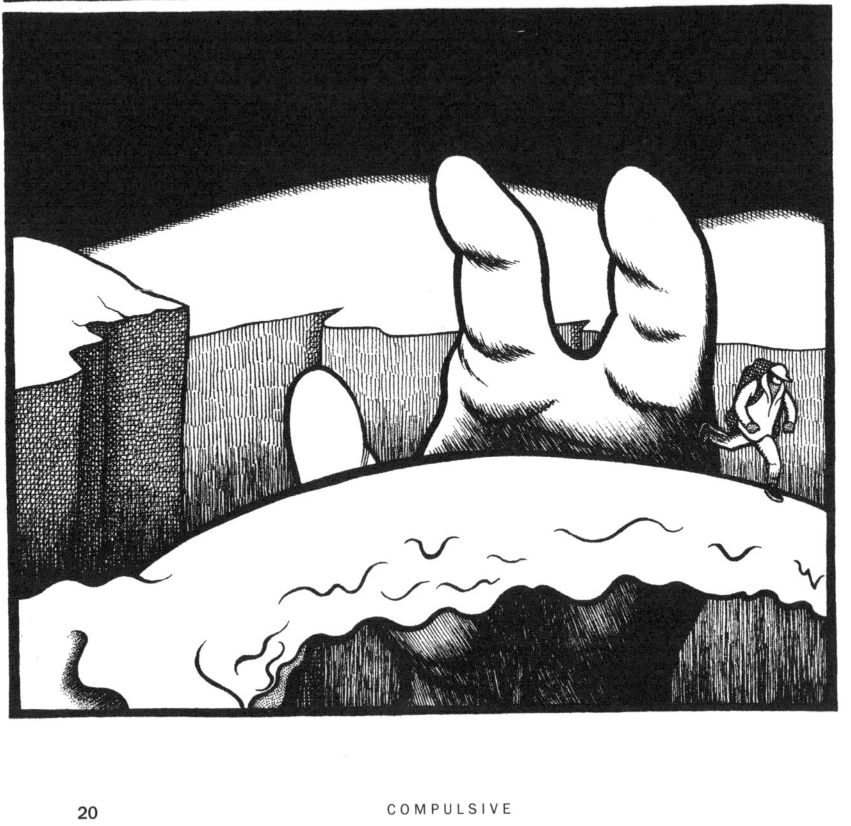

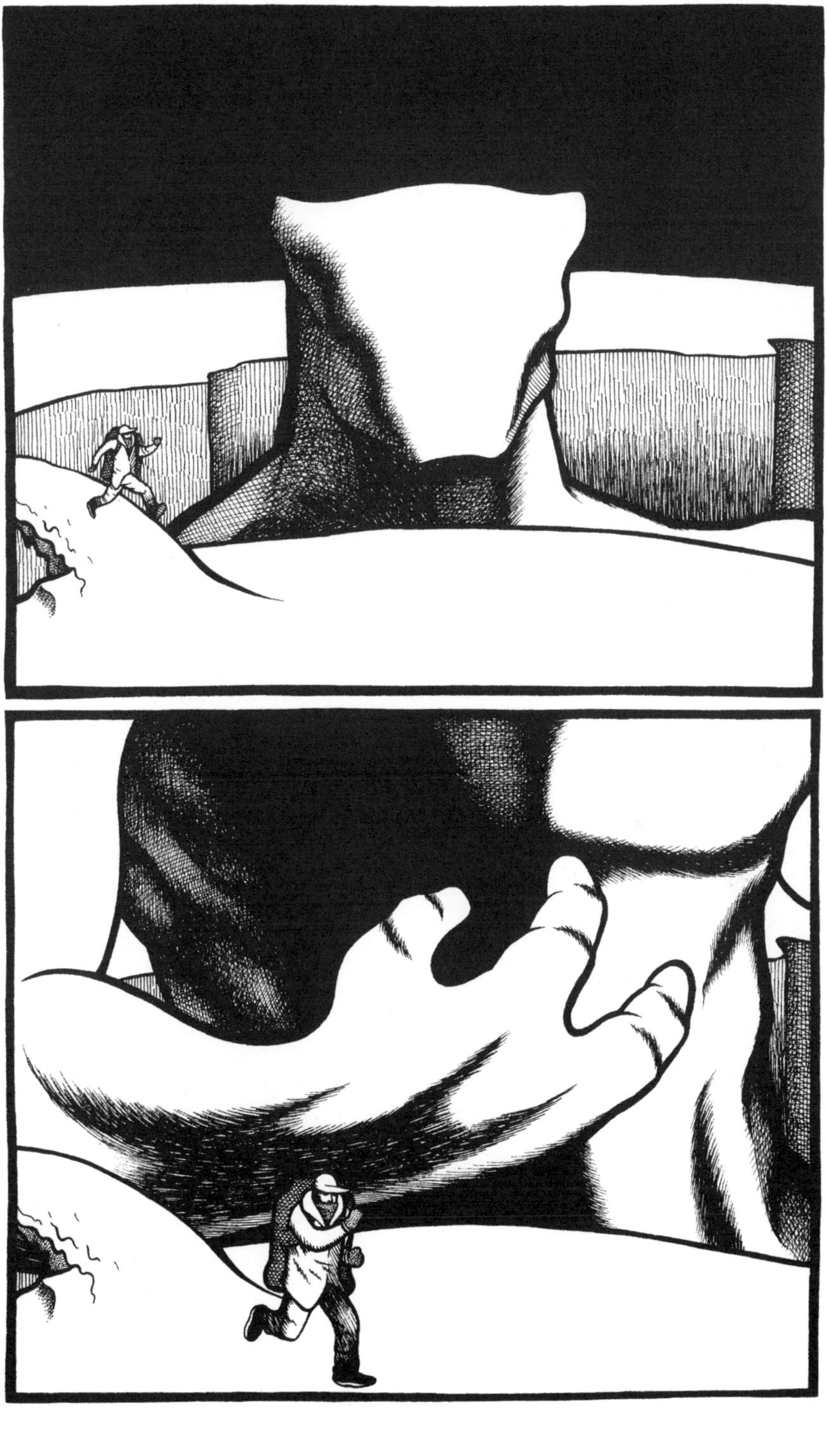

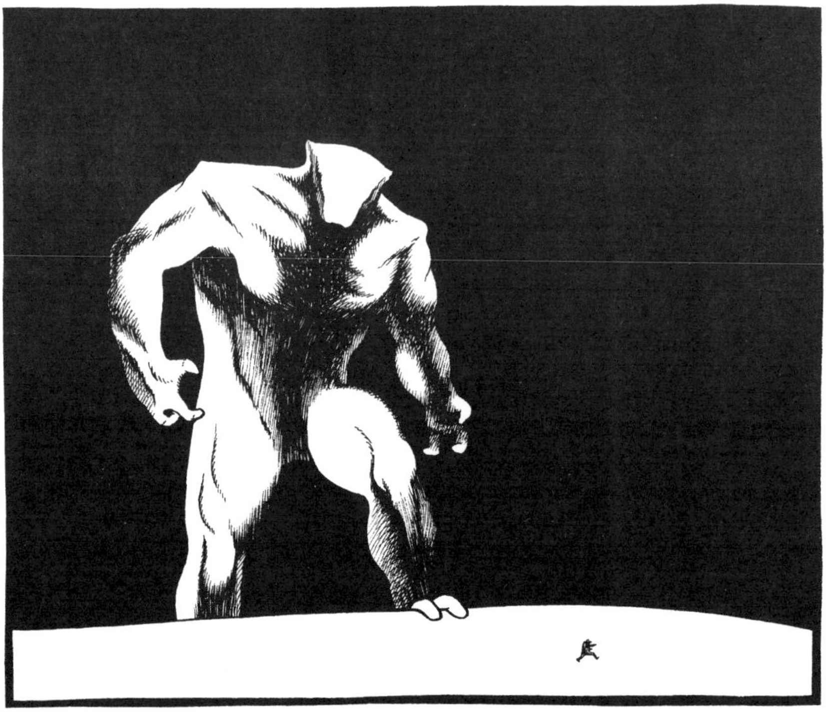

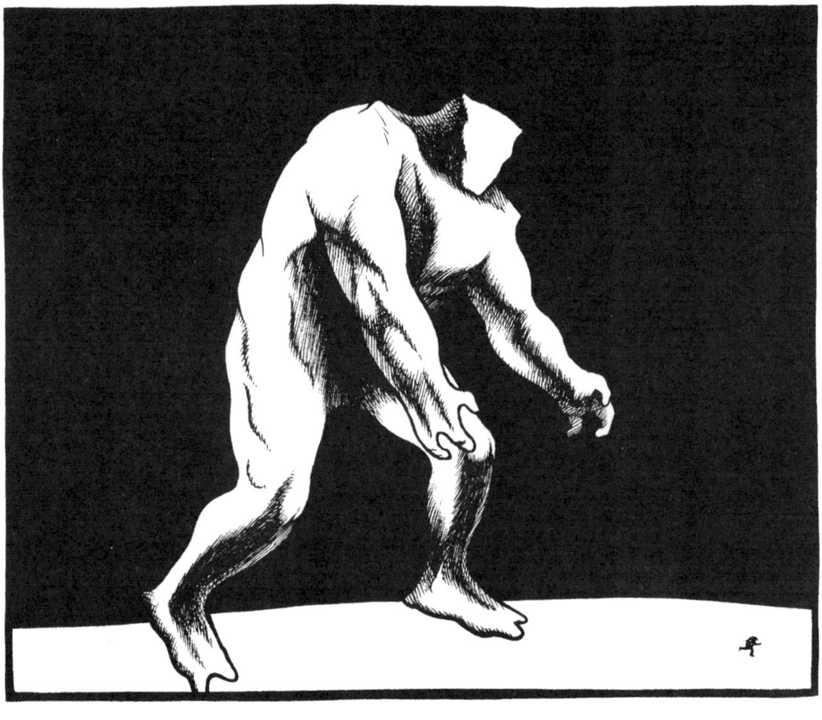

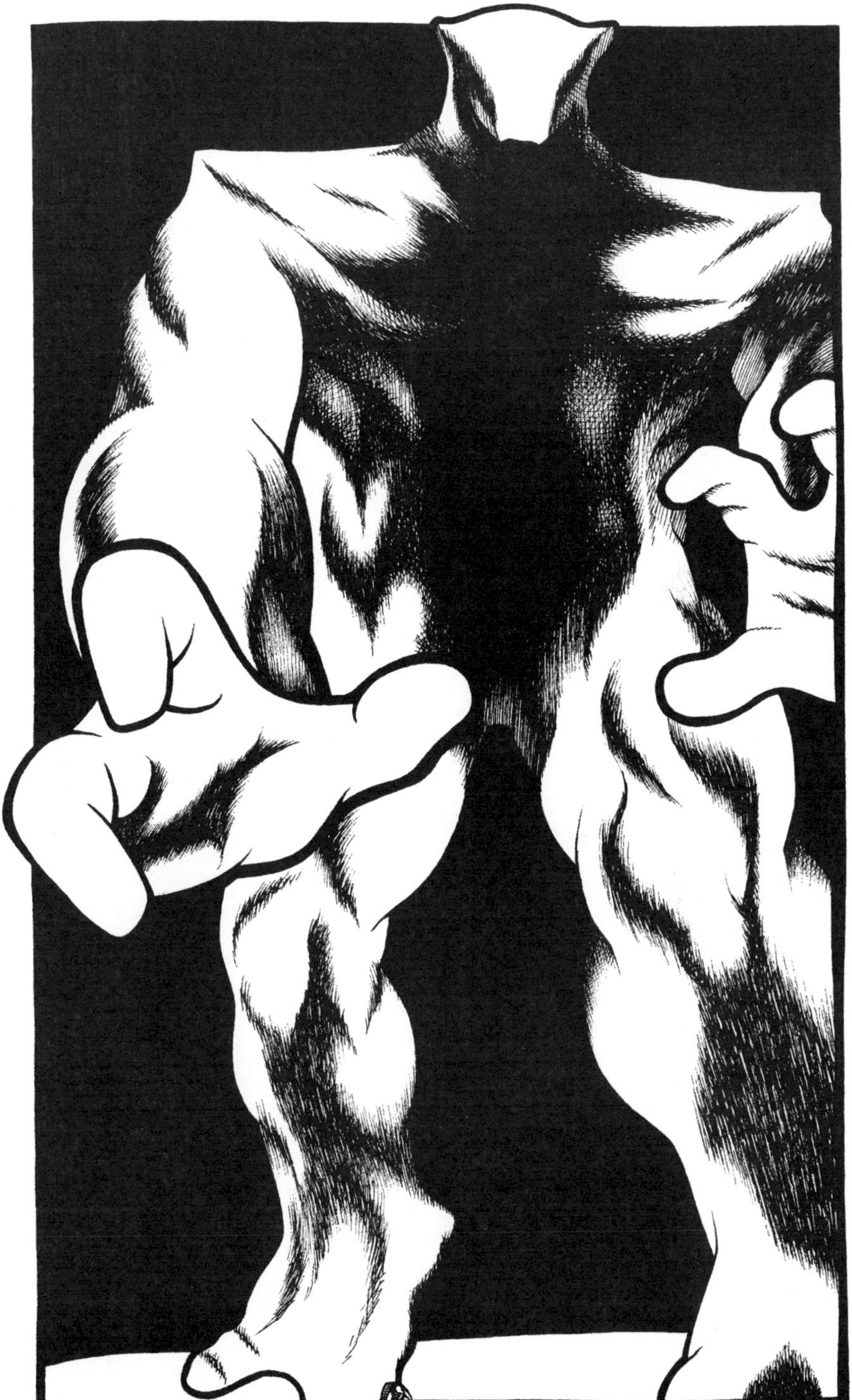

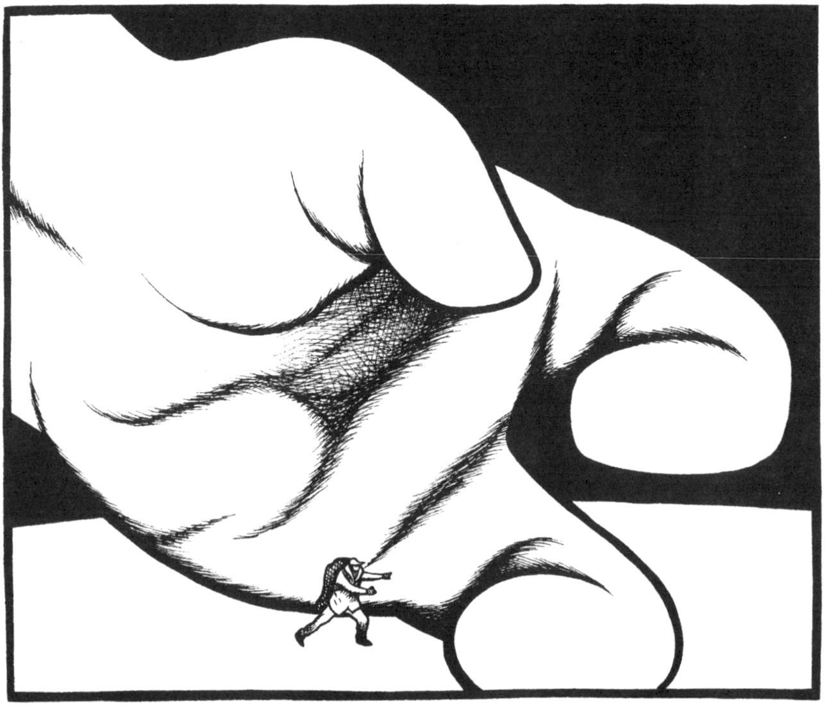

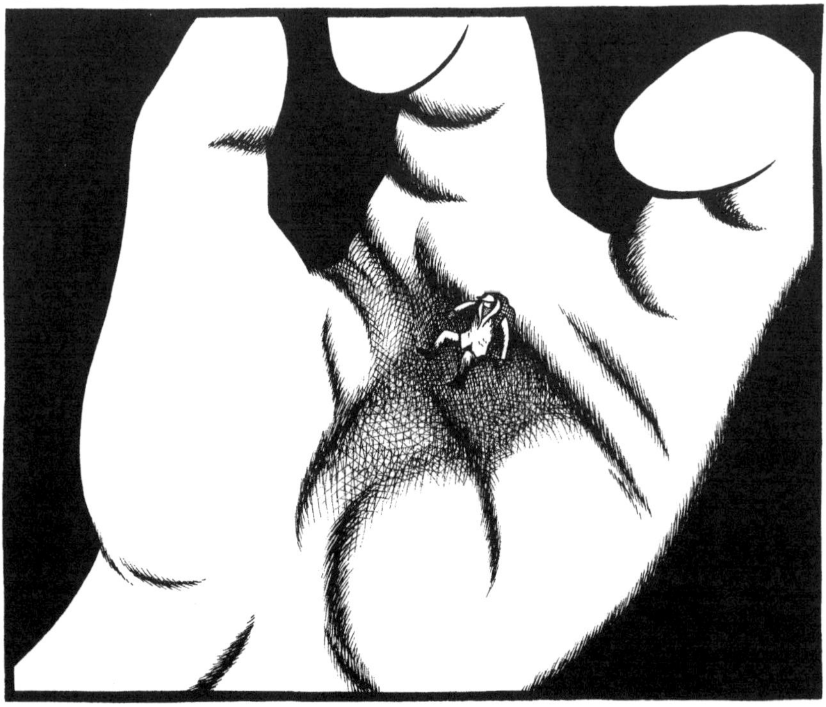

I AWOKE TOO SOON. I SEE YOU ARE NOT QUITE READY.*
*TRANSLATED FROM A THOUGHT PROCESS FAR TOO ADVANCED, FAR TOO COMPLEX TO BE COMPREHENDED BY A PUNY HUMAN BRAIN.

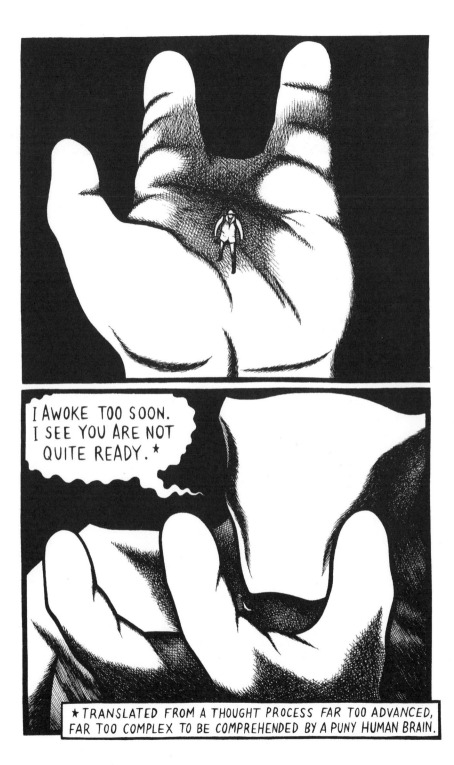

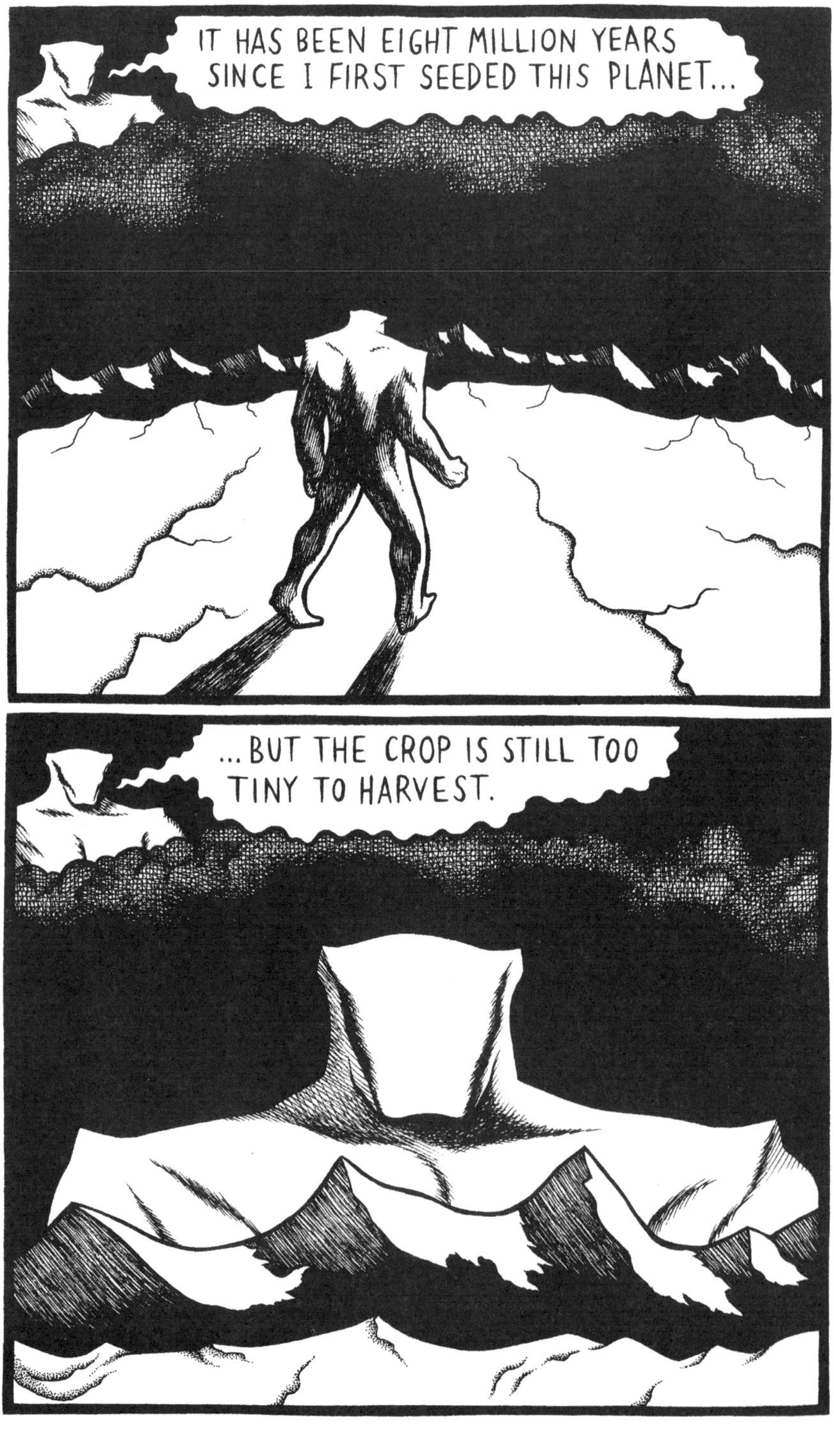
IT HAS BEEN EIGHT MILLION YEARS SINCE I FIRST SEEDED THIS PLANET...
...BUT THE CROP IS STILL TOO TINY TO HARVEST.

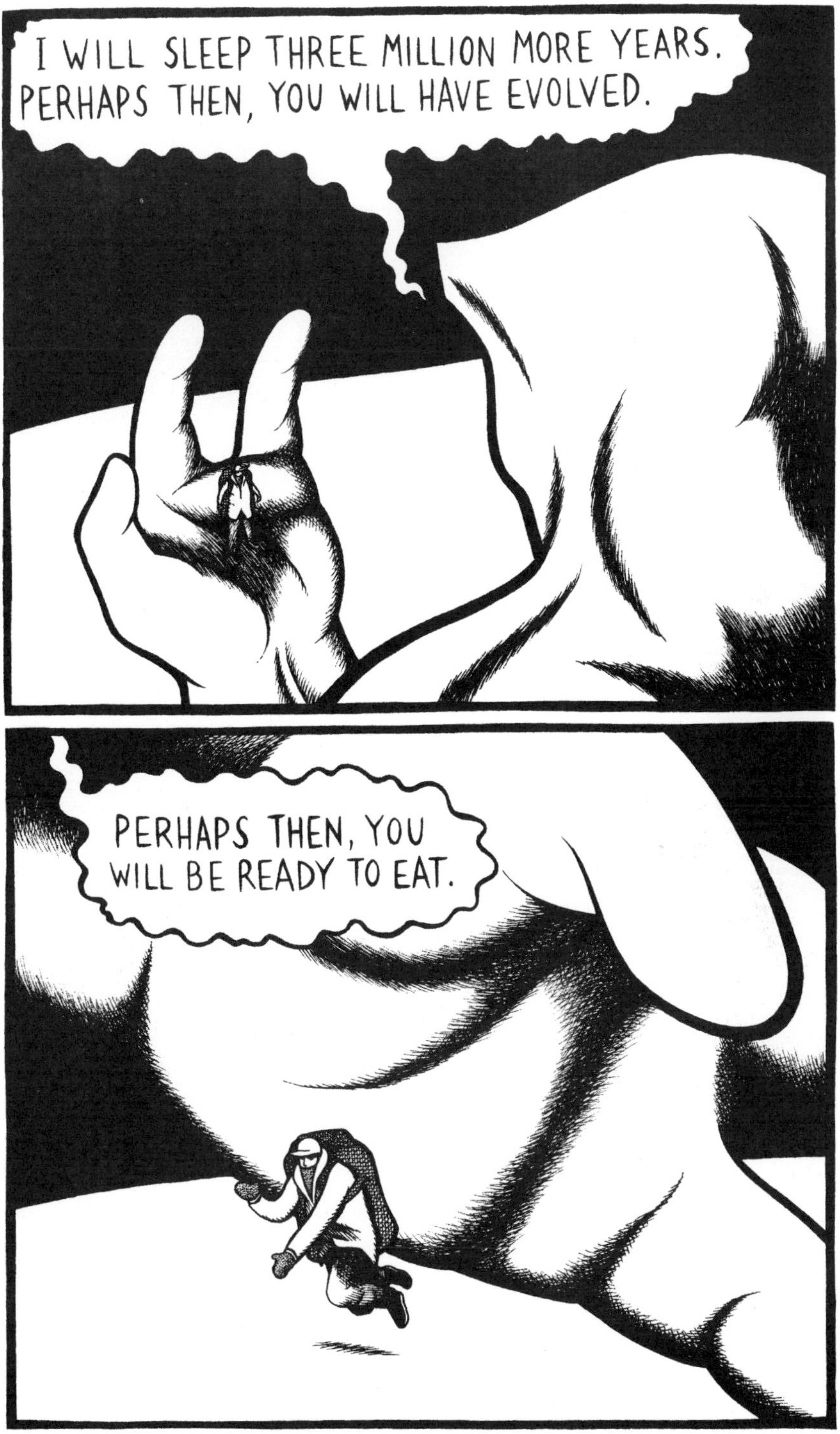
I WILL SLEEP THREE MILLION MORE YEARS. PERHAPS THEN, YOU WILL HAVE EVOLVED.
PERHAPS THEN, YOU WILL BE READY TO EAT.

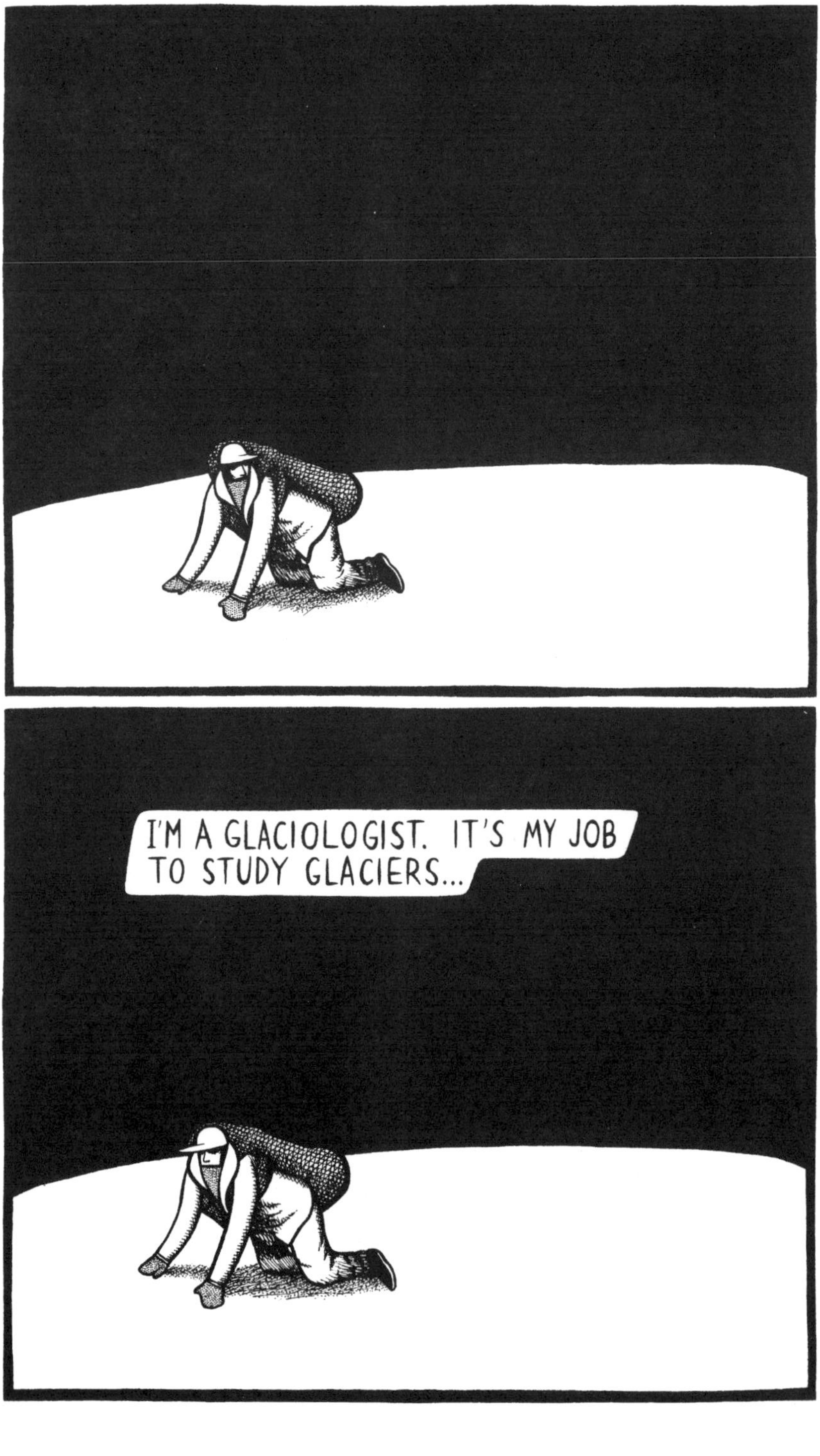
I'M A GLACIOLOGIST. IT'S MY JOB TO STUDY GLACIERS...

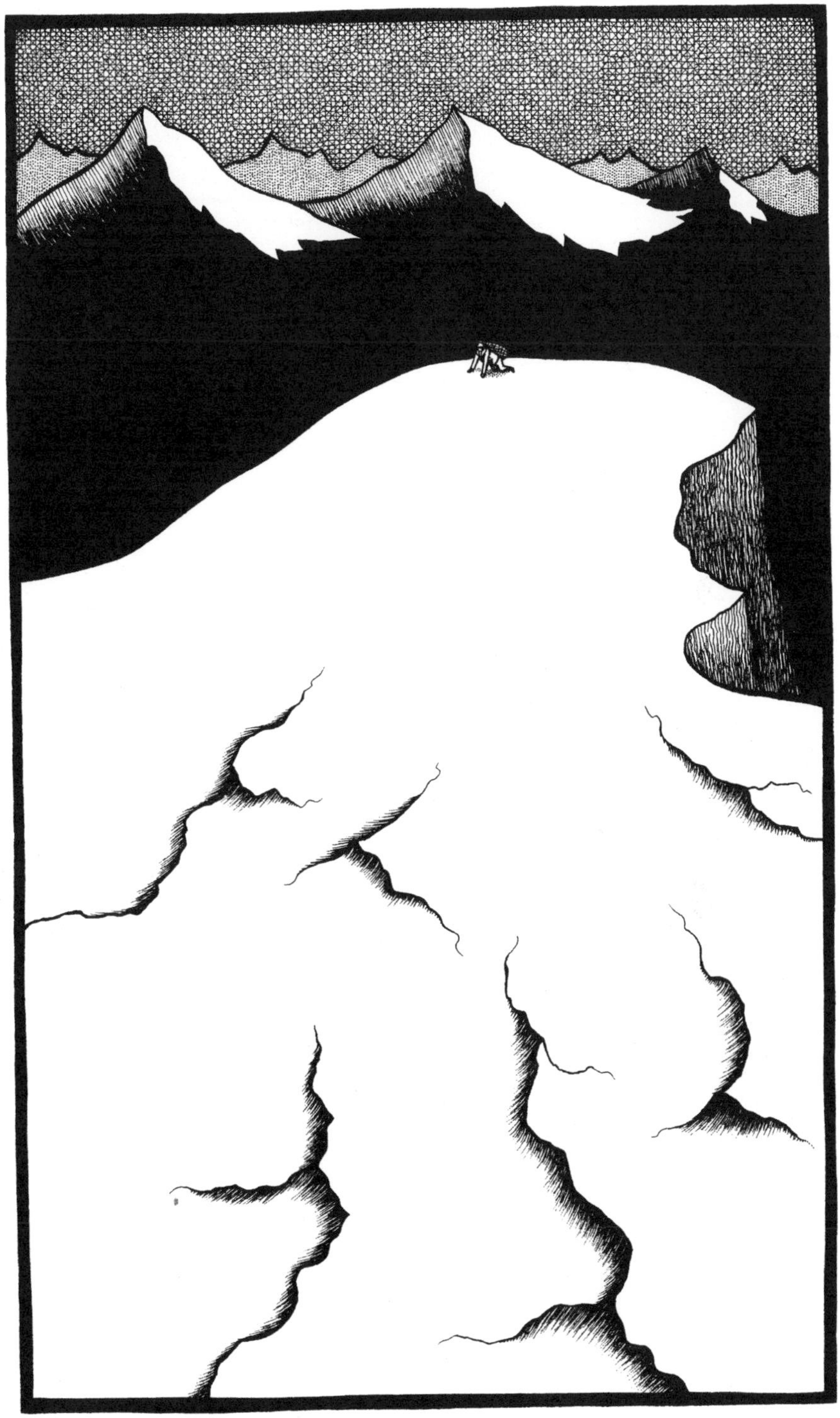

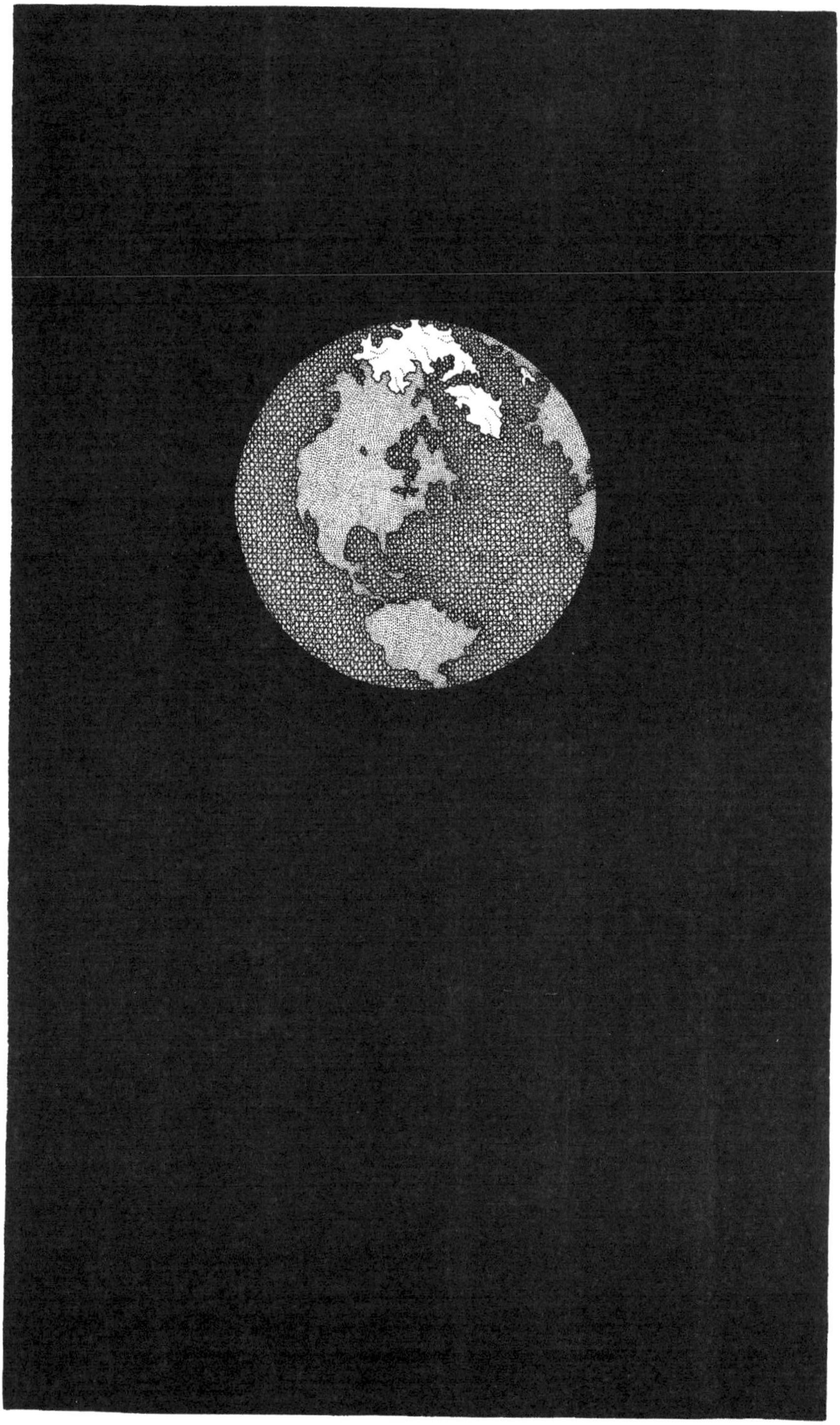

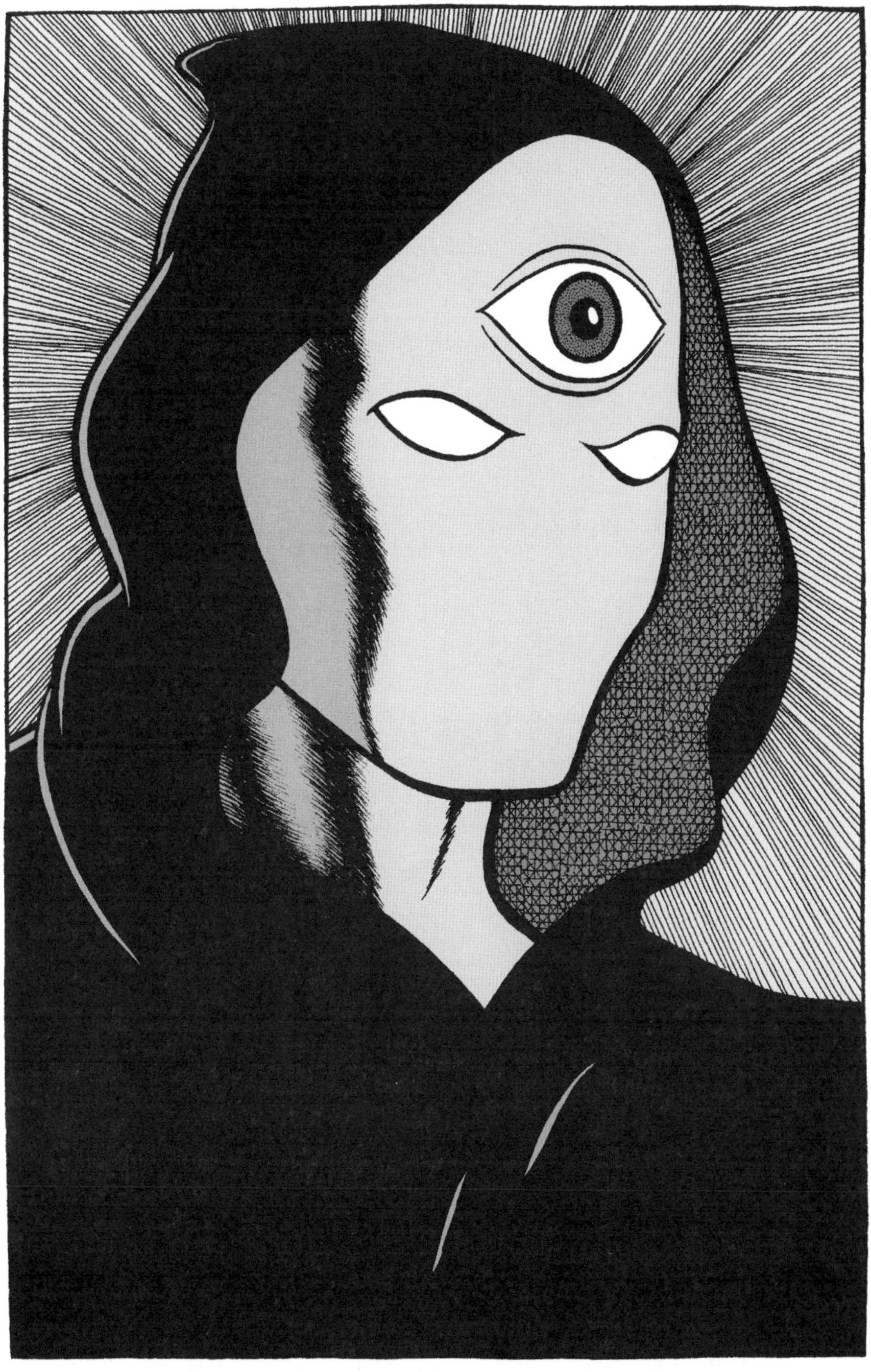

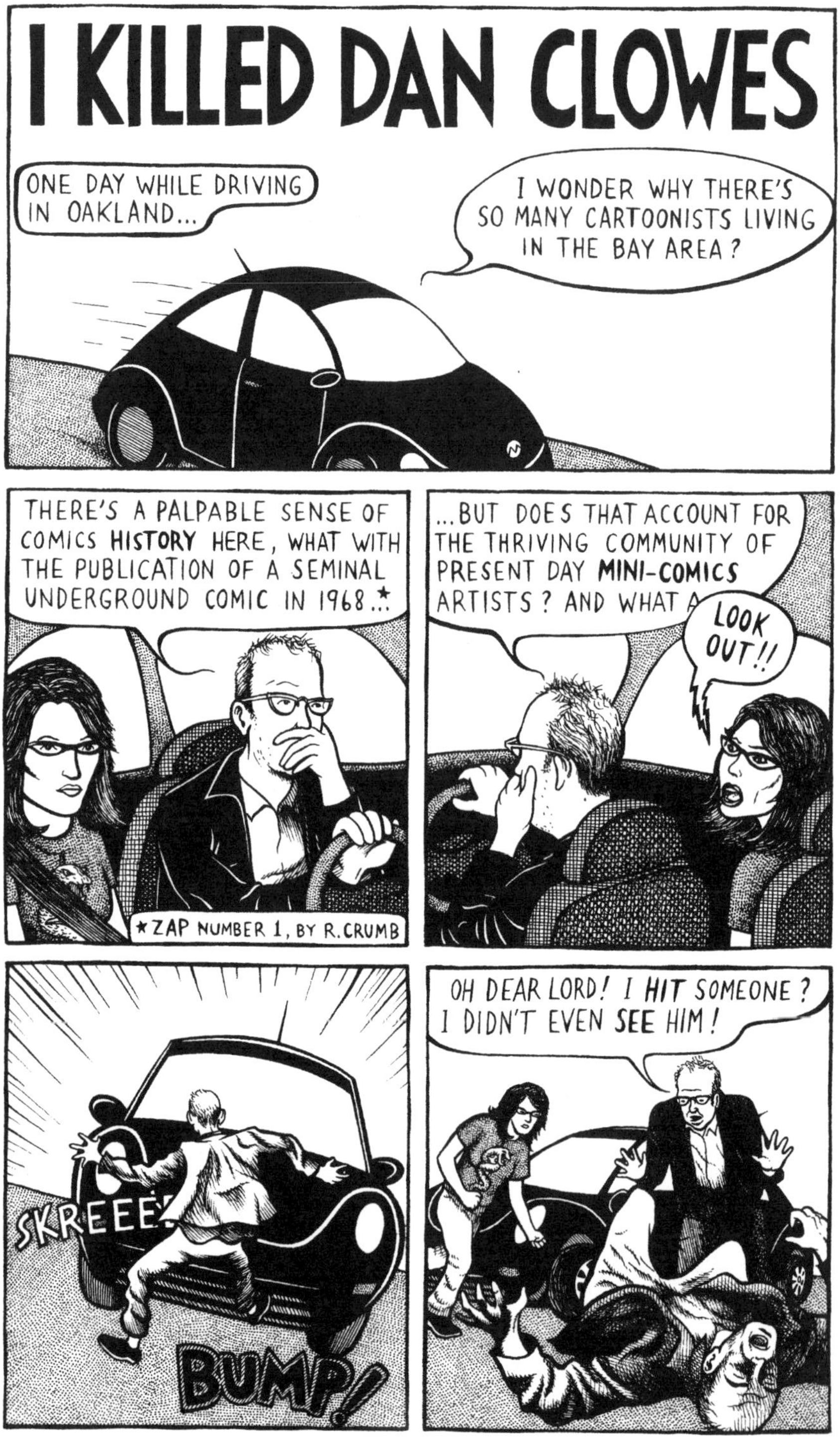
I KILLED DAN CLOWES
ONE DAY WHILE DRIVING IN OAKLAND...
I WONDER WHY THERE'S SO MANY CARTOONISTS LIVING IN THE BAY AREA?
THERE'S A PALPABLE SENSE OF COMICS HISTORY HERE, WHAT WITH THE PUBLICATION OF A SEMINAL UNDERGROUND COMIC IN 1968...*
*ZAP NUMBER 1, BY R. CRUMB
...BUT DOES THAT ACCOUNT FOR THE THRIVING COMMUNITY OF PRESENT DAY MINI-COMICS ARTISTS? AND WHAT A
LOOK OUT!!
SKREEEE
BUMP!
OH DEAR LORD! I HIT SOMEONE? I DIDN'T EVEN SEE HIM!

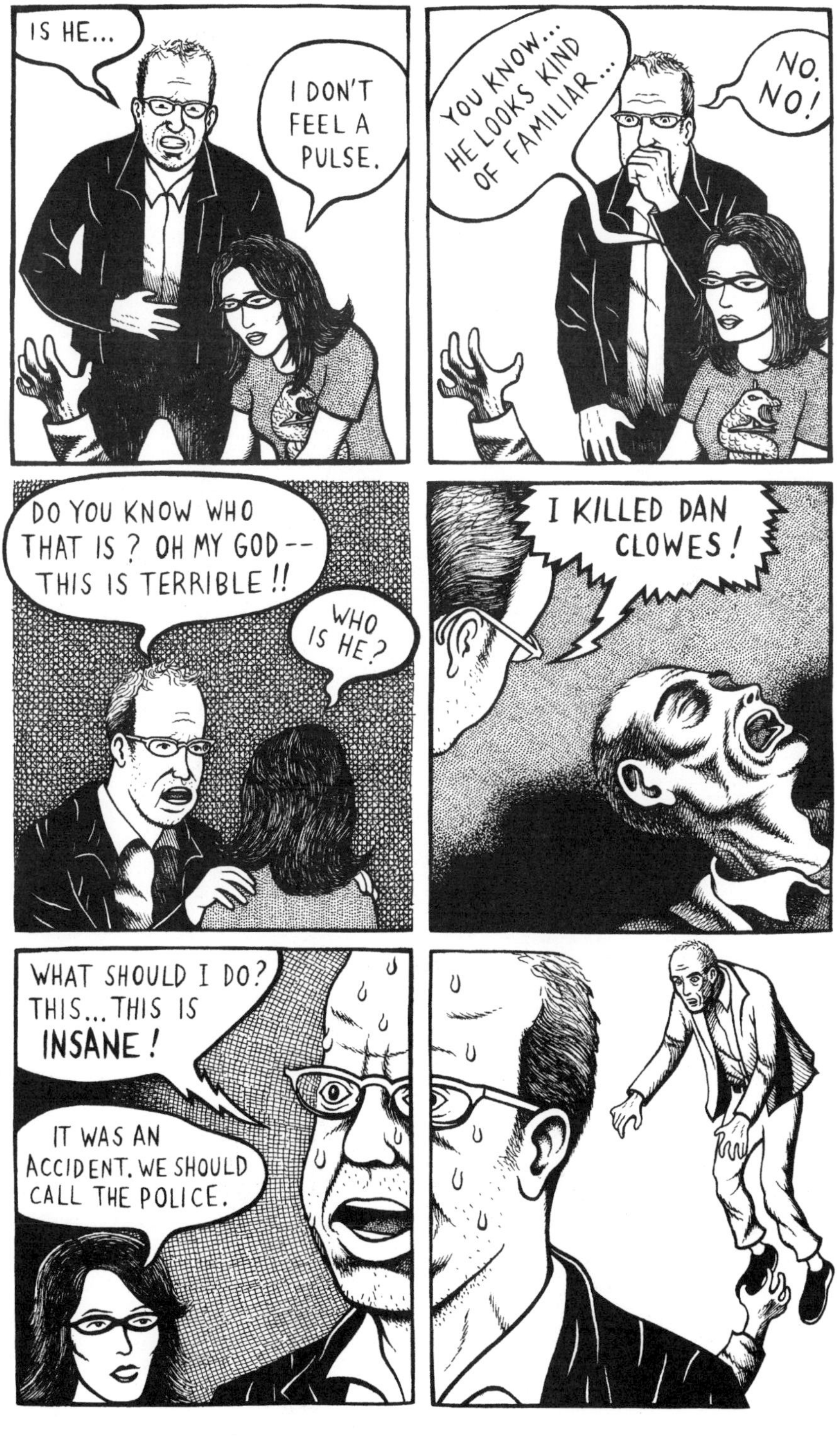
IS HE...
I DON'T FEEL A PULSE.
YOU KNOW... HE LOOKS KIND OF FAMILIAR...
NO. NO!
DO YOU KNOW WHO THAT IS? OH MY GOD -- THIS IS TERRIBLE!!
WHO IS HE?
I KILLED DAN CLOWES!
WHAT SHOULD I DO? THIS... THIS IS INSANE!
IT WAS AN ACCIDENT. WE SHOULD CALL THE POLICE.

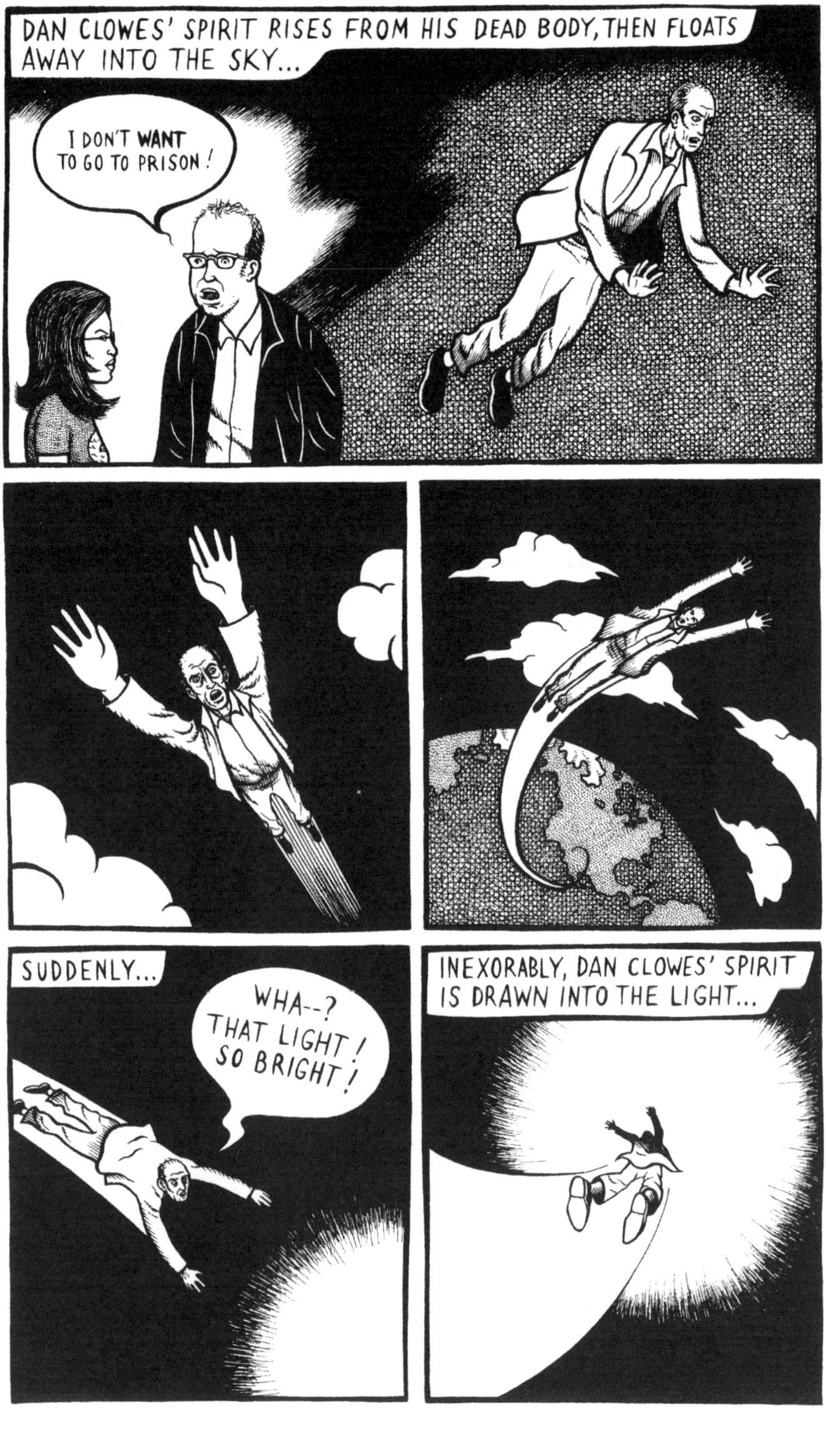
DAN CLOWES' SPIRIT RISES FROM HIS DEAD BODY, THEN FLOATS AWAY INTO THE SKY...
I DON'T **WANT** TO GO TO PRISON!
SUDDENLY...
WHA--? THAT LIGHT! SO BRIGHT!
INEXORABLY, DAN CLOWES' SPIRIT IS DRAWN INTO THE LIGHT...

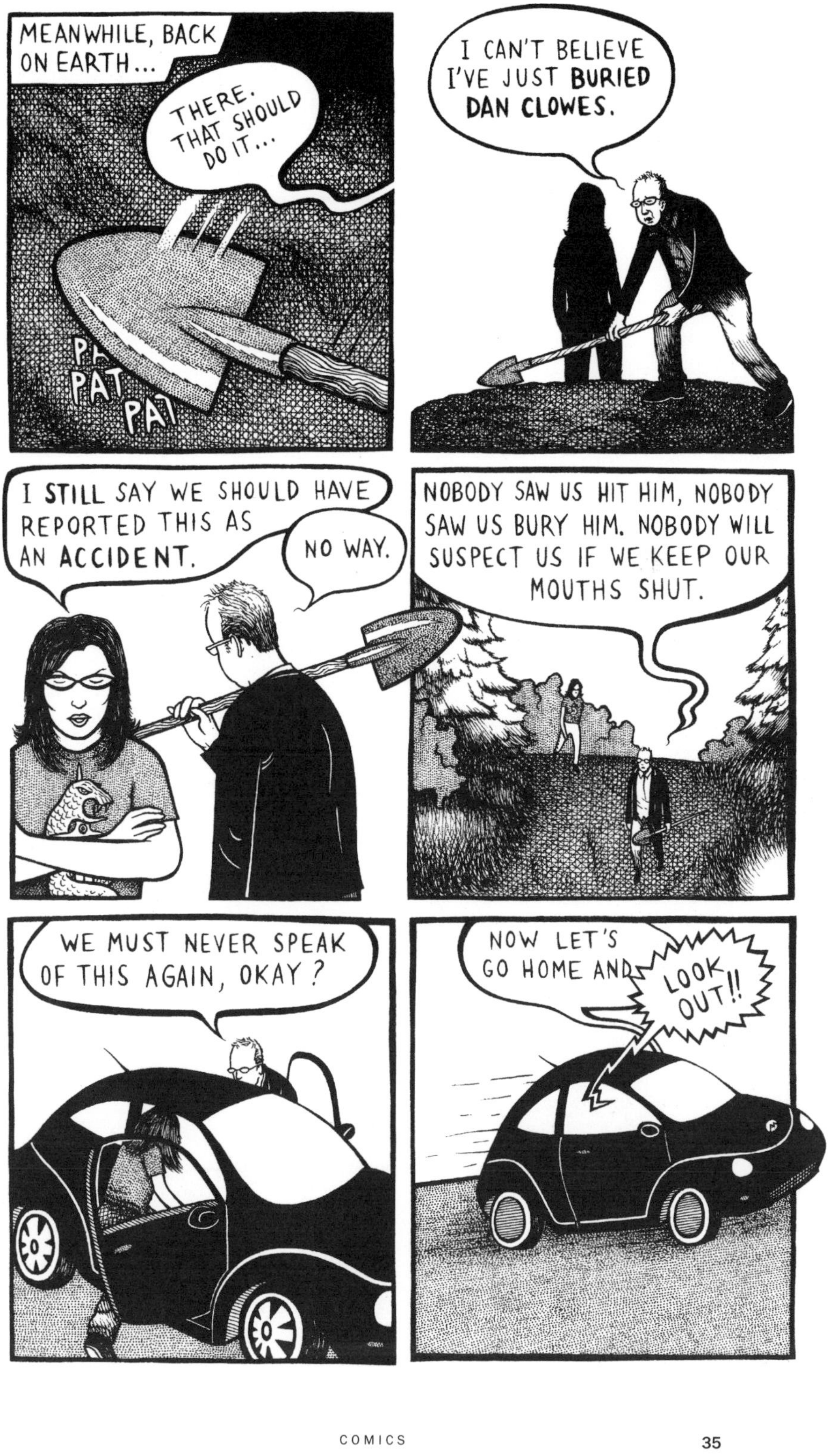
MEANWHILE, BACK ON EARTH...
THERE. THAT SHOULD DO IT...
PAT
I CAN'T BELIEVE I'VE JUST **BURIED DAN CLOWES**.
I **STILL** SAY WE SHOULD HAVE REPORTED THIS AS AN **ACCIDENT**.
NO WAY.
NOBODY SAW US HIT HIM, NOBODY SAW US BURY HIM. NOBODY WILL SUSPECT US IF WE KEEP OUR MOUTHS SHUT.
WE MUST NEVER SPEAK OF THIS AGAIN, OKAY?
NOW LET'S GO HOME AND
LOOK OUT!!

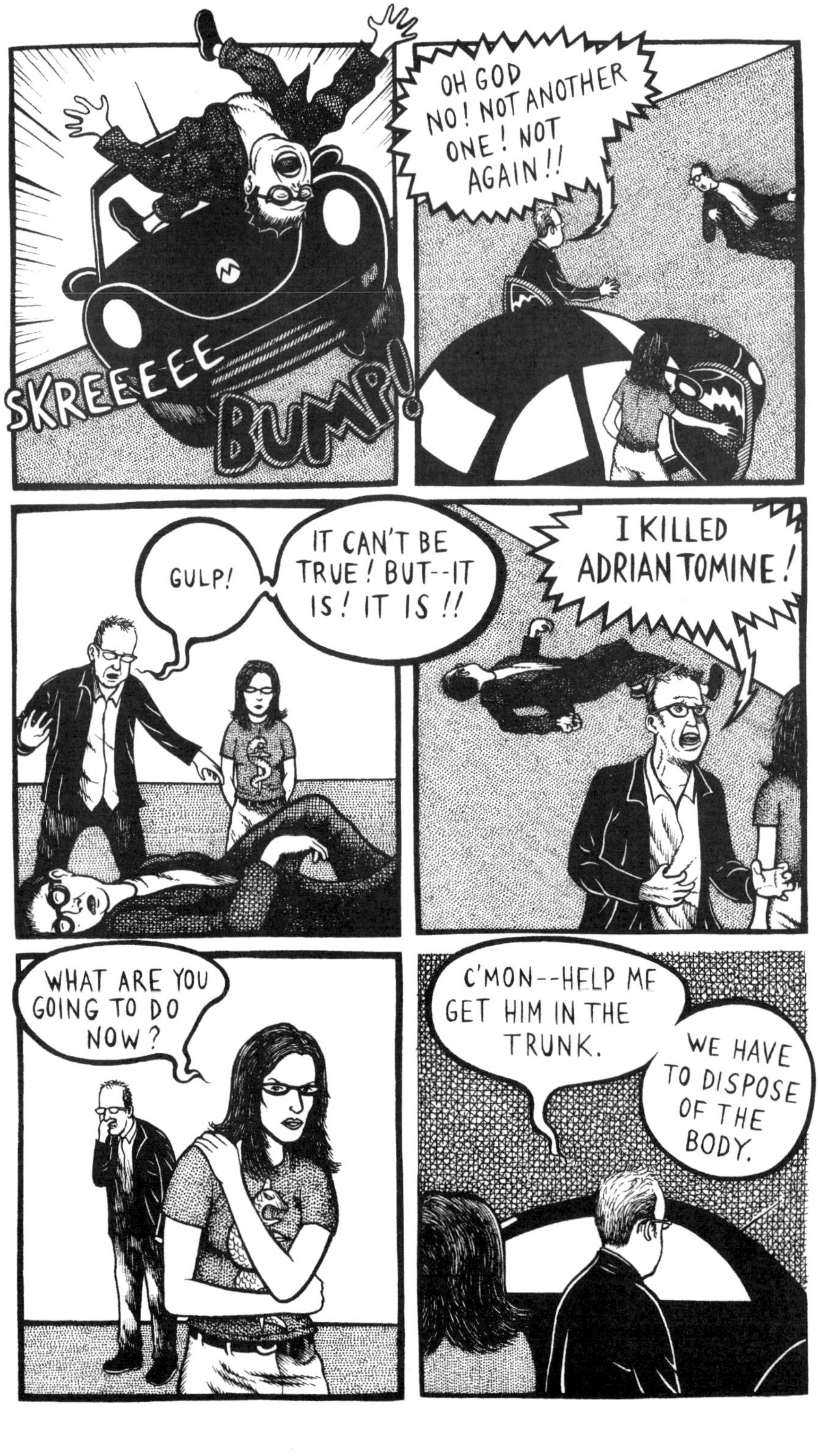
SKREEEEEE
BUMP!
OH GOD NO! NOT ANOTHER ONE! NOT AGAIN!!
GULP!
IT CAN'T BE TRUE! BUT--IT IS! IT IS!!
I KILLED ADRIAN TOMINE!
WHAT ARE YOU GOING TO DO NOW?
C'MON--HELP ME GET HIM IN THE TRUNK.
WE HAVE TO DISPOSE OF THE BODY.

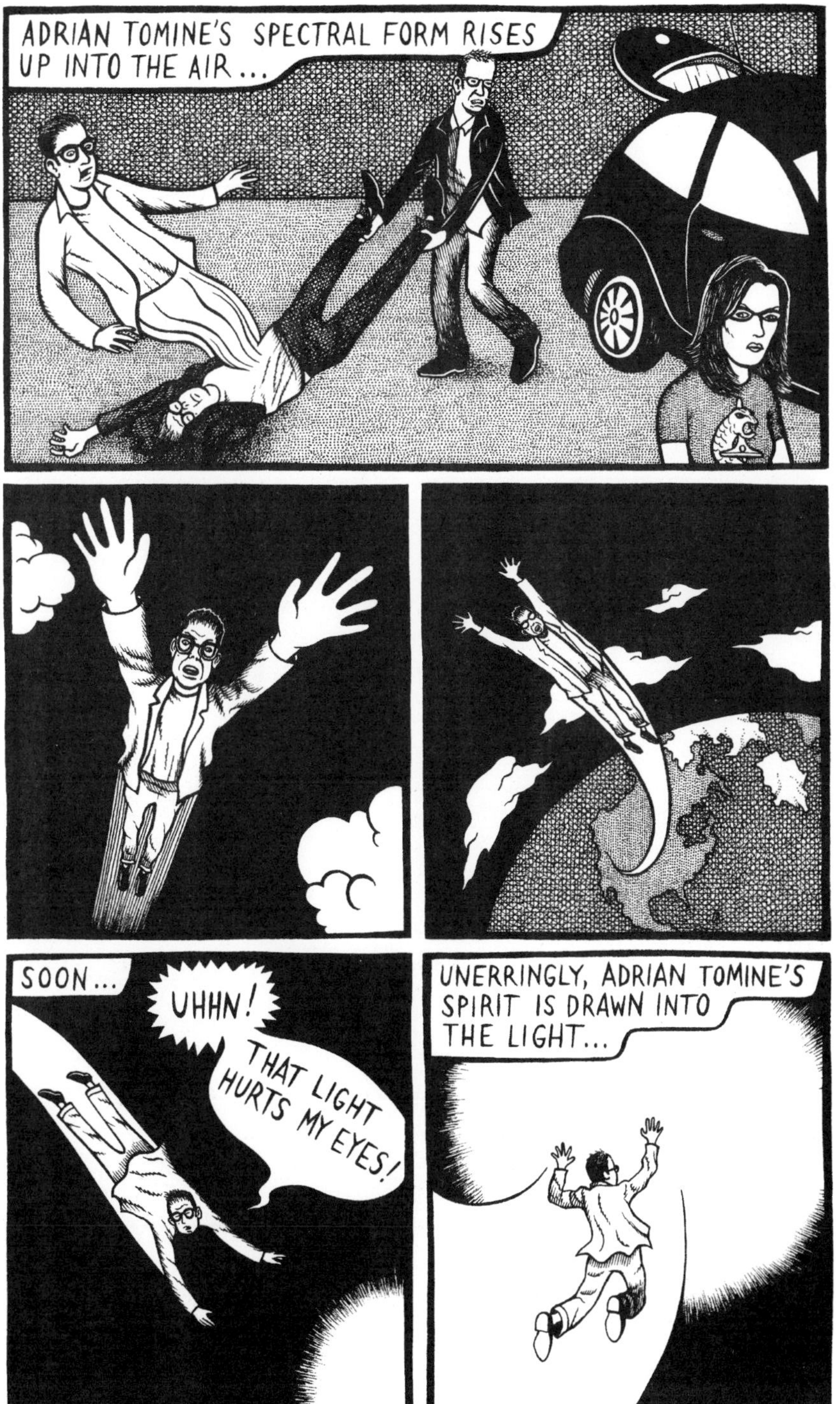

ADRIAN TOMINE'S SPECTRAL FORM RISES UP INTO THE AIR...
SOON...
UHHN!
THAT LIGHT HURTS MY EYES!
UNERRINGLY, ADRIAN TOMINE'S SPIRIT IS DRAWN INTO THE LIGHT...

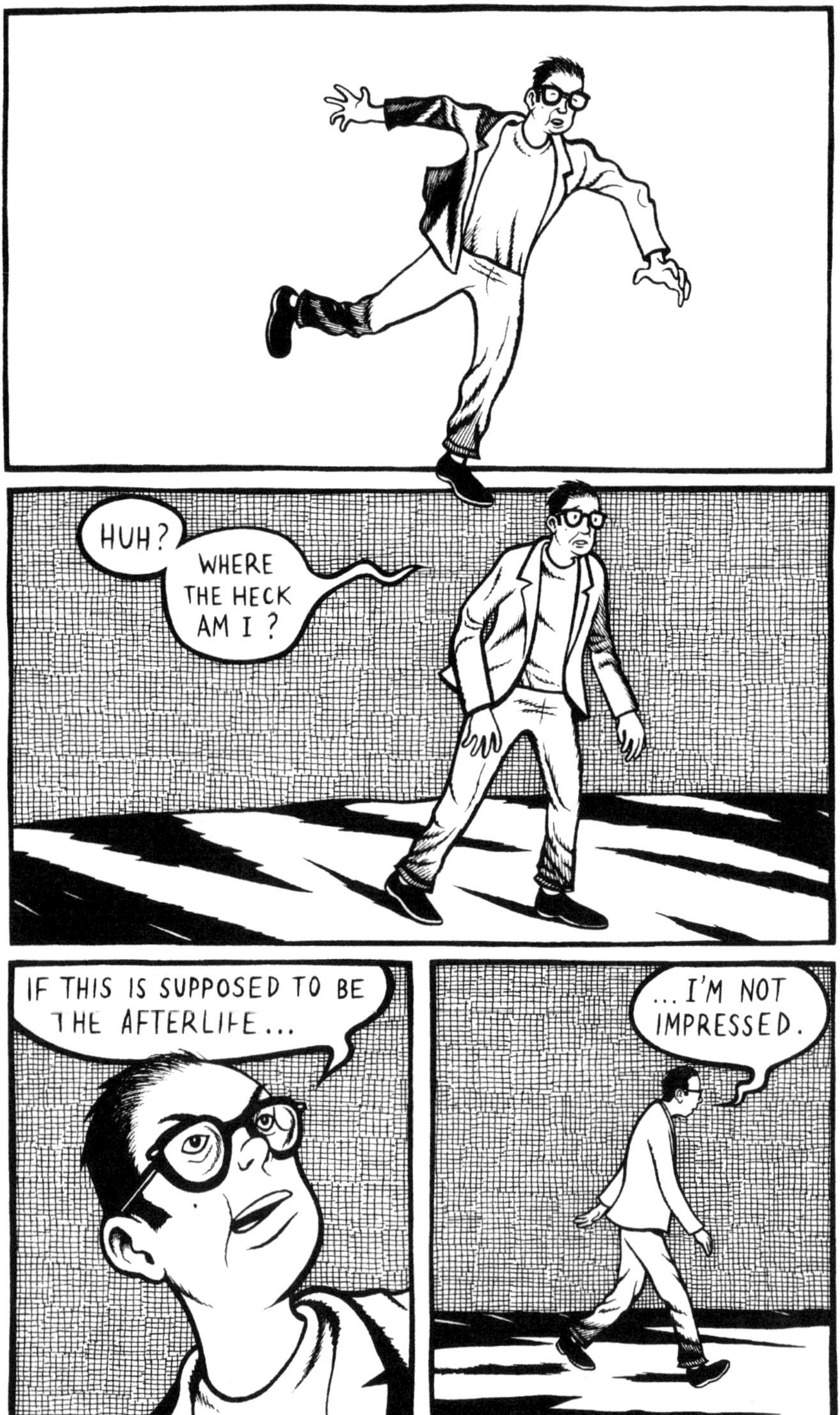
HUH?
WHERE THE HECK AM I ?
IF THIS IS SUPPOSED TO BE THE AFTERLIFE...
...I'M NOT IMPRESSED.

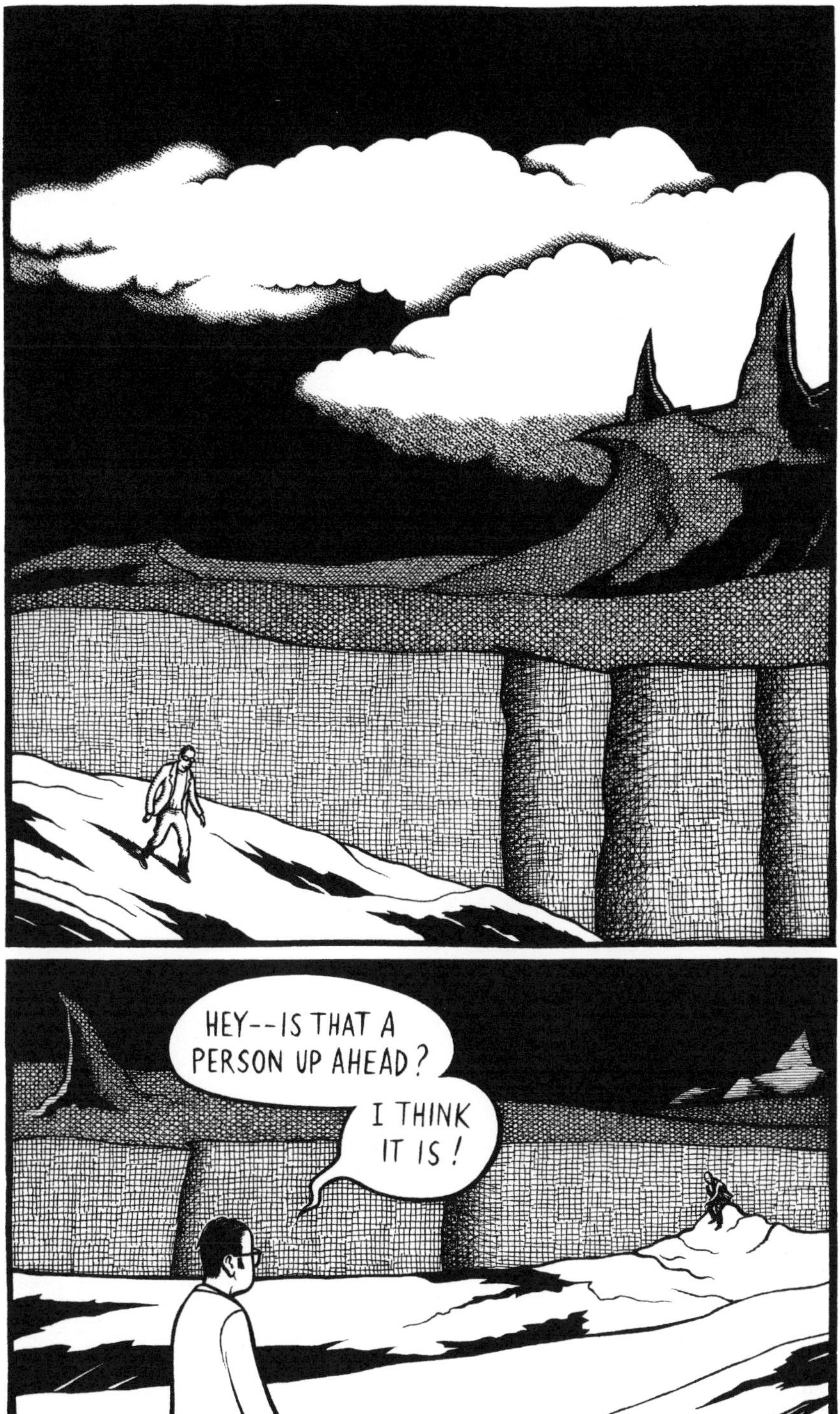
HEY--IS THAT A PERSON UP AHEAD?
I THINK IT IS!

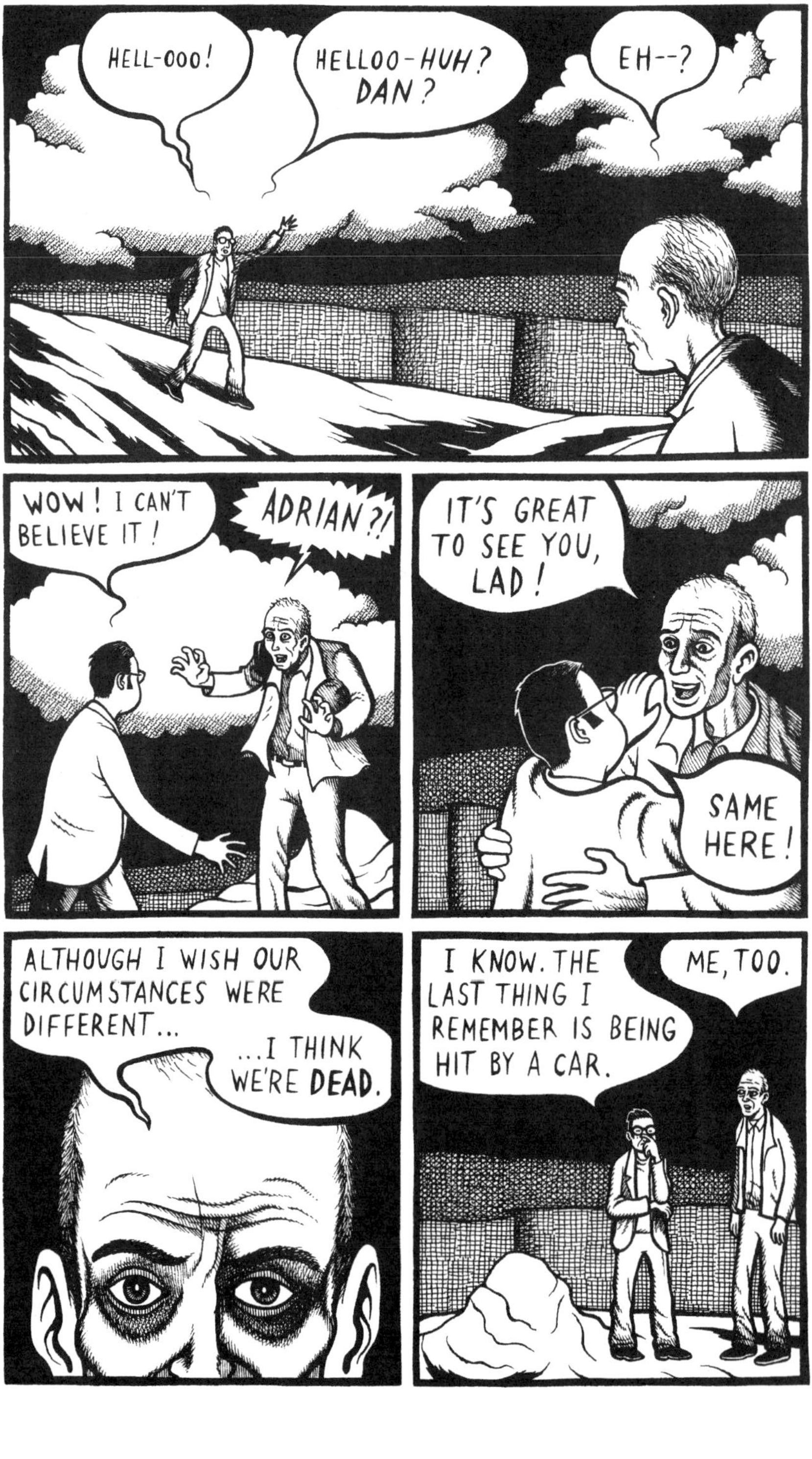
HELL-OOO!
HELLOO-HUH? DAN?
EH--?
WOW! I CAN'T BELIEVE IT!
ADRIAN?!
IT'S GREAT TO SEE YOU, LAD!
SAME HERE!
ALTHOUGH I WISH OUR CIRCUMSTANCES WERE DIFFERENT...
...I THINK WE'RE **DEAD**.
I KNOW. THE LAST THING I REMEMBER IS BEING HIT BY A CAR.
ME, TOO.

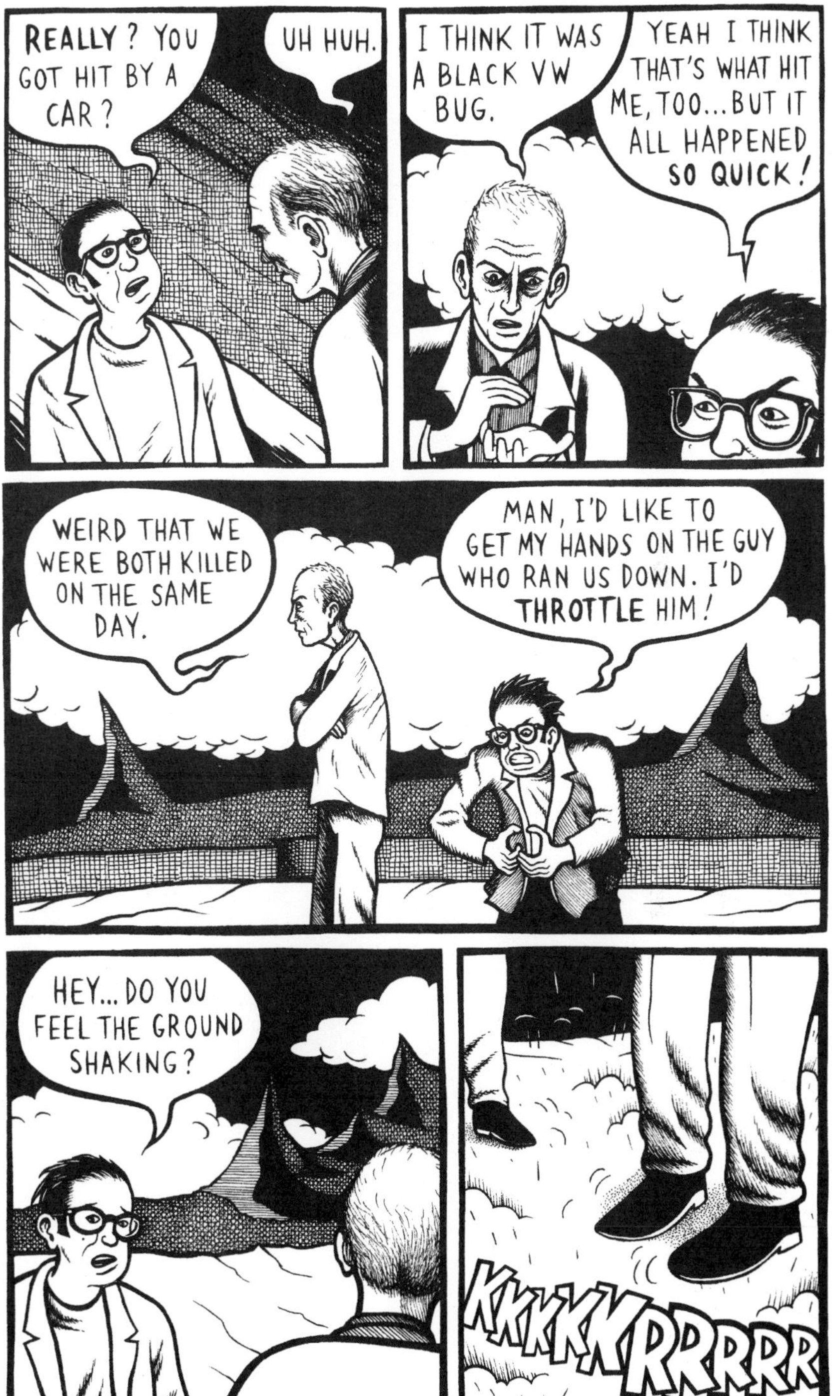
REALLY? YOU GOT HIT BY A CAR?
UH HUH.
I THINK IT WAS A BLACK VW BUG.
YEAH I THINK THAT'S WHAT HIT ME, TOO... BUT IT ALL HAPPENED SO QUICK!
WEIRD THAT WE WERE BOTH KILLED ON THE SAME DAY.
MAN, I'D LIKE TO GET MY HANDS ON THE GUY WHO RAN US DOWN. I'D THROTTLE HIM!
HEY... DO YOU FEEL THE GROUND SHAKING?
KKKKKRRRRR

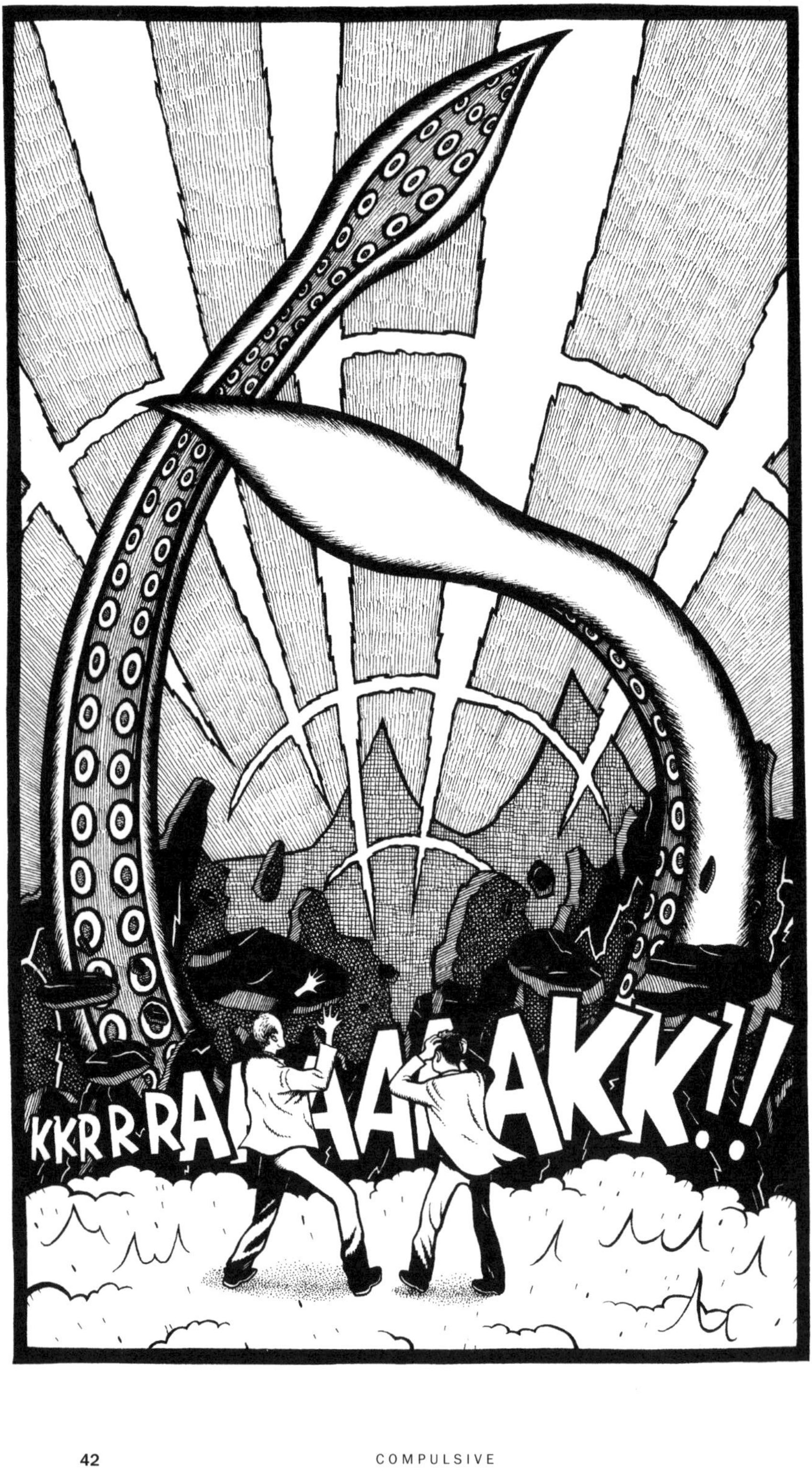
KKRRRA AA AKK!!

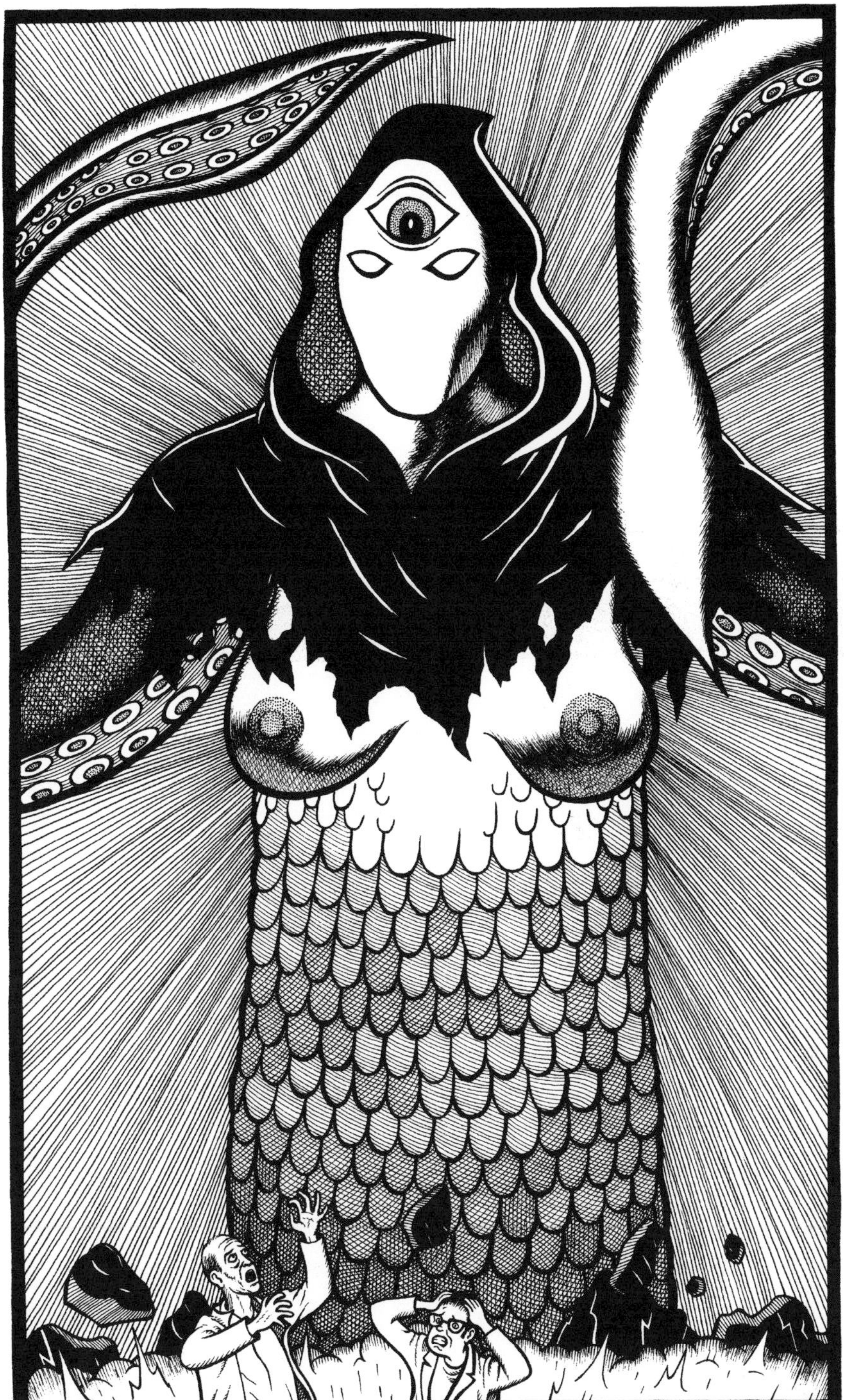

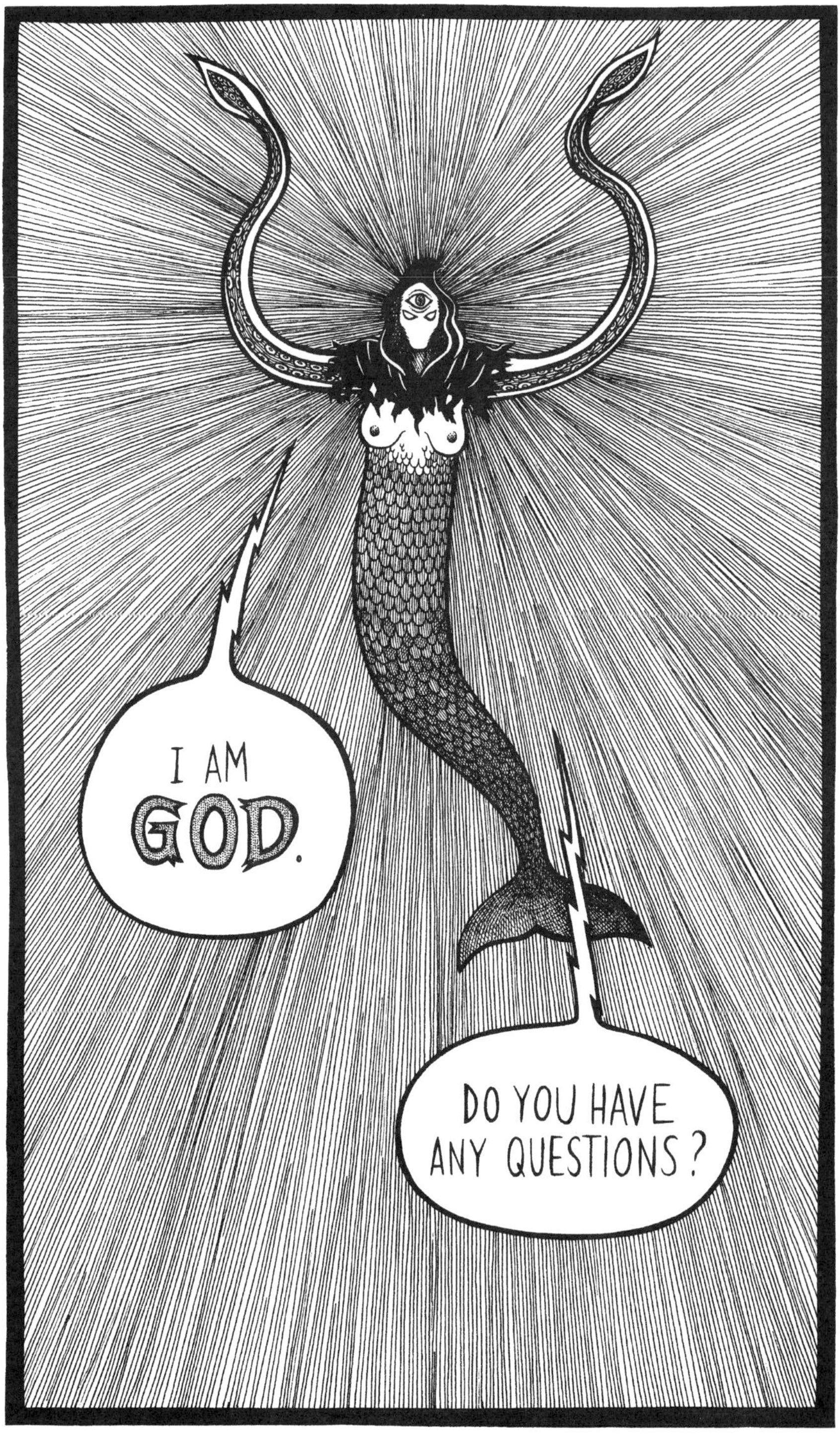
I AM GOD.
DO YOU HAVE ANY QUESTIONS?

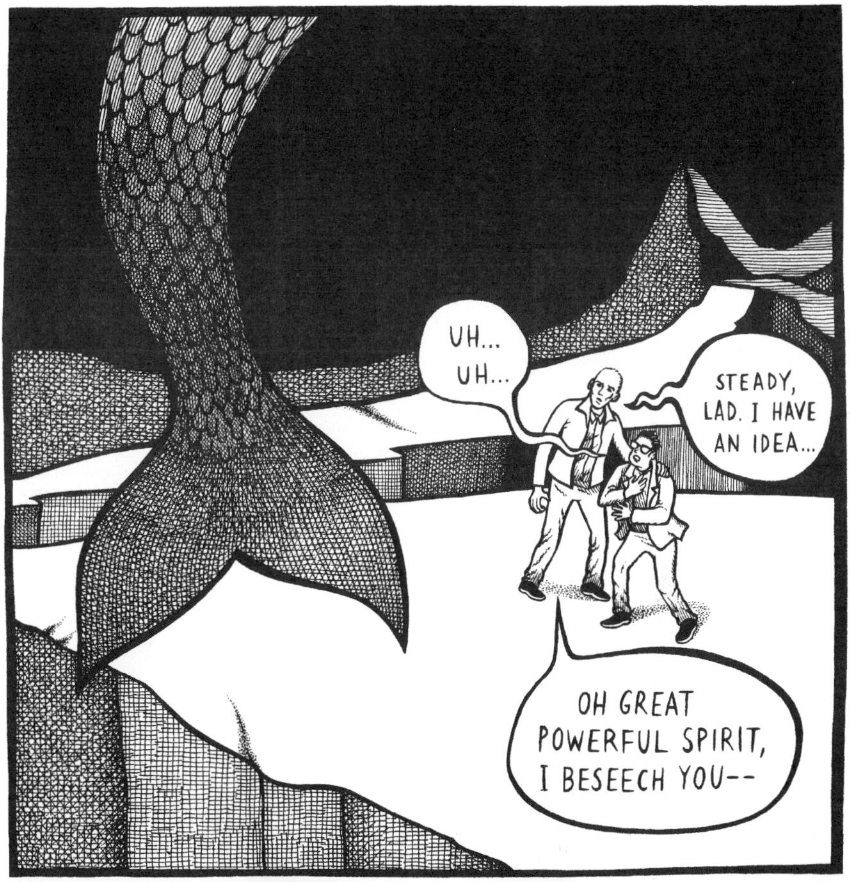
UH... UH...
STEADY, LAD. I HAVE AN IDEA...
OH GREAT POWERFUL SPIRIT, I BESEECH YOU--

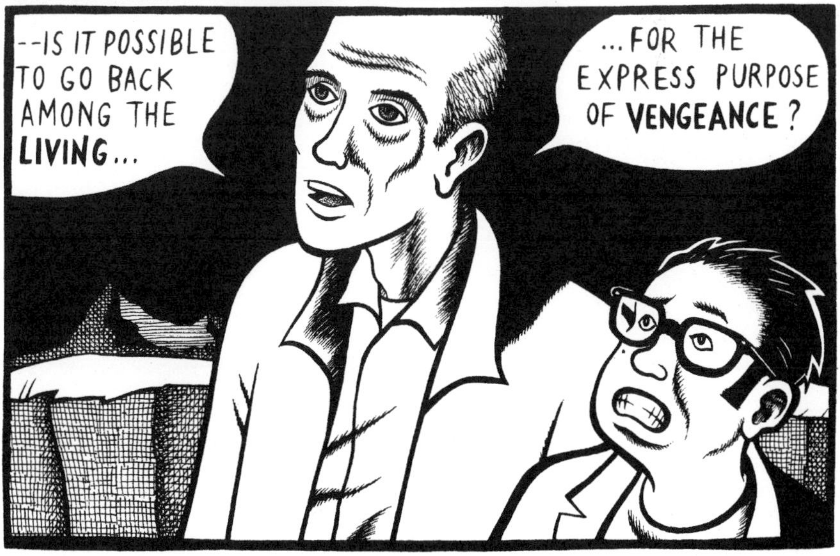
--IS IT POSSIBLE TO GO BACK AMONG THE LIVING...
...FOR THE EXPRESS PURPOSE OF VENGEANCE?

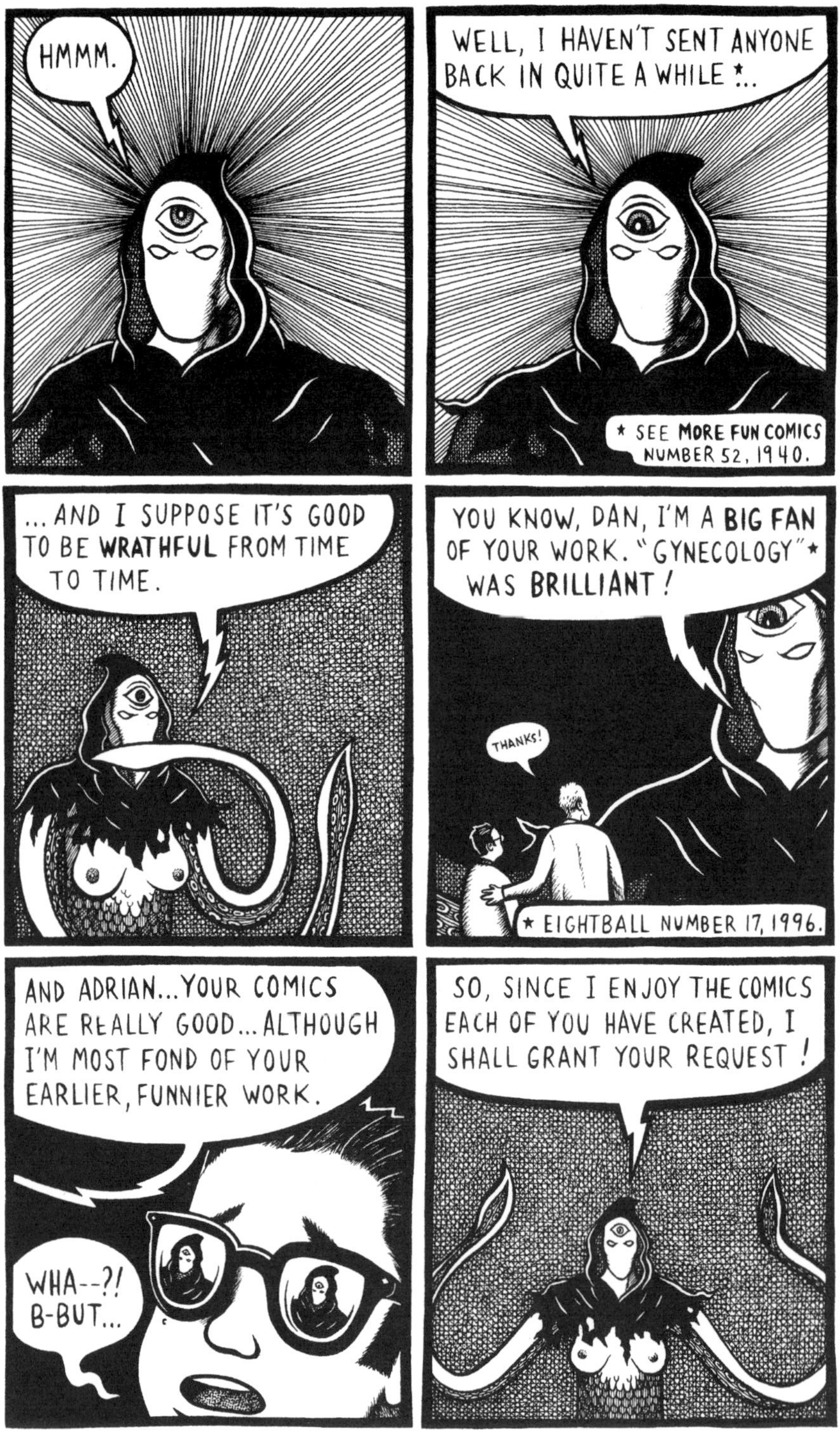
HMMM.
WELL, I HAVEN'T SENT ANYONE BACK IN QUITE A WHILE*...
* SEE MORE FUN COMICS NUMBER 52, 1940.
... AND I SUPPOSE IT'S GOOD TO BE WRATHFUL FROM TIME TO TIME.
YOU KNOW, DAN, I'M A BIG FAN OF YOUR WORK. "GYNECOLOGY"* WAS BRILLIANT!
THANKS!
* EIGHTBALL NUMBER 17, 1996.
AND ADRIAN... YOUR COMICS ARE REALLY GOOD... ALTHOUGH I'M MOST FOND OF YOUR EARLIER, FUNNIER WORK.
WHA--?! B-BUT...
SO, SINCE I ENJOY THE COMICS EACH OF YOU HAVE CREATED, I SHALL GRANT YOUR REQUEST!

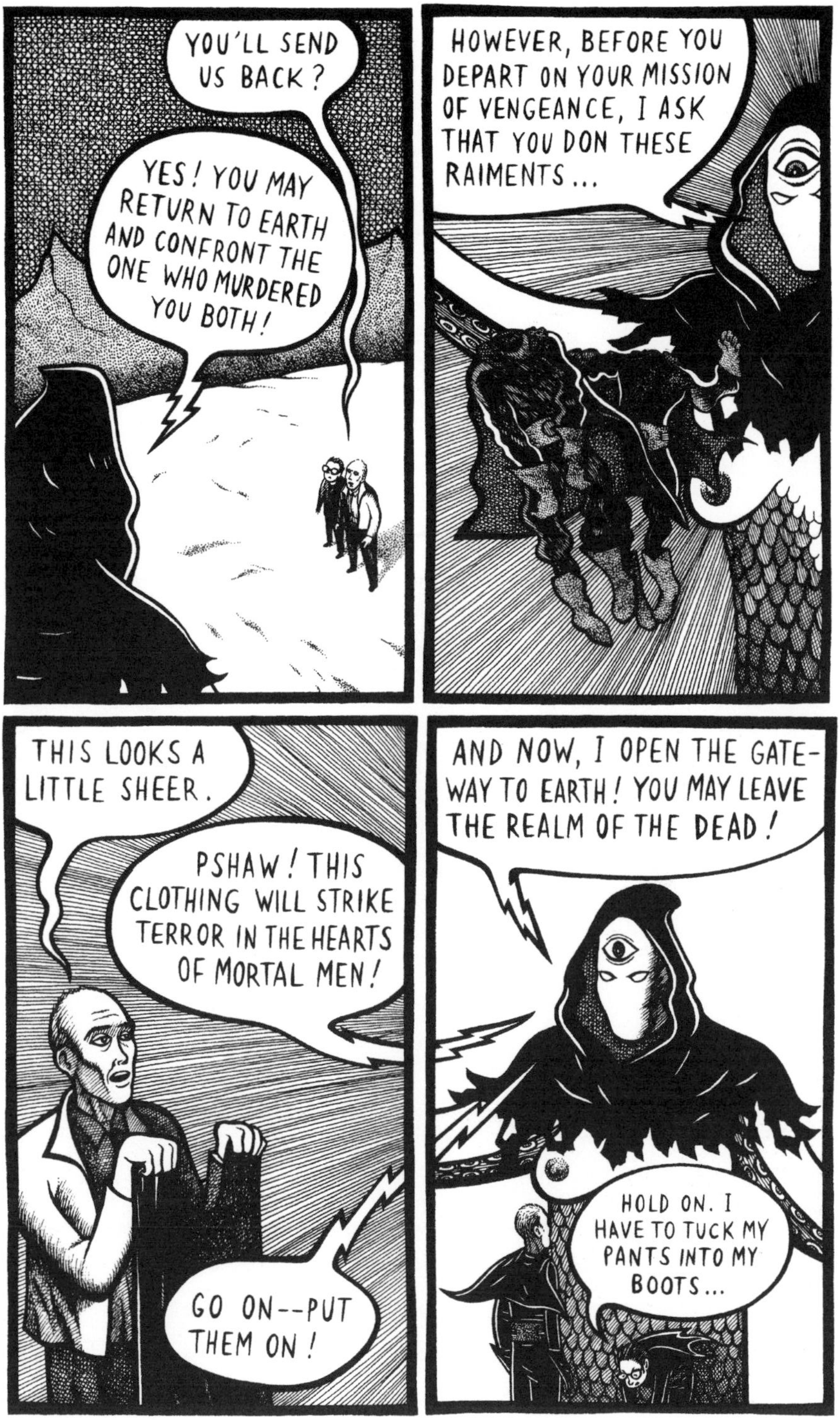
YOU'LL SEND US BACK?
YES! YOU MAY RETURN TO EARTH AND CONFRONT THE ONE WHO MURDERED YOU BOTH!
HOWEVER, BEFORE YOU DEPART ON YOUR MISSION OF VENGEANCE, I ASK THAT YOU DON THESE RAIMENTS...
THIS LOOKS A LITTLE SHEER.
PSHAW! THIS CLOTHING WILL STRIKE TERROR IN THE HEARTS OF MORTAL MEN!
GO ON--PUT THEM ON!
AND NOW, I OPEN THE GATE-WAY TO EARTH! YOU MAY LEAVE THE REALM OF THE DEAD!
HOLD ON. I HAVE TO TUCK MY PANTS INTO MY BOOTS...

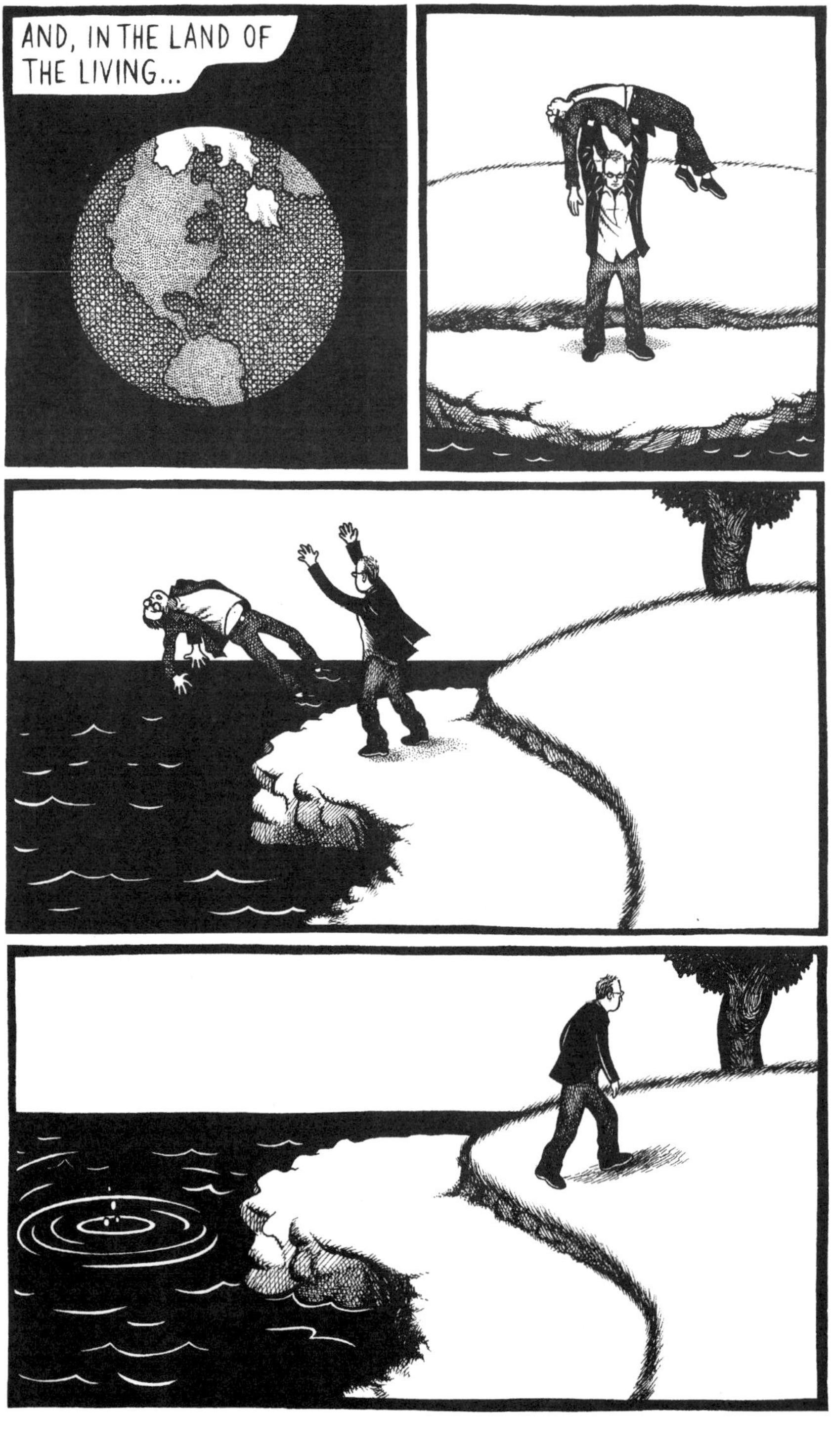
AND, IN THE LAND OF THE LIVING...

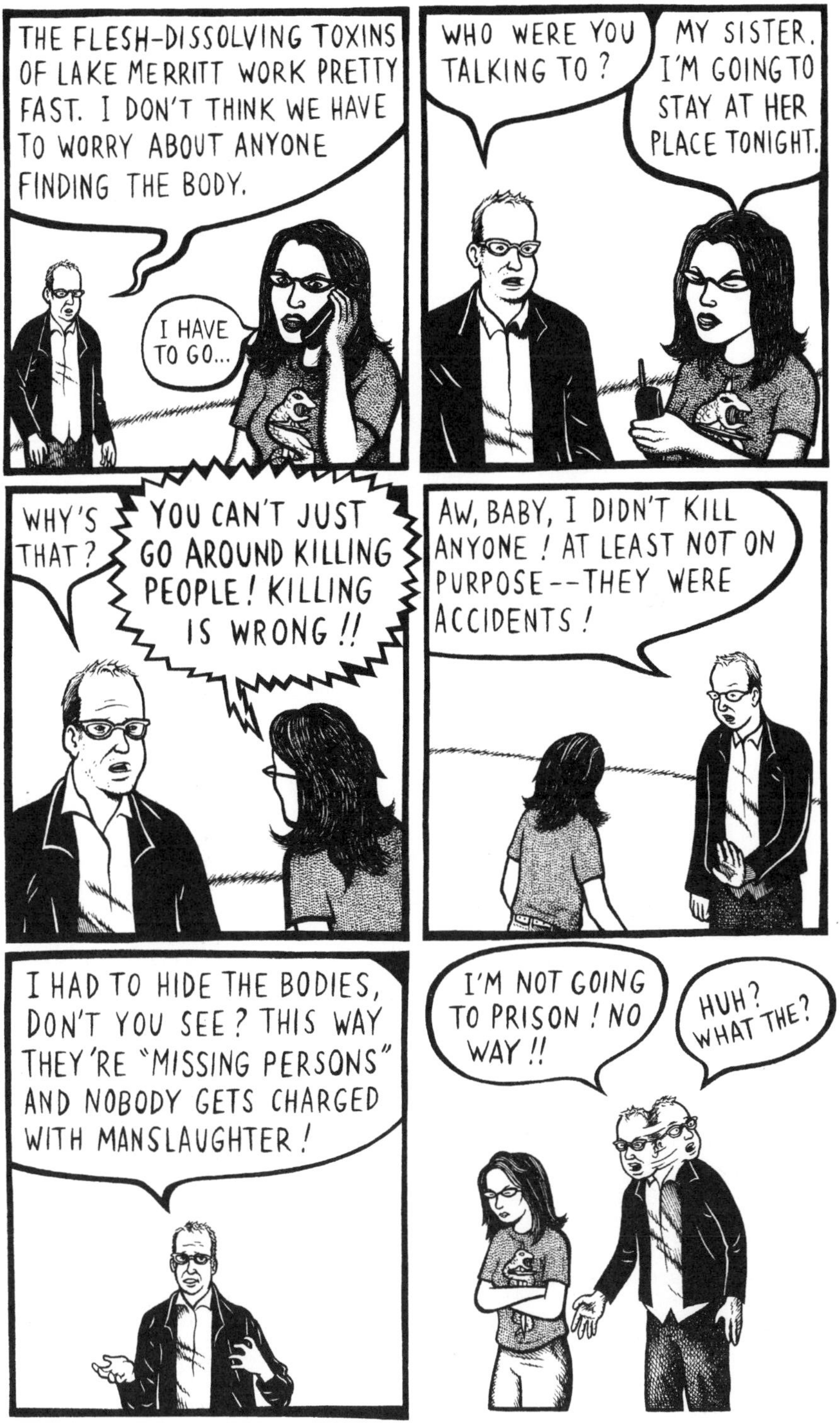

THE FLESH-DISSOLVING TOXINS OF LAKE MERRITT WORK PRETTY FAST. I DON'T THINK WE HAVE TO WORRY ABOUT ANYONE FINDING THE BODY.
I HAVE TO GO...
WHO WERE YOU TALKING TO?
MY SISTER. I'M GOING TO STAY AT HER PLACE TONIGHT.
WHY'S THAT?
YOU CAN'T JUST GO AROUND KILLING PEOPLE! KILLING IS WRONG!!
AW, BABY, I DIDN'T KILL ANYONE! AT LEAST NOT ON PURPOSE--THEY WERE ACCIDENTS!
I HAD TO HIDE THE BODIES, DON'T YOU SEE? THIS WAY THEY'RE "MISSING PERSONS" AND NOBODY GETS CHARGED WITH MANSLAUGHTER!
I'M NOT GOING TO PRISON! NO WAY!!
HUH? WHAT THE?

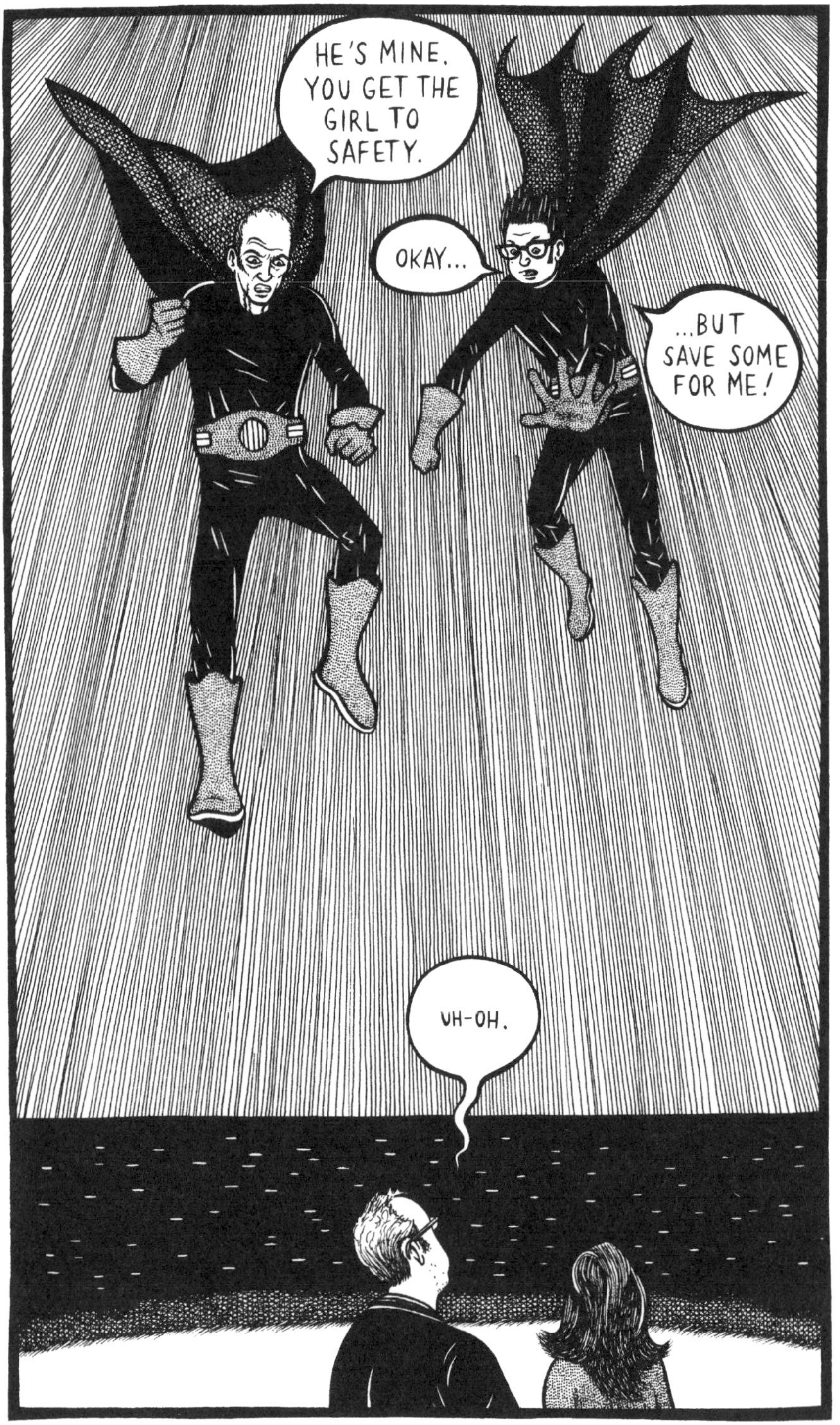
HE'S MINE. YOU GET THE GIRL TO SAFETY.
OKAY...
...BUT SAVE SOME FOR ME!
UH-OH.

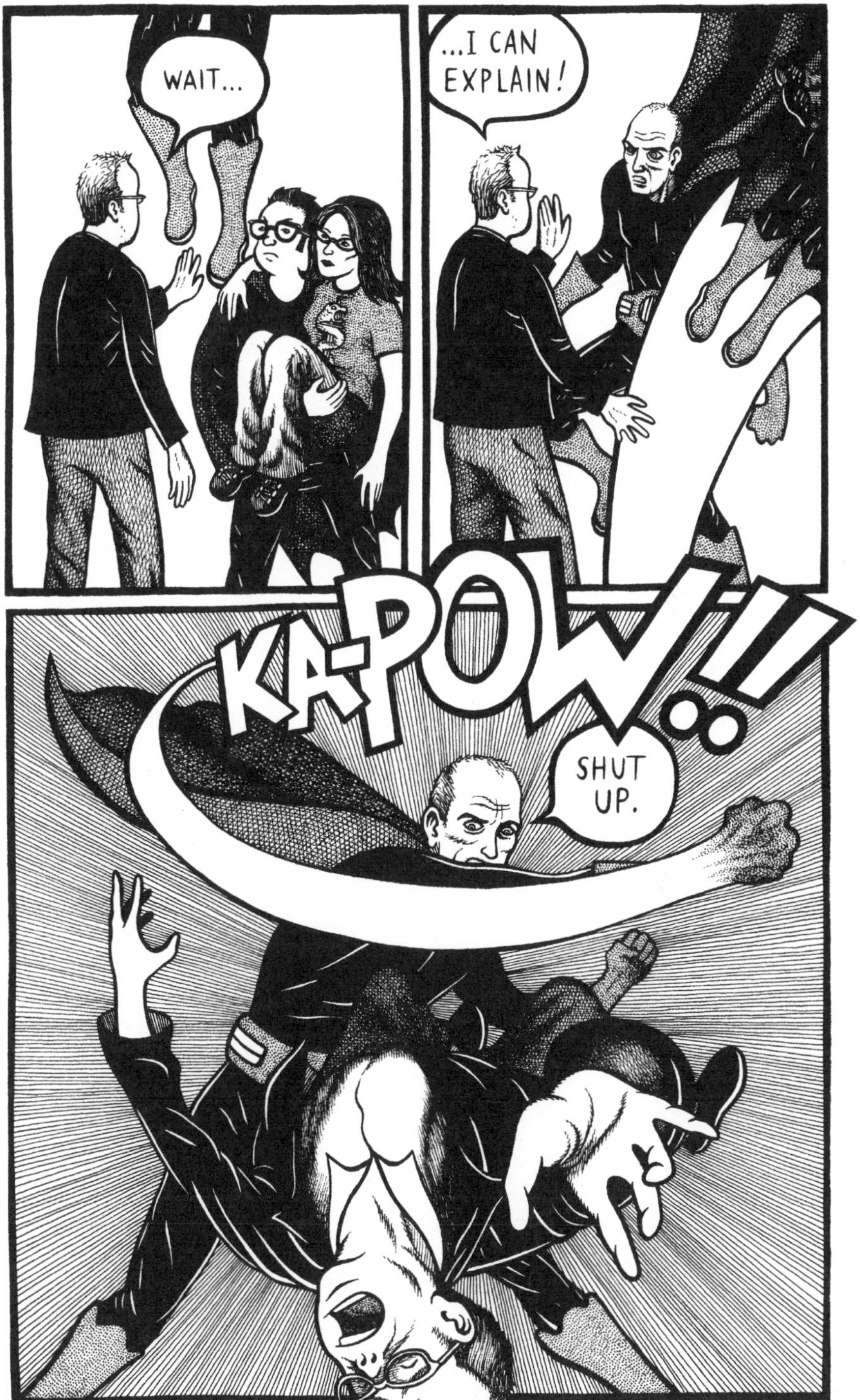
WAIT...
...I CAN EXPLAIN!
KA-POW!!
SHUT UP.

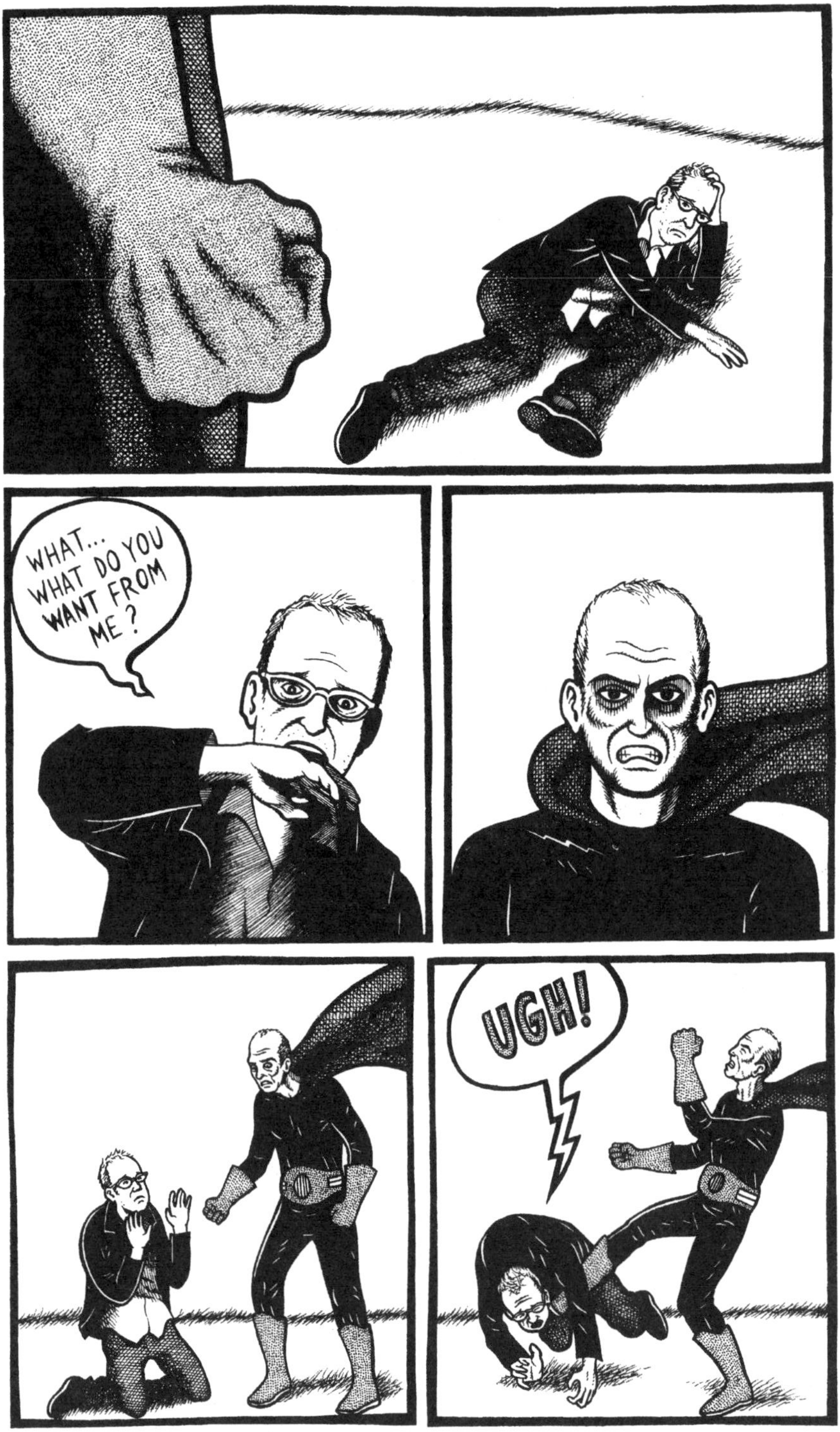
WHAT...
WHAT DO YOU WANT FROM ME?
UGH!

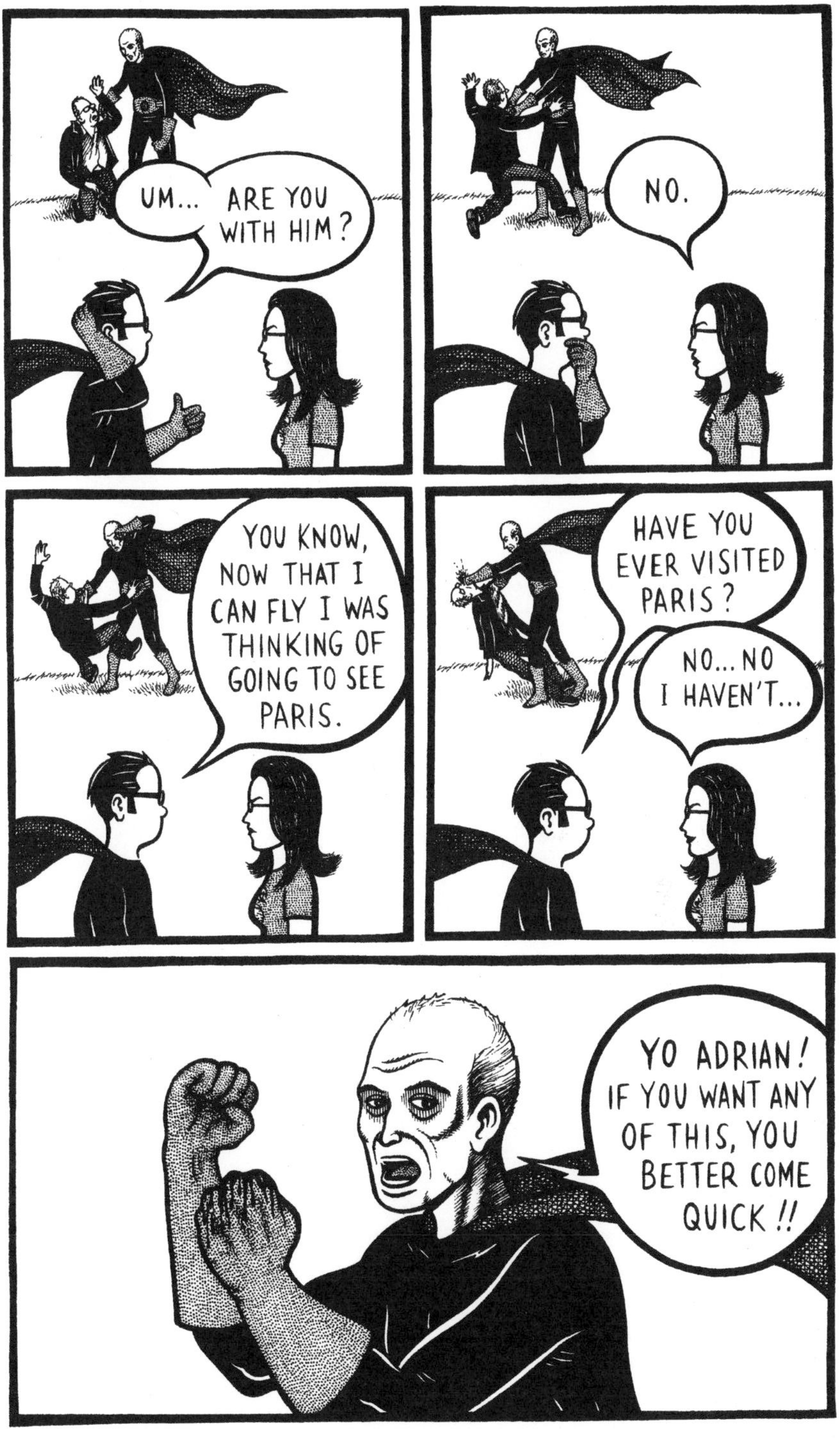
UM... ARE YOU WITH HIM?
NO.
YOU KNOW, NOW THAT I CAN FLY I WAS THINKING OF GOING TO SEE PARIS.
HAVE YOU EVER VISITED PARIS?
NO... NO I HAVEN'T...
YO ADRIAN! IF YOU WANT ANY OF THIS, YOU BETTER COME QUICK!!

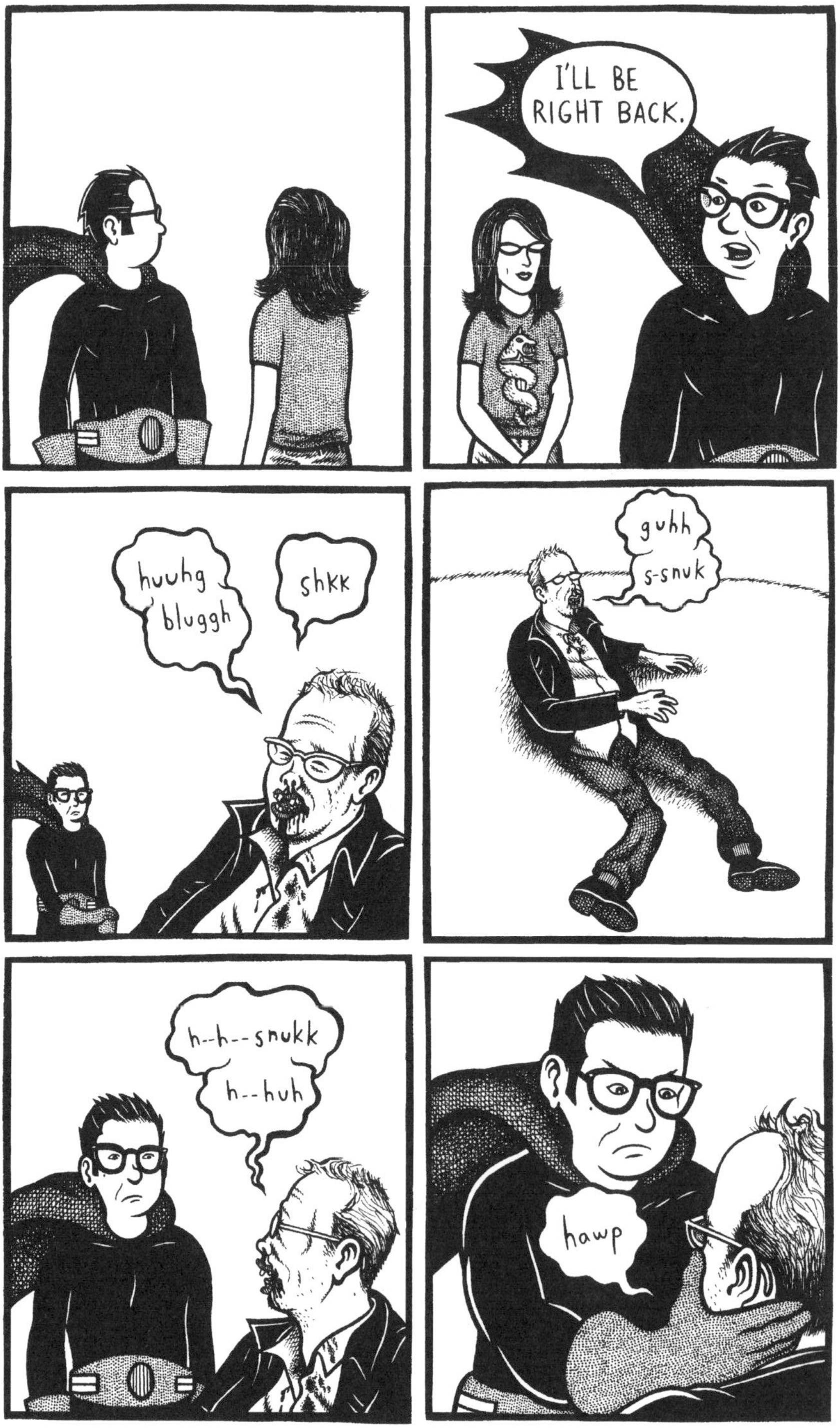
I'LL BE RIGHT BACK.
huuhg bluggh
shkk
guhh s-snuk
h--h--snukk h--huh
hawp

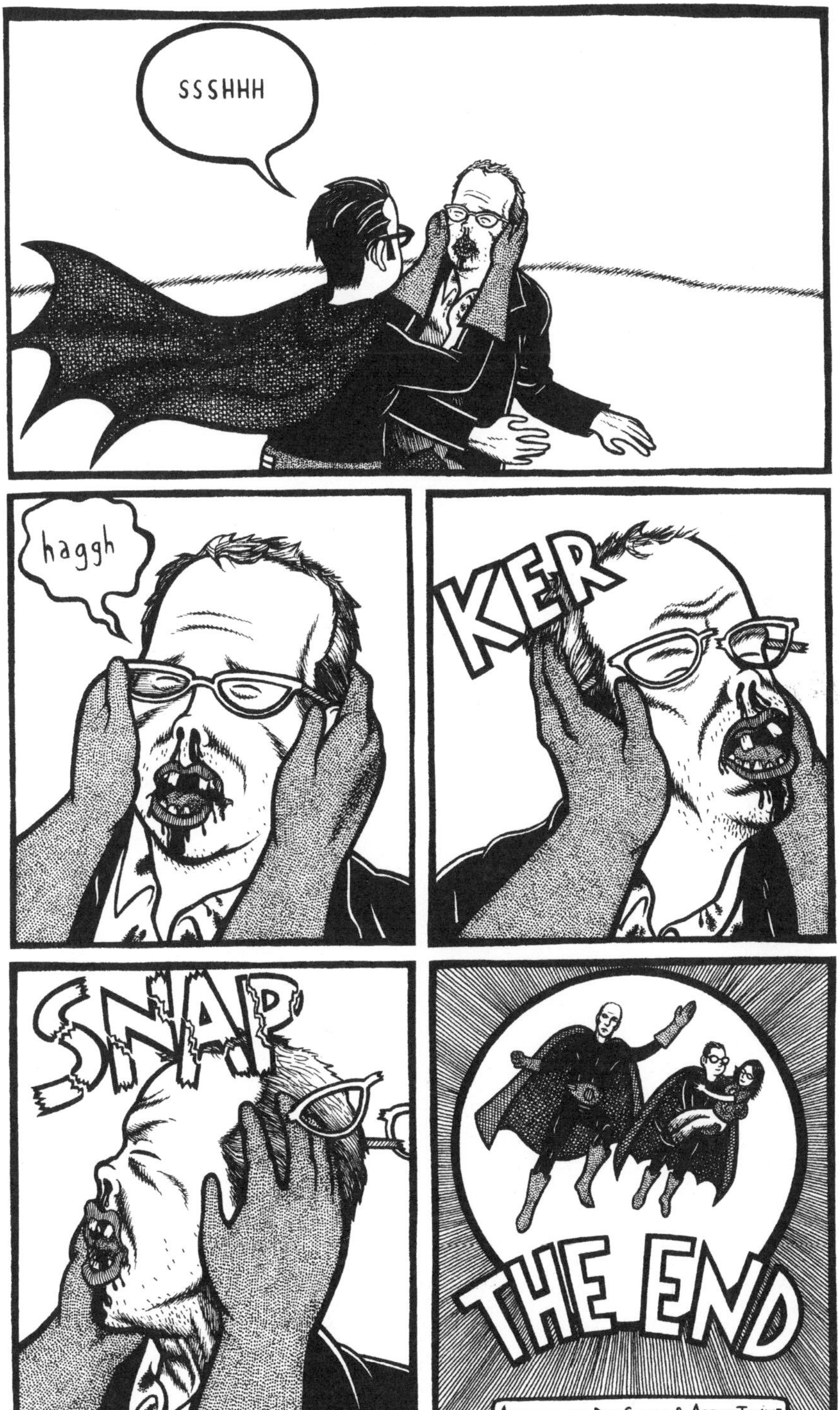
SSSHHH
hagggh
KER
SNAP
THE END
Apologies to Dan Clowes & Adrian Tomine

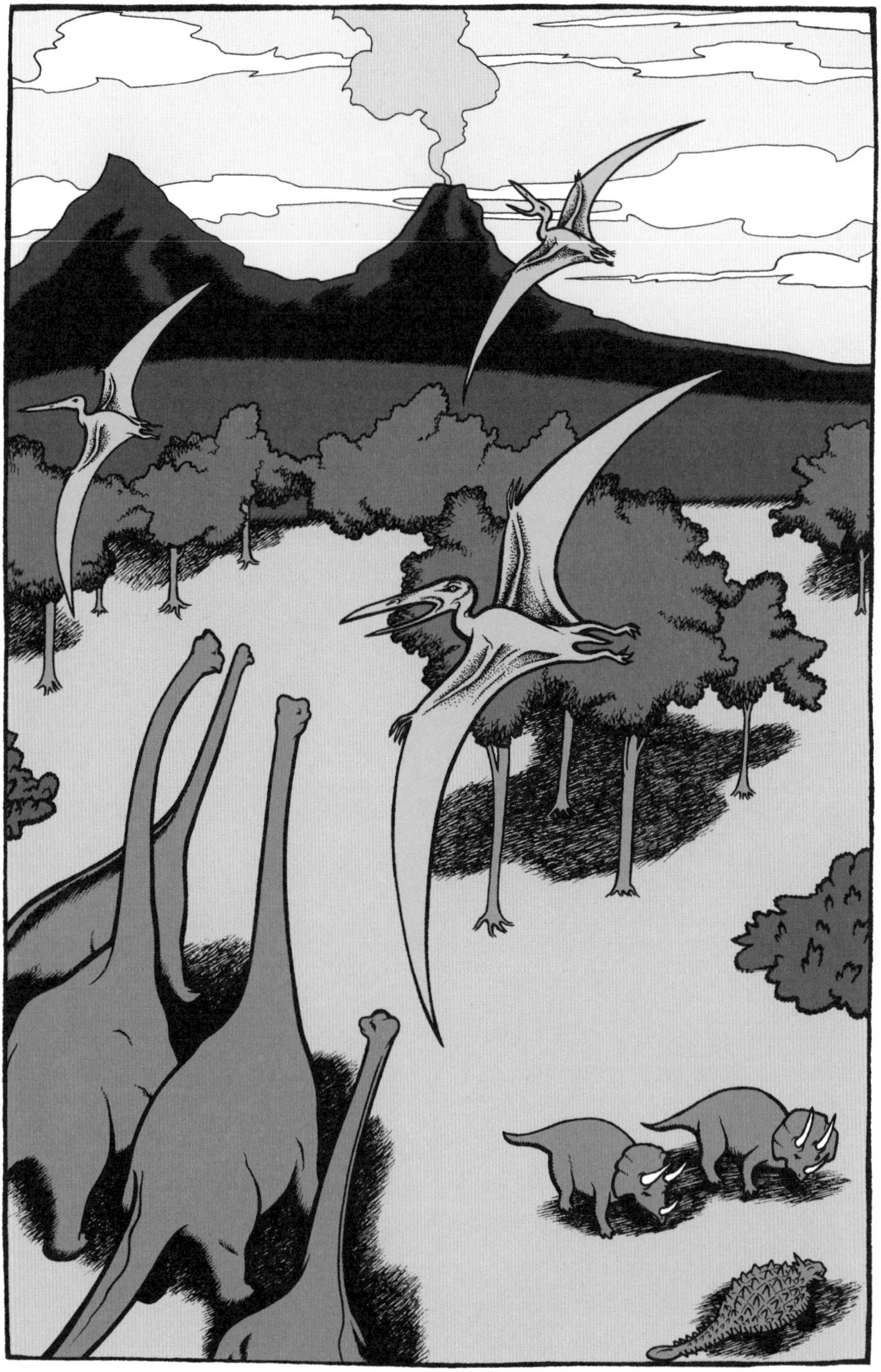

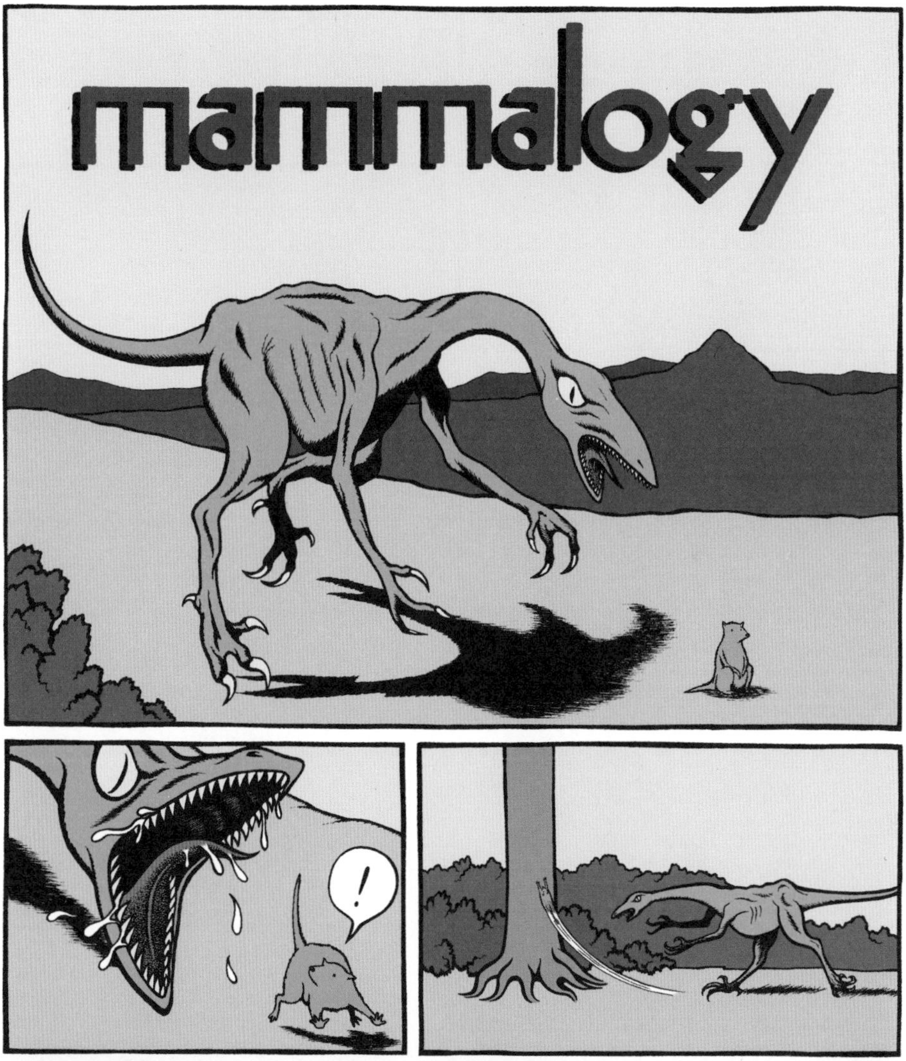
mammalogy
!

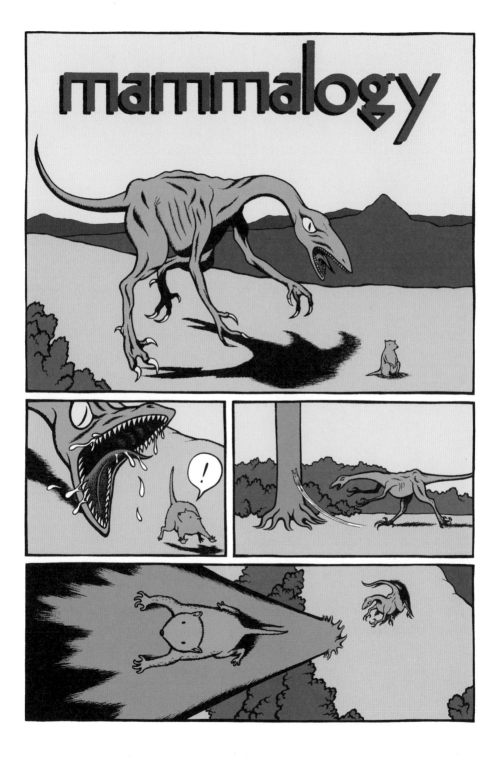

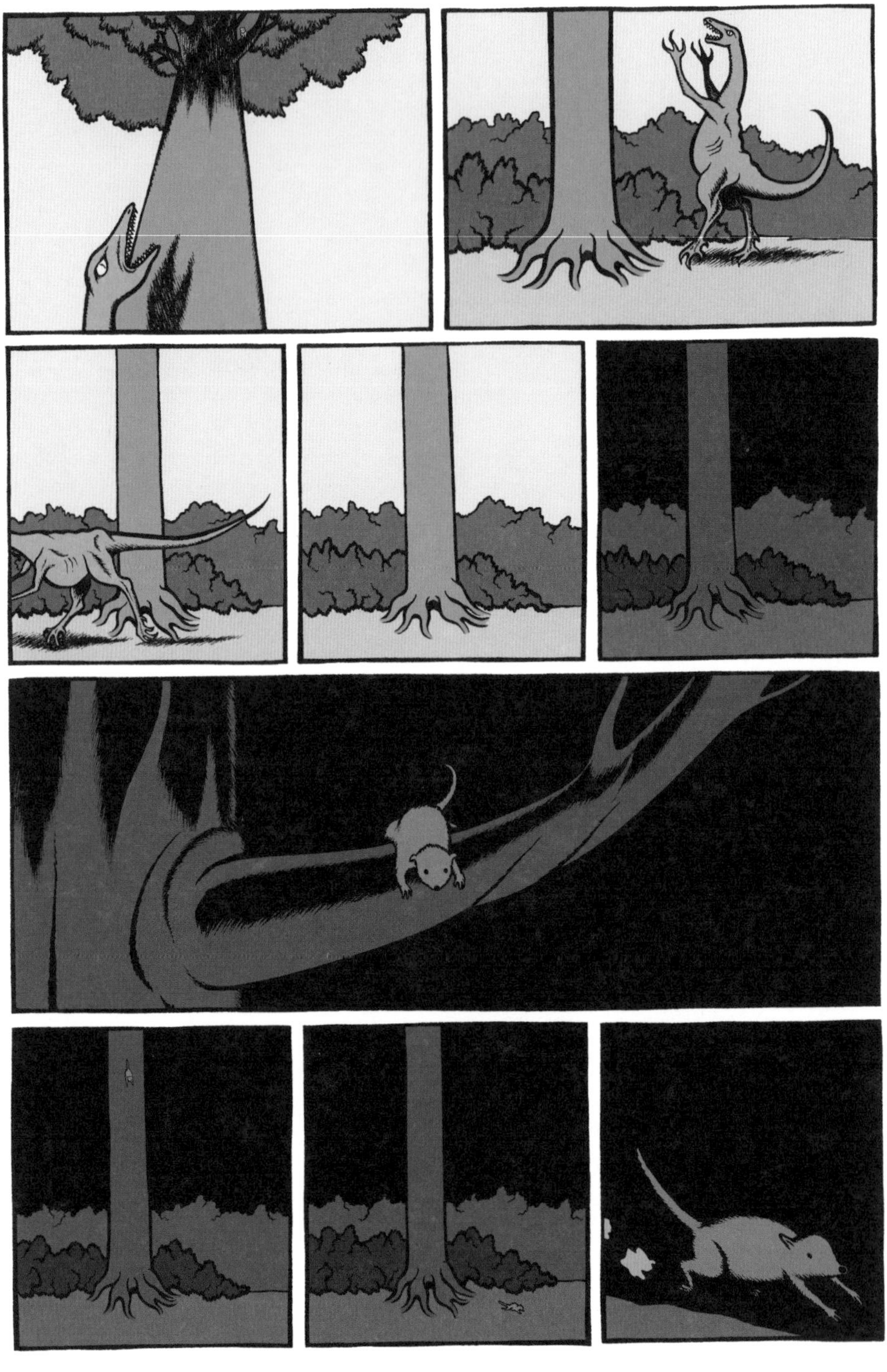

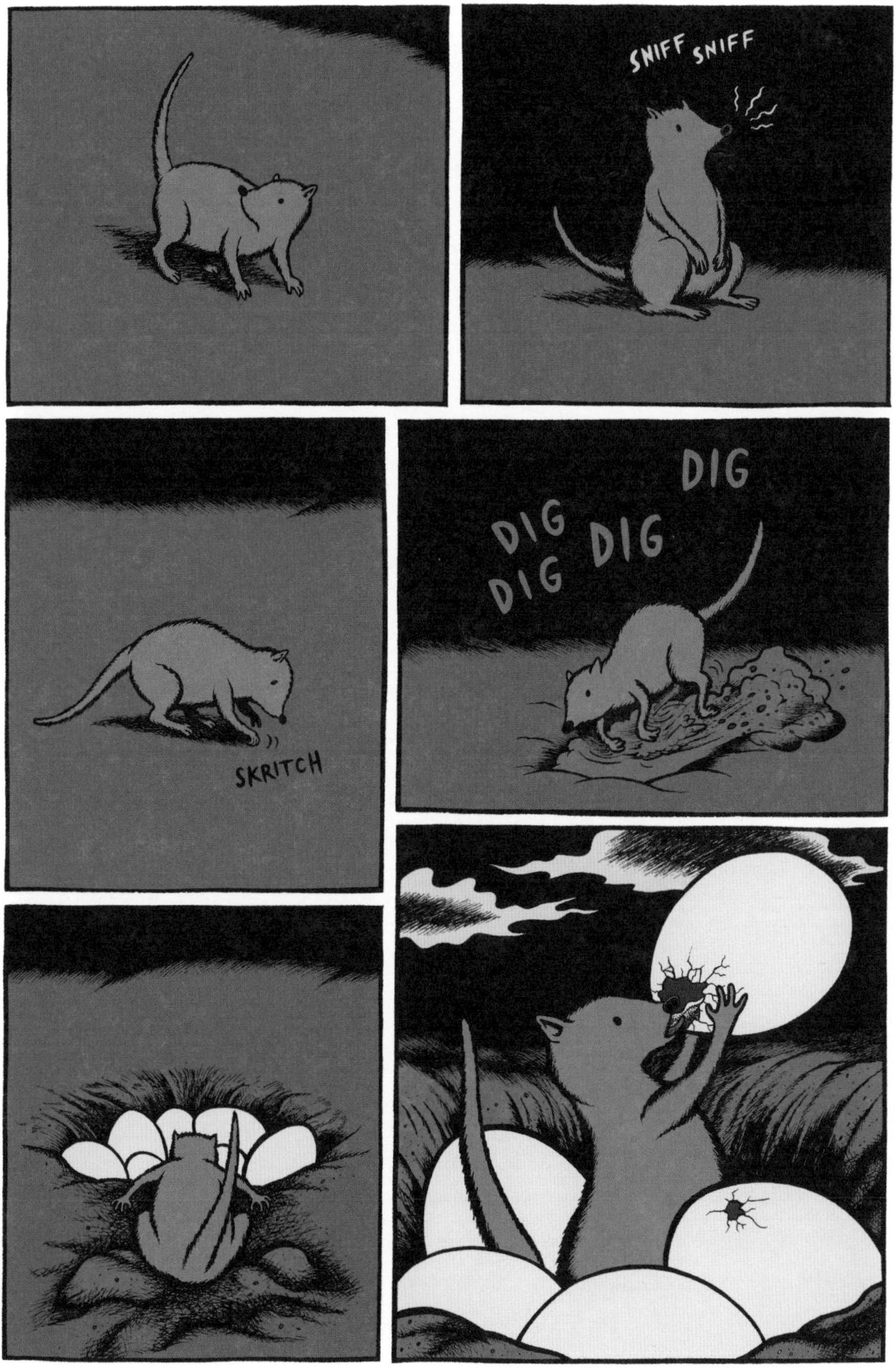
SNIFF SNIFF
SKRITCH
DIG
DIG
DIG
DIG

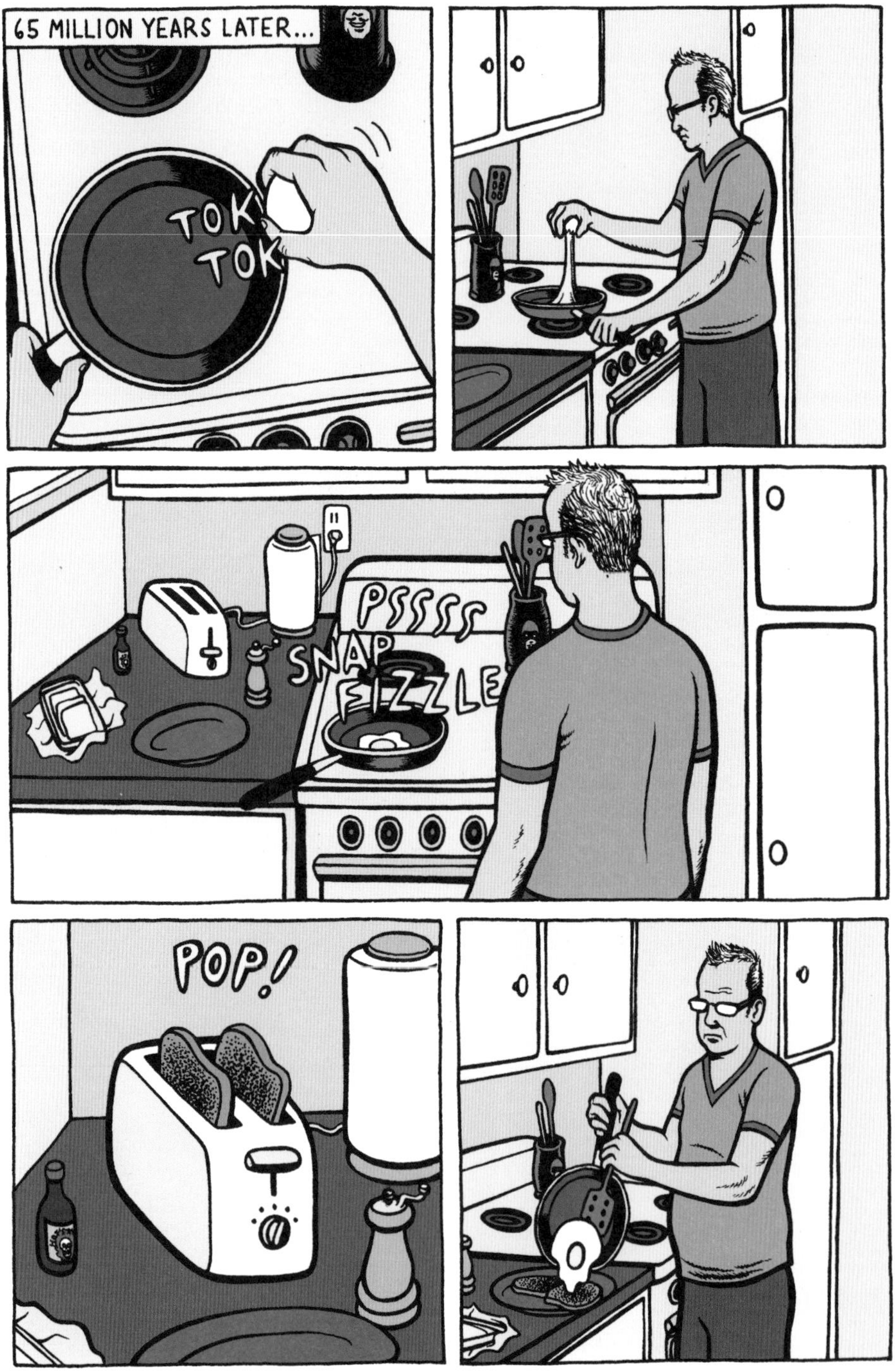
65 MILLION YEARS LATER...
TOK TOK
PSSSS
SNAP
FIZZLE
POP!

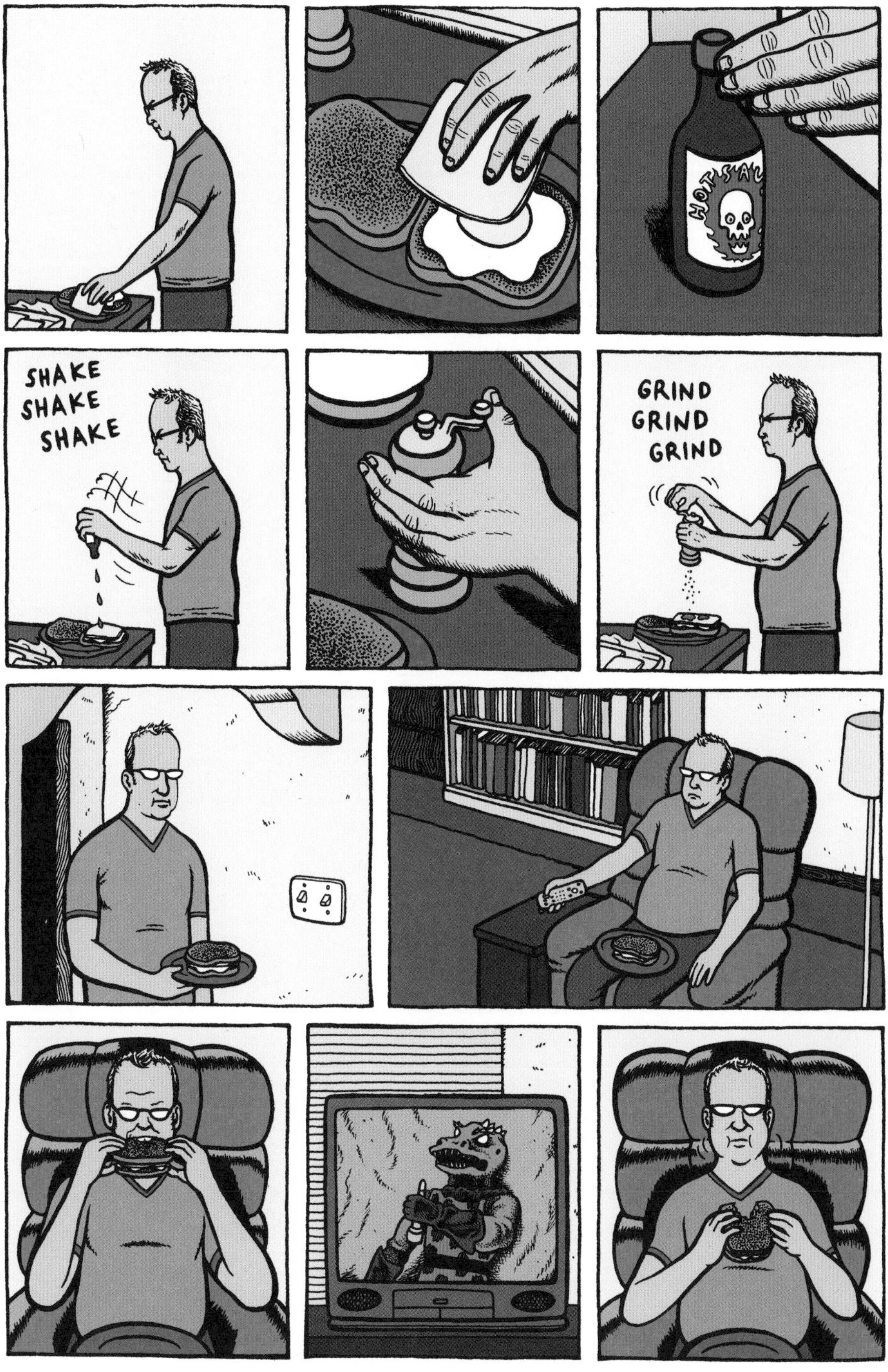
HOT SAUCE
SHAKE
SHAKE
SHAKE
GRIND
GRIND
GRIND

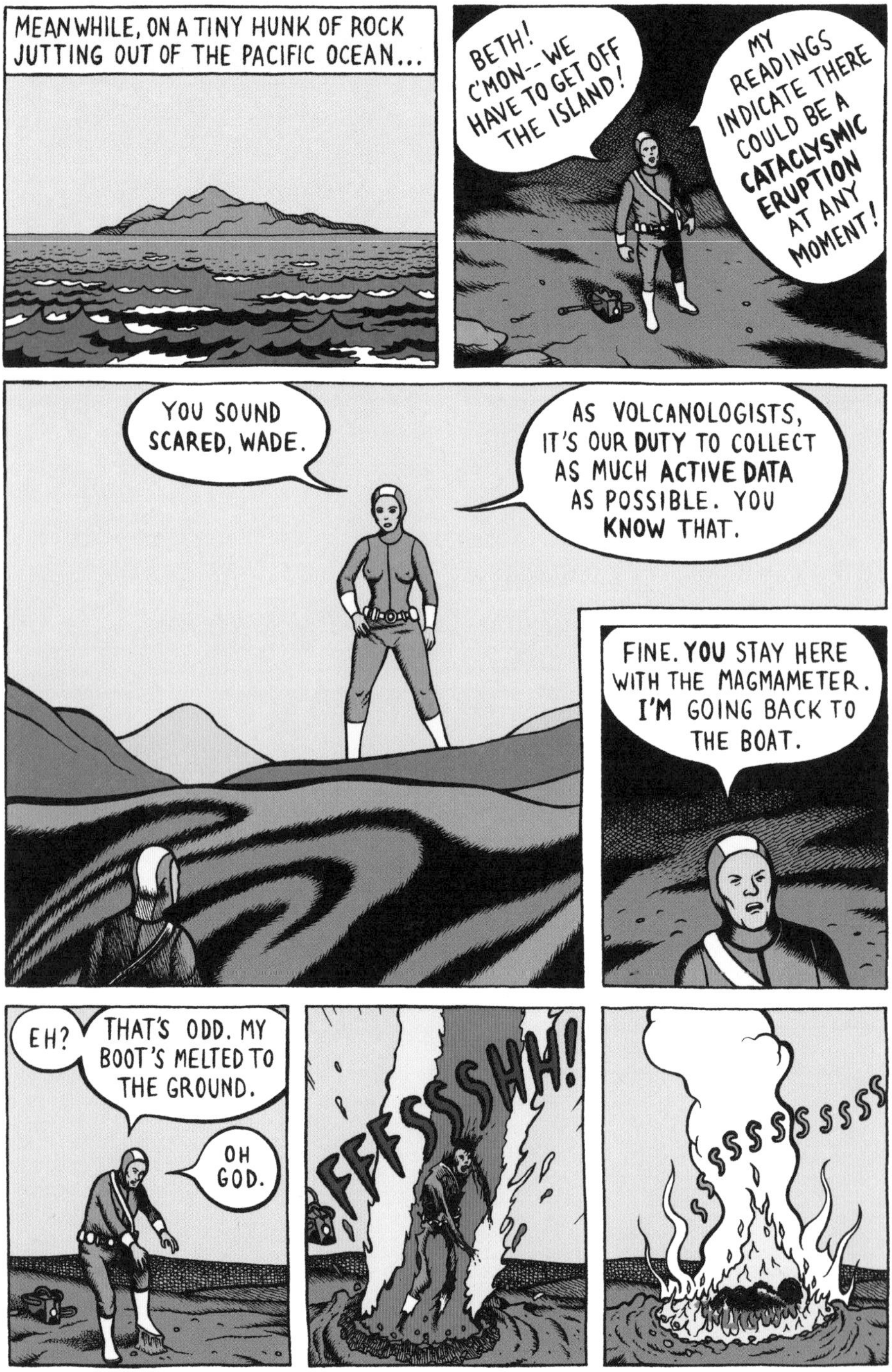
MEANWHILE, ON A TINY HUNK OF ROCK JUTTING OUT OF THE PACIFIC OCEAN...
BETH! C'MON-- WE HAVE TO GET OFF THE ISLAND!
MY READINGS INDICATE THERE COULD BE A CATACLYSMIC ERUPTION AT ANY MOMENT!
YOU SOUND SCARED, WADE.
AS VOLCANOLOGISTS, IT'S OUR DUTY TO COLLECT AS MUCH ACTIVE DATA AS POSSIBLE. YOU KNOW THAT.
FINE. YOU STAY HERE WITH THE MAGMAMETER. I'M GOING BACK TO THE BOAT.
EH?
THAT'S ODD. MY BOOT'S MELTED TO THE GROUND.
OH GOD.
FFFSSSHH!
SSSSSSSSSS

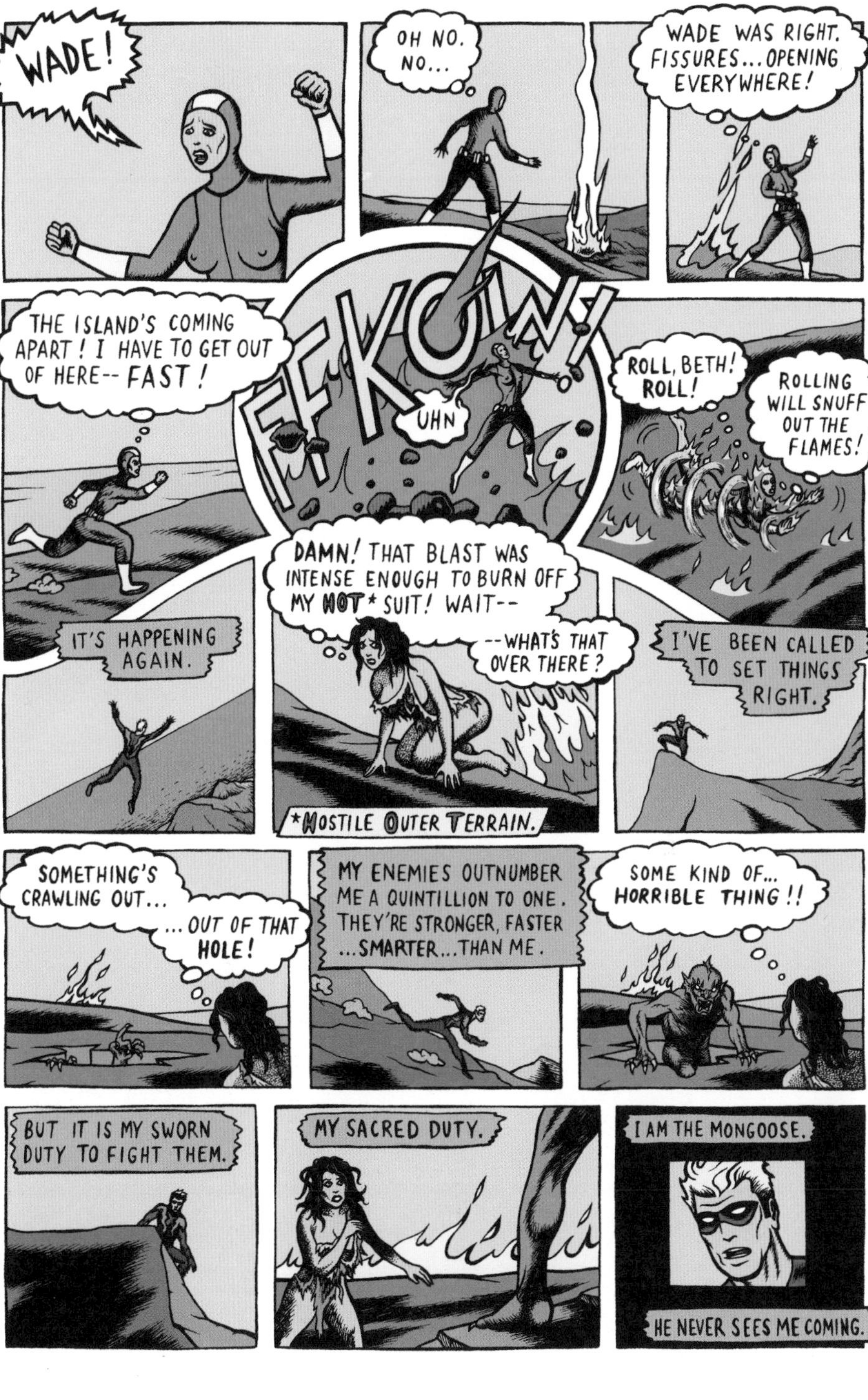
WADE!
OH NO. NO...
WADE WAS RIGHT. FISSURES...OPENING EVERYWHERE!
THE ISLAND'S COMING APART! I HAVE TO GET OUT OF HERE-- FAST!
FFKOOM!
UHN
ROLL, BETH! ROLL!
ROLLING WILL SNUFF OUT THE FLAMES!
IT'S HAPPENING AGAIN.
DAMN! THAT BLAST WAS INTENSE ENOUGH TO BURN OFF MY HOT* SUIT! WAIT--
--WHAT'S THAT OVER THERE?
*HOSTILE OUTER TERRAIN.
I'VE BEEN CALLED TO SET THINGS RIGHT.
SOMETHING'S CRAWLING OUT...
...OUT OF THAT HOLE!
MY ENEMIES OUTNUMBER ME A QUINTILLION TO ONE. THEY'RE STRONGER, FASTER ...SMARTER...THAN ME.
SOME KIND OF... HORRIBLE THING!!
BUT IT IS MY SWORN DUTY TO FIGHT THEM.
MY SACRED DUTY.
I AM THE MONGOOSE.
HE NEVER SEES ME COMING.

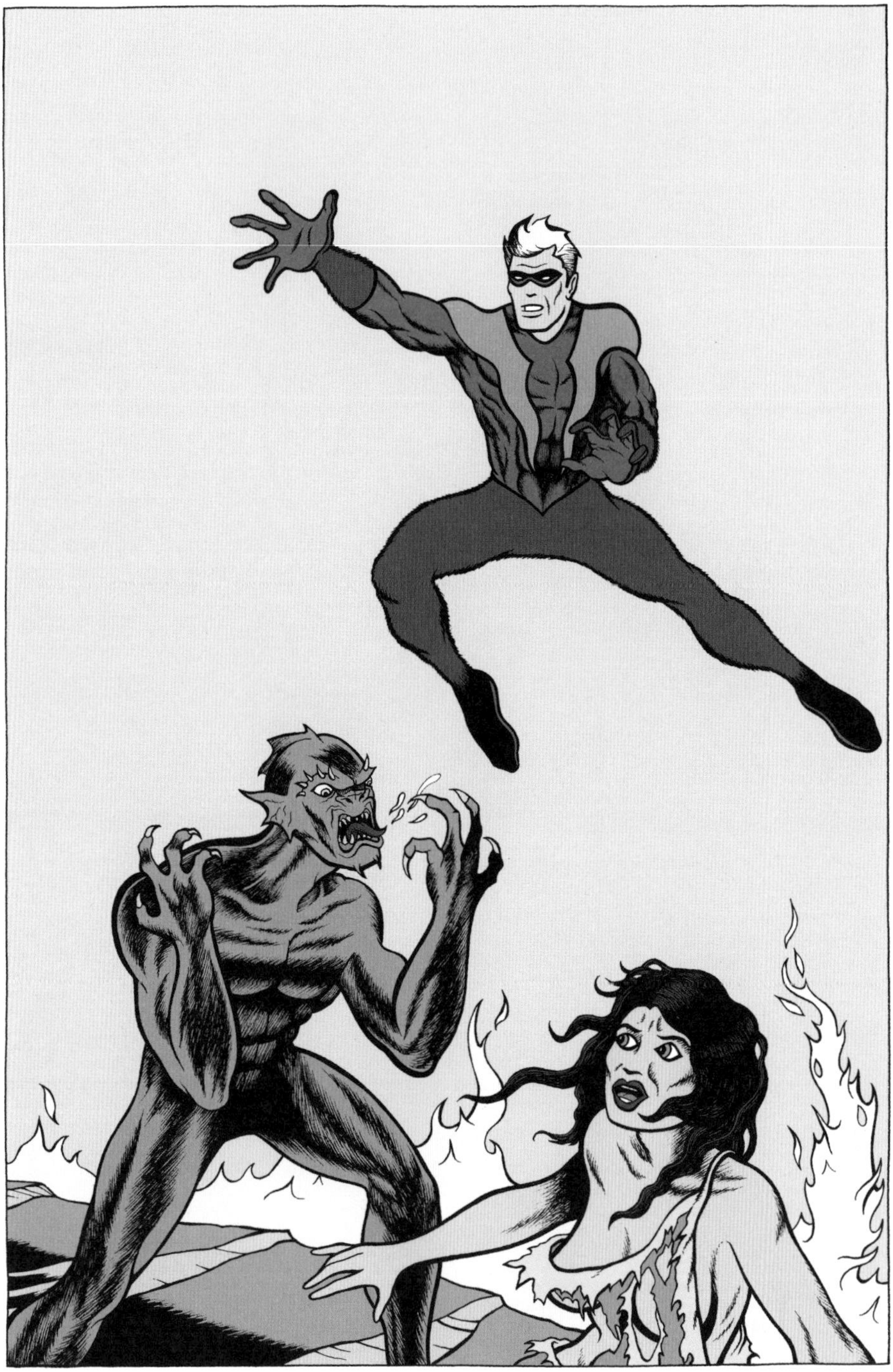

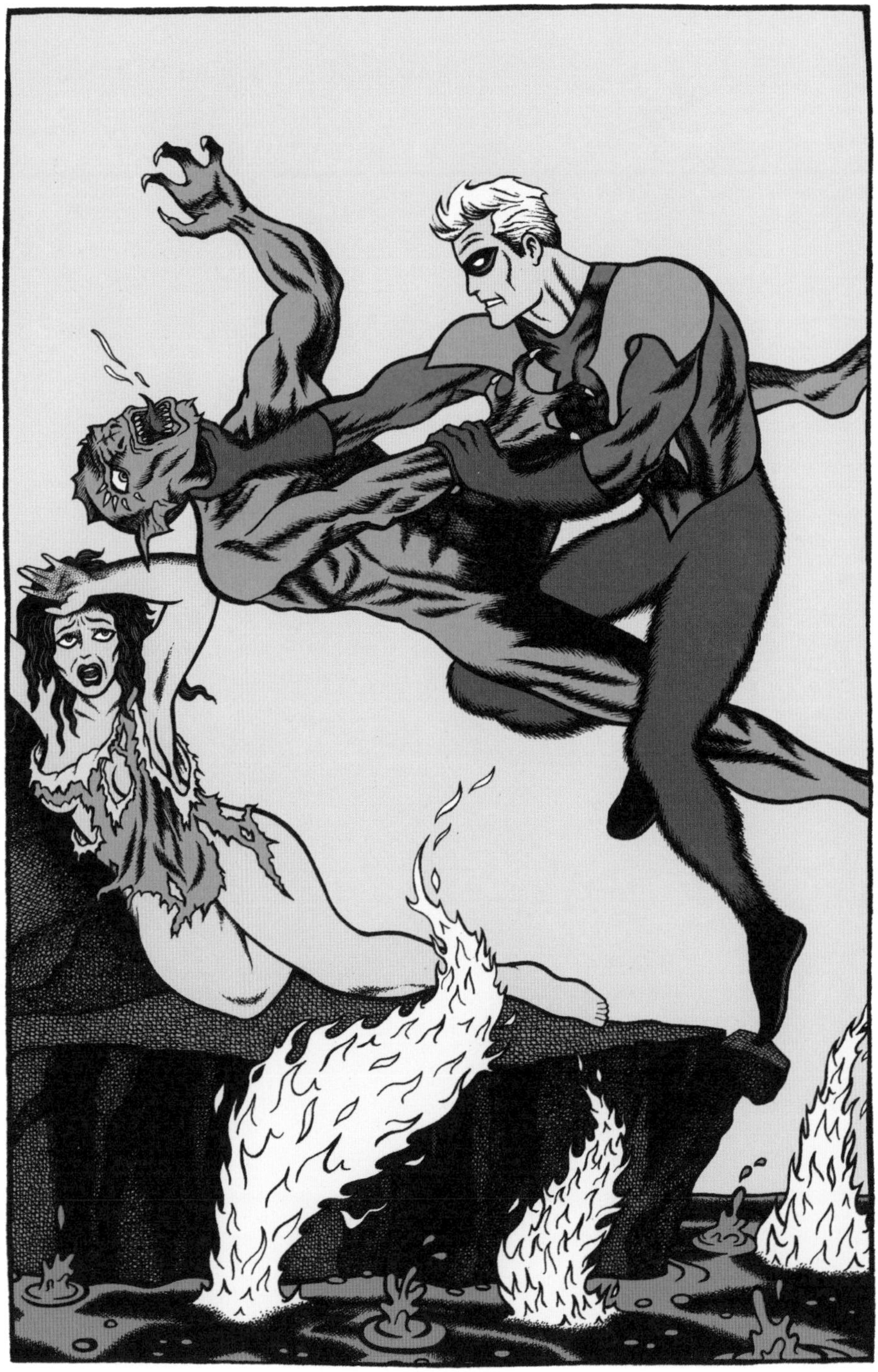

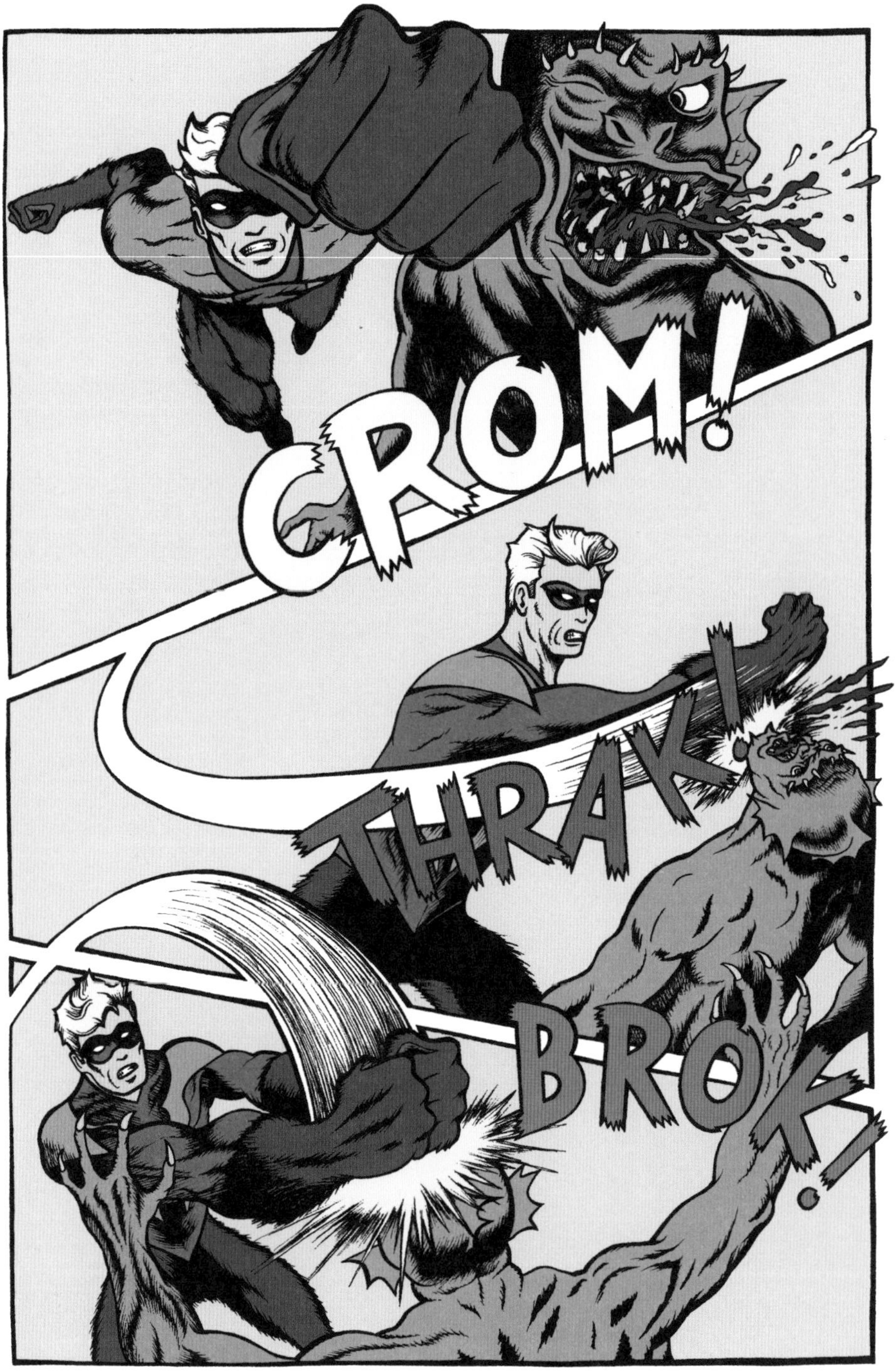
CROM!
THRAK!
BROK!

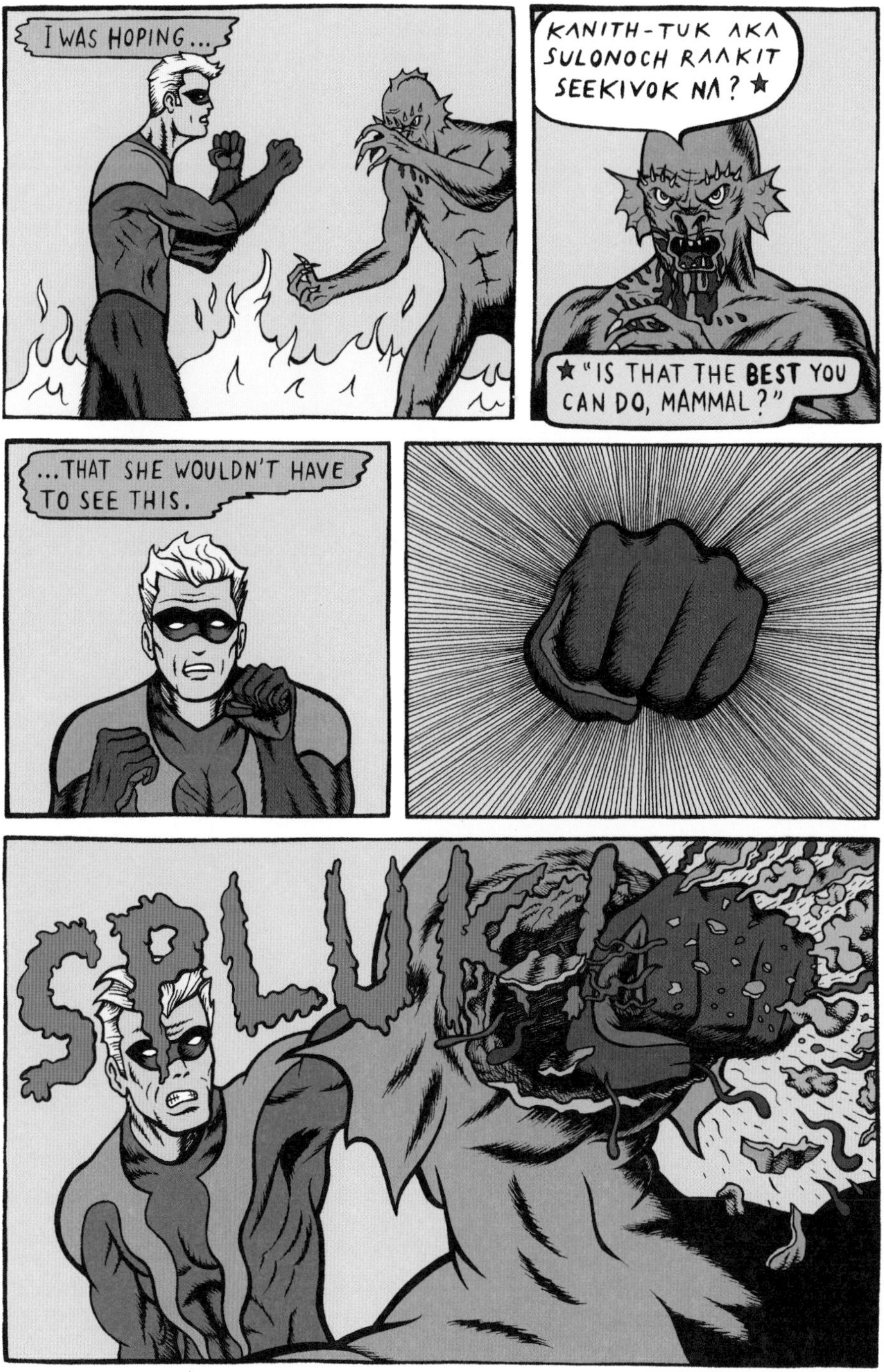
I WAS HOPING...
KANITH-TUK AKA SULONOCH RAAKIT SEEKIVOK NA? ★
★ "IS THAT THE BEST YOU CAN DO, MAMMAL?"
...THAT SHE WOULDN'T HAVE TO SEE THIS.
SPLU

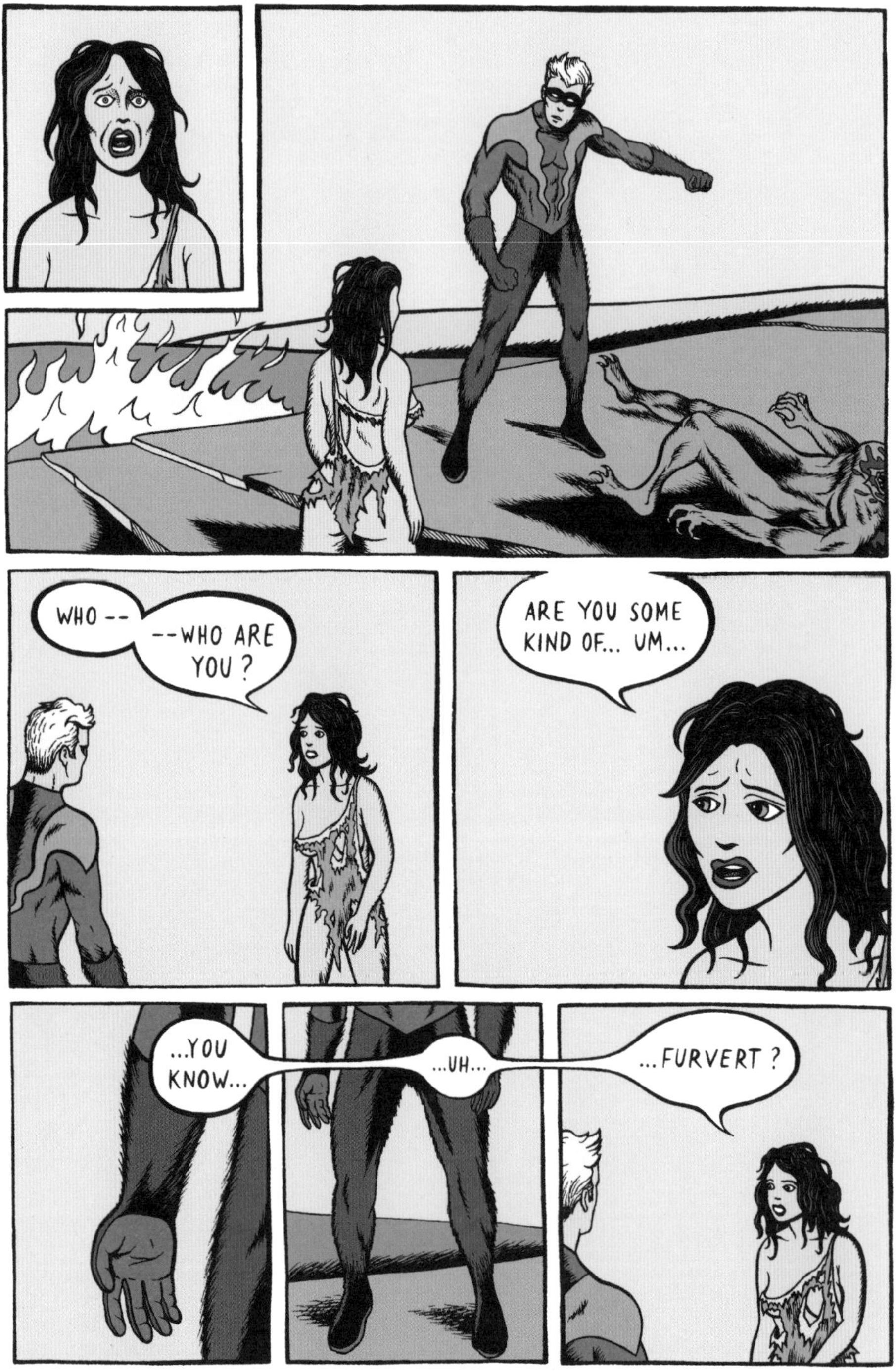
WHO --
--WHO ARE YOU ?
ARE YOU SOME KIND OF... UM...
...YOU KNOW...
...UH...
...FURVERT ?

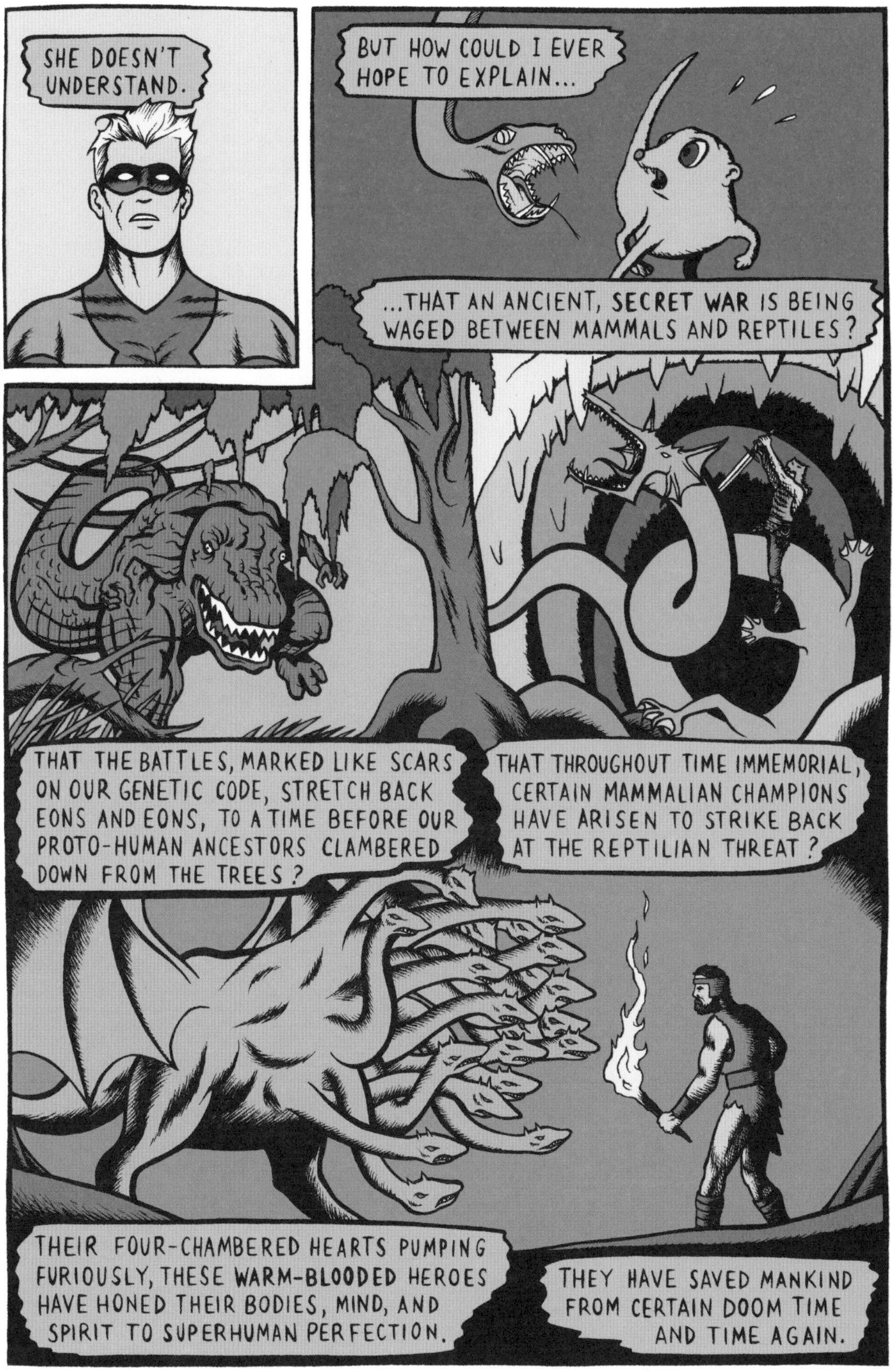
SHE DOESN'T UNDERSTAND.
BUT HOW COULD I EVER HOPE TO EXPLAIN...
...THAT AN ANCIENT, SECRET WAR IS BEING WAGED BETWEEN MAMMALS AND REPTILES?
THAT THE BATTLES, MARKED LIKE SCARS ON OUR GENETIC CODE, STRETCH BACK EONS AND EONS, TO A TIME BEFORE OUR PROTO-HUMAN ANCESTORS CLAMBERED DOWN FROM THE TREES?
THAT THROUGHOUT TIME IMMEMORIAL, CERTAIN MAMMALIAN CHAMPIONS HAVE ARISEN TO STRIKE BACK AT THE REPTILIAN THREAT?
THEIR FOUR-CHAMBERED HEARTS PUMPING FURIOUSLY, THESE WARM-BLOODED HEROES HAVE HONED THEIR BODIES, MIND, AND SPIRIT TO SUPERHUMAN PERFECTION.
THEY HAVE SAVED MANKIND FROM CERTAIN DOOM TIME AND TIME AGAIN.

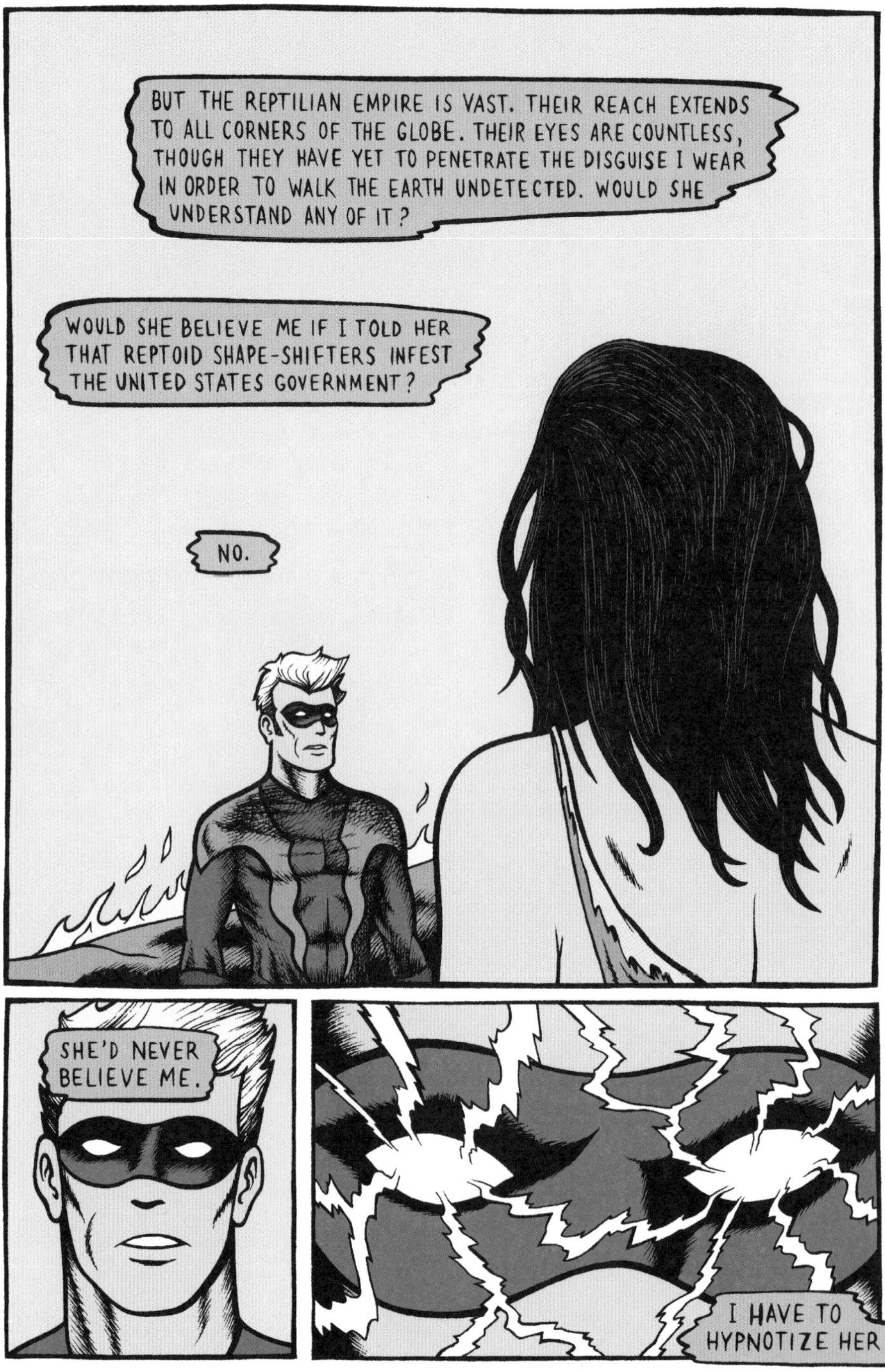
BUT THE REPTILIAN EMPIRE IS VAST. THEIR REACH EXTENDS TO ALL CORNERS OF THE GLOBE. THEIR EYES ARE COUNTLESS, THOUGH THEY HAVE YET TO PENETRATE THE DISGUISE I WEAR IN ORDER TO WALK THE EARTH UNDETECTED. WOULD SHE UNDERSTAND ANY OF IT?
WOULD SHE BELIEVE ME IF I TOLD HER THAT REPTOID SHAPE-SHIFTERS INFEST THE UNITED STATES GOVERNMENT?
NO.
SHE'D NEVER BELIEVE ME.
I HAVE TO HYPNOTIZE HER.

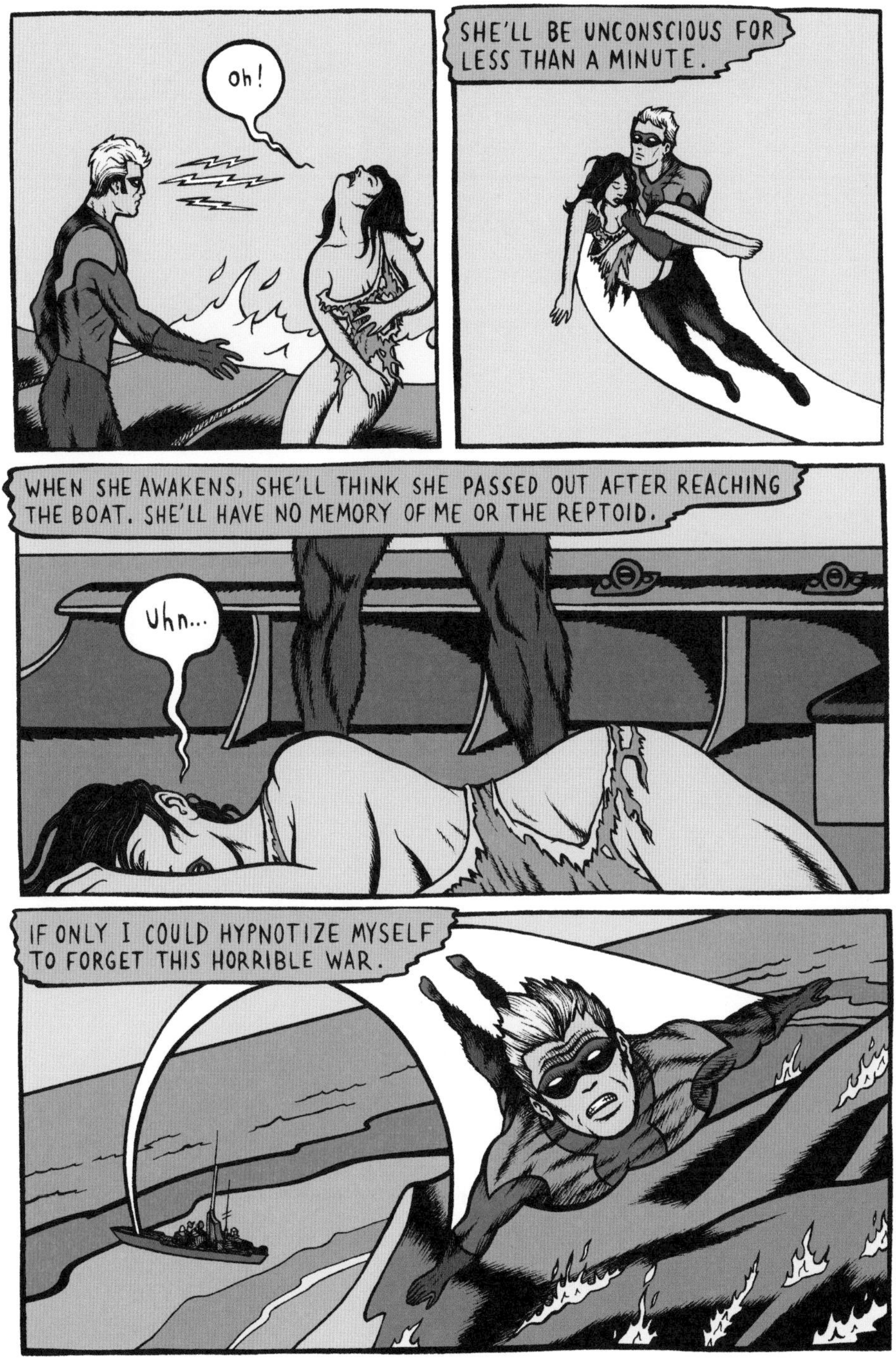
Oh!
SHE'LL BE UNCONSCIOUS FOR LESS THAN A MINUTE.
WHEN SHE AWAKENS, SHE'LL THINK SHE PASSED OUT AFTER REACHING THE BOAT. SHE'LL HAVE NO MEMORY OF ME OR THE REPTOID.
Uhn...
IF ONLY I COULD HYPNOTIZE MYSELF TO FORGET THIS HORRIBLE WAR.

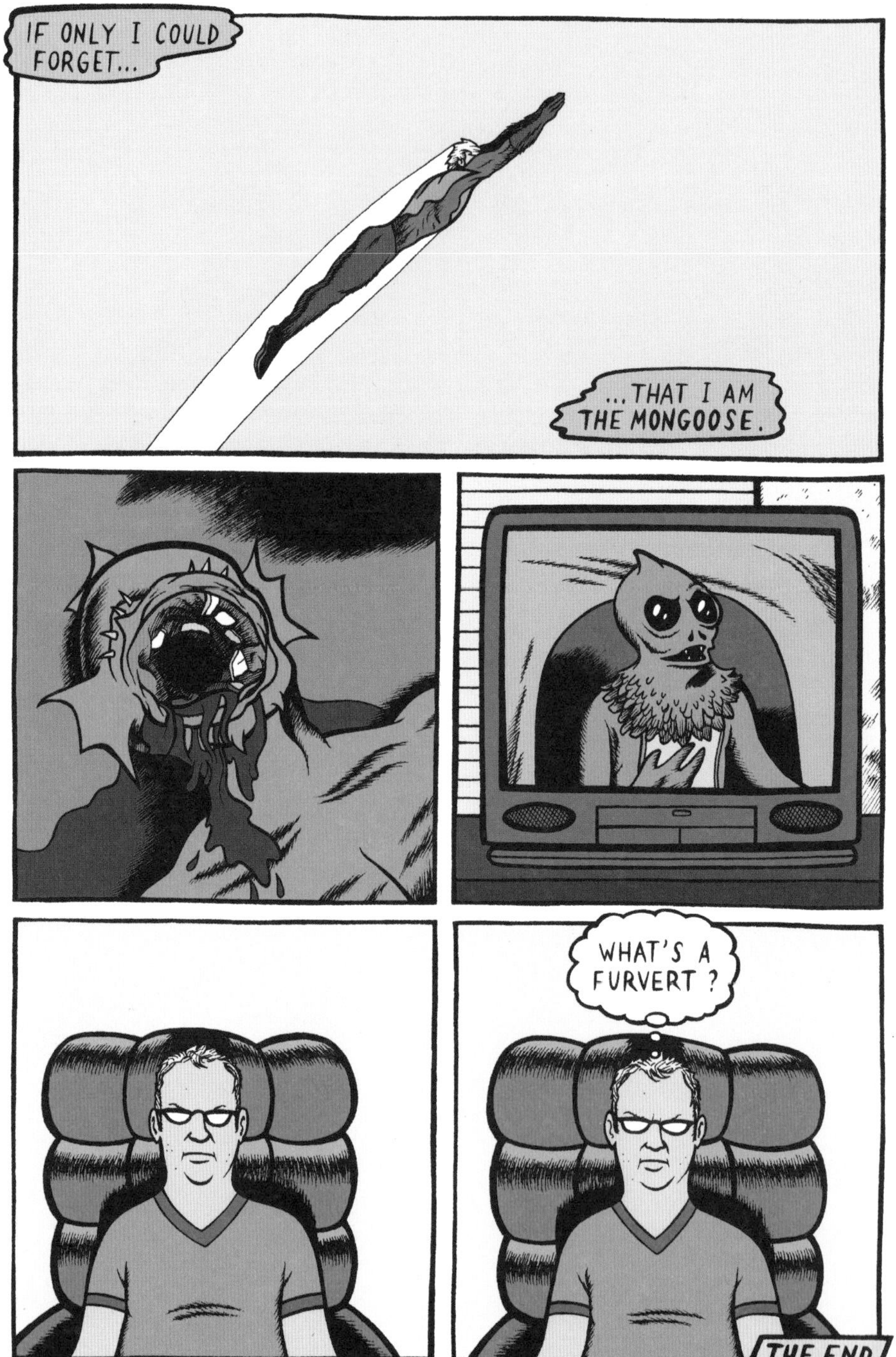
IF ONLY I COULD FORGET...
...THAT I AM THE MONGOOSE.
WHAT'S A FURVERT ?
THE END

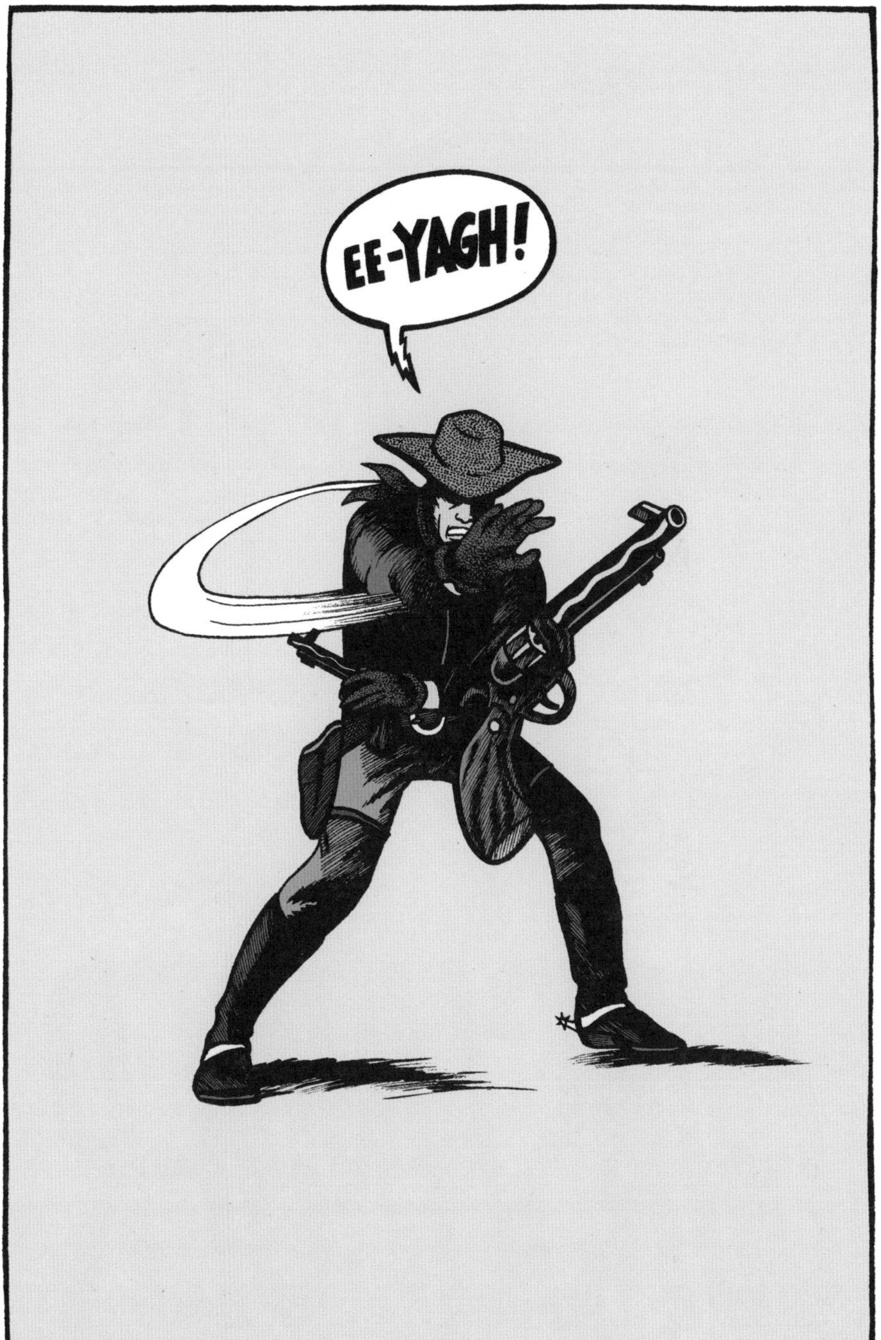
EE-YAGH!

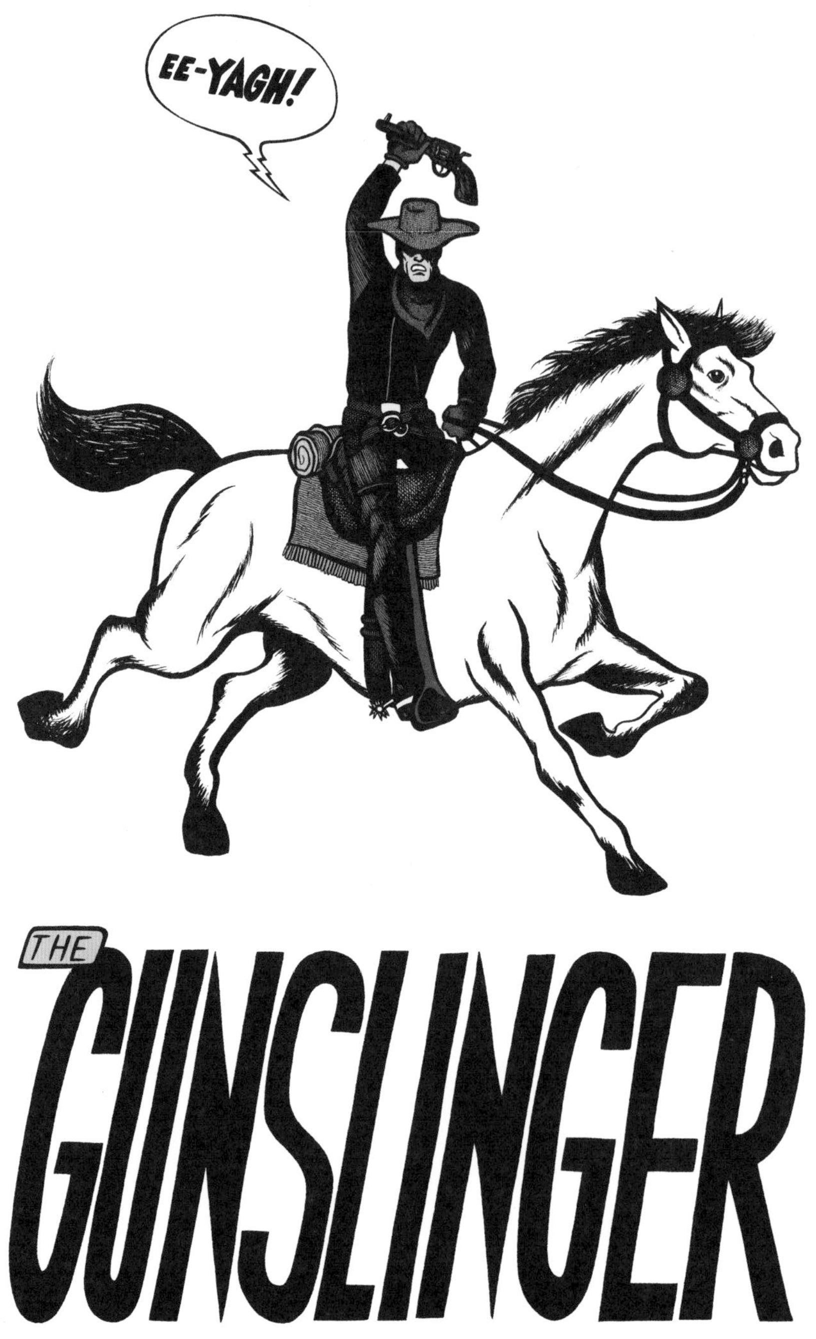
EE-YAGH!

THE GUNSLINGER

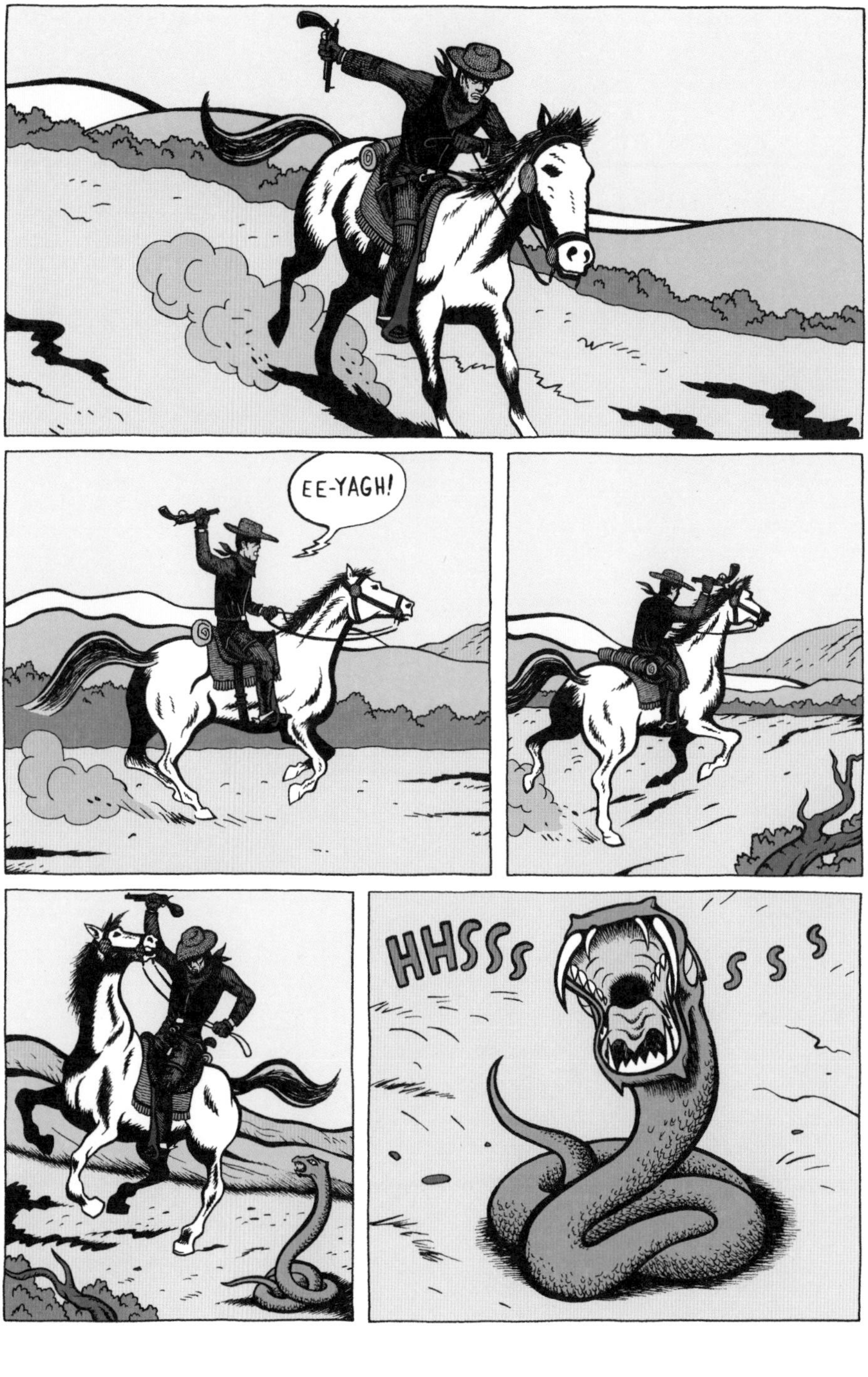
EE-YAGH!
HHSSSS
SSS

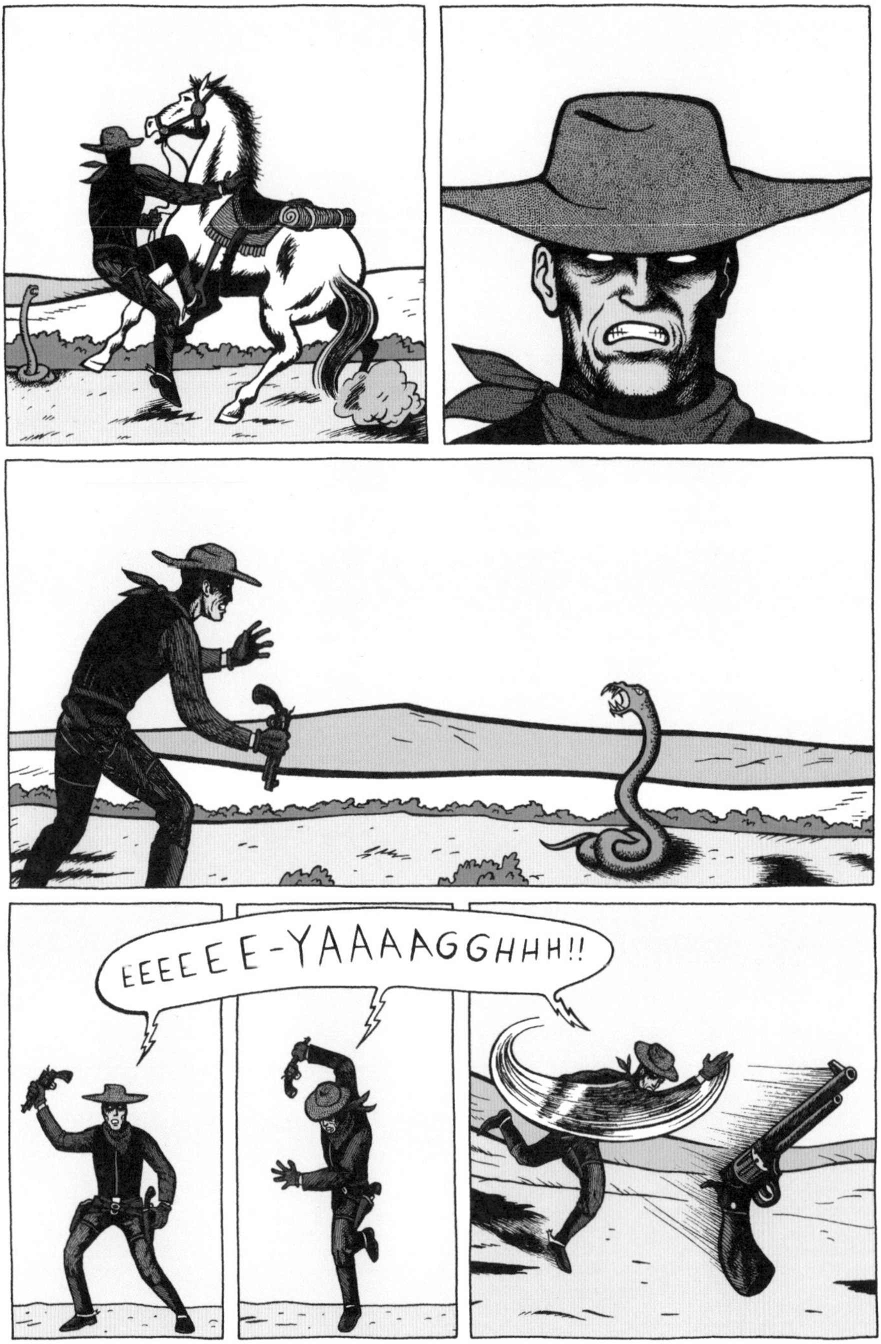
EEEEEE-YAAAAGGHHH!!

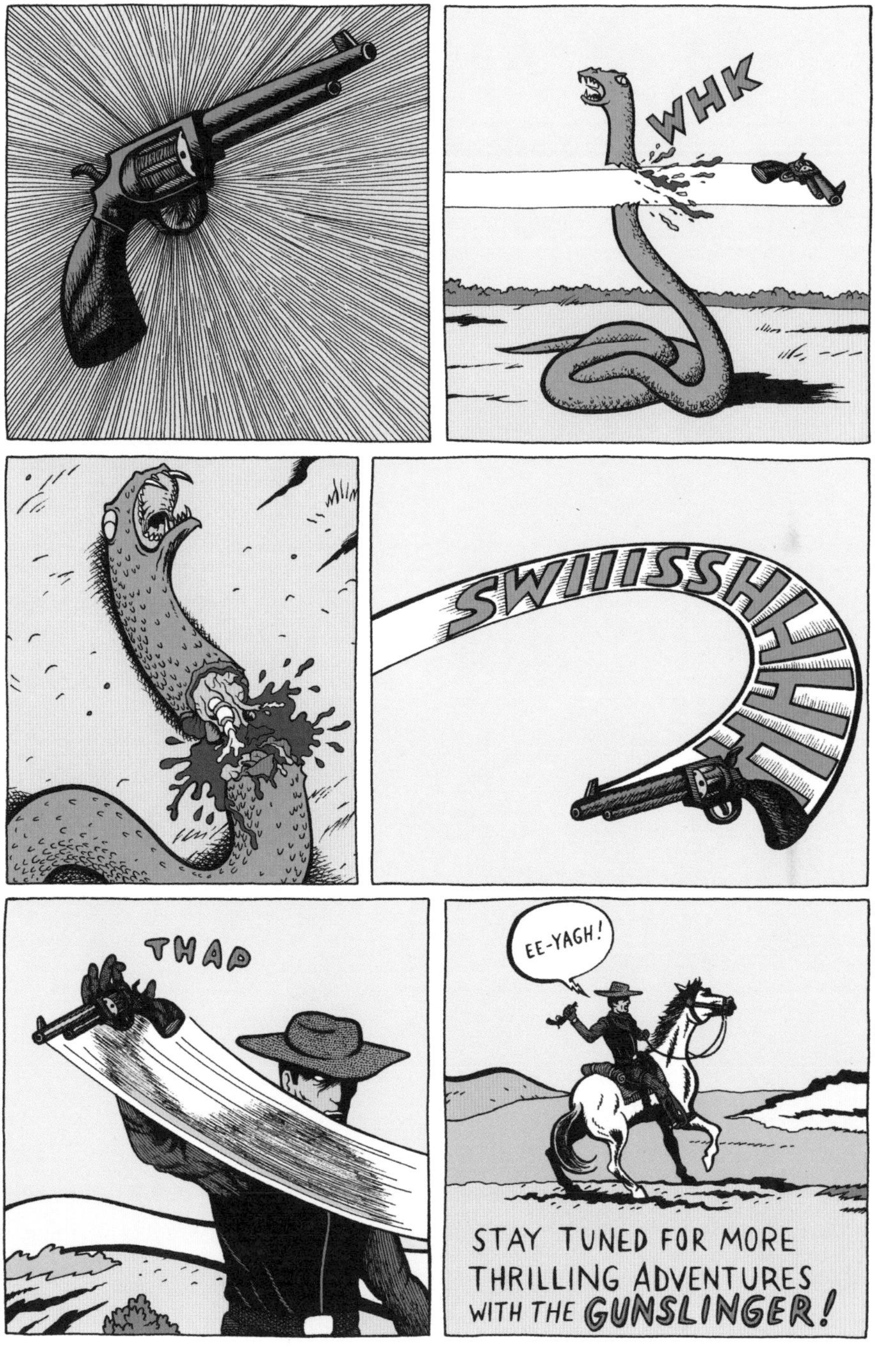
WHK
SWIIISSHHHHH
THAP
EE-YAGH!
STAY TUNED FOR MORE THRILLING ADVENTURES WITH THE GUNSLINGER!

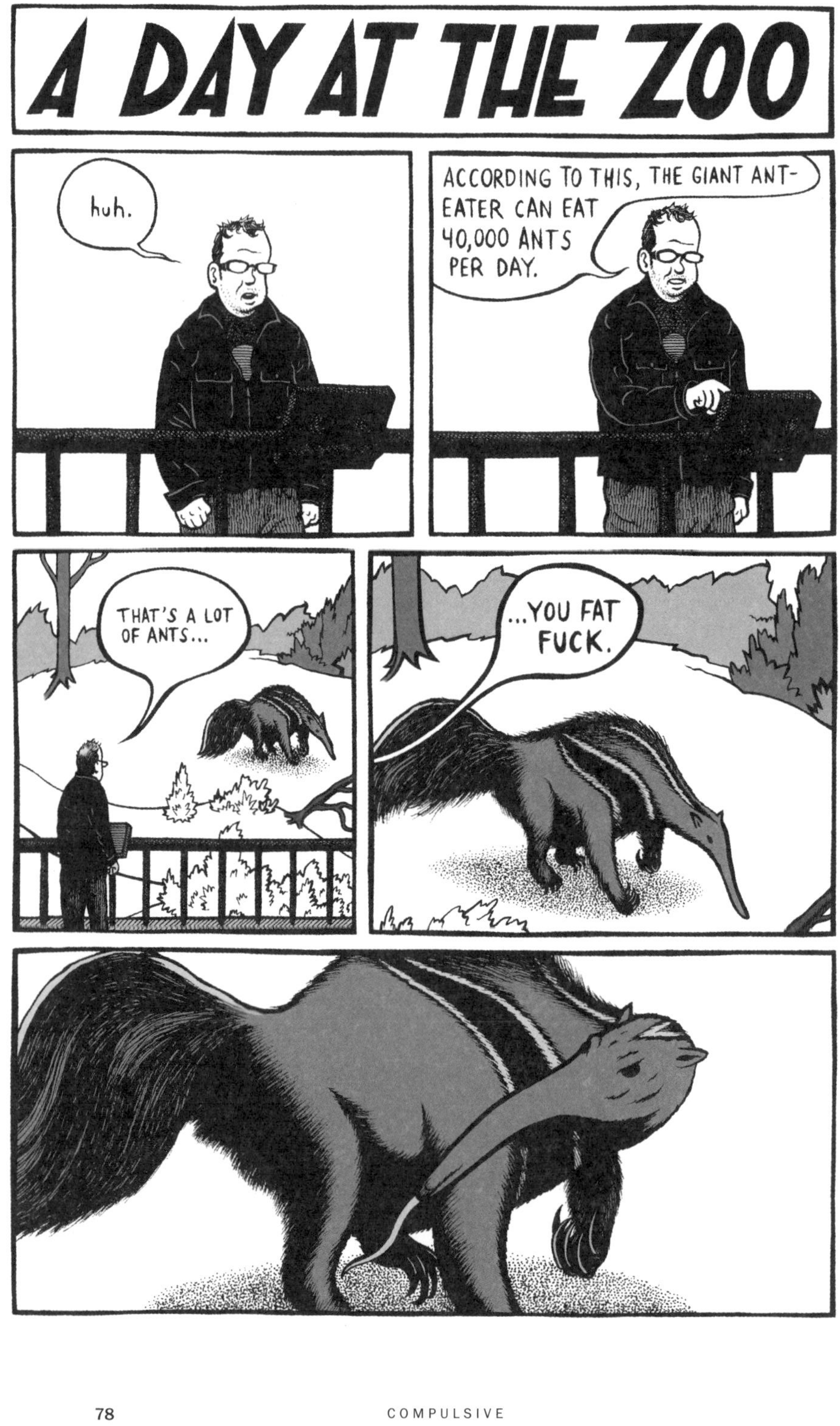
A DAY AT THE ZOO
huh.
ACCORDING TO THIS, THE GIANT ANT-EATER CAN EAT 40,000 ANTS PER DAY.
THAT'S A LOT OF ANTS...
...YOU FAT FUCK.

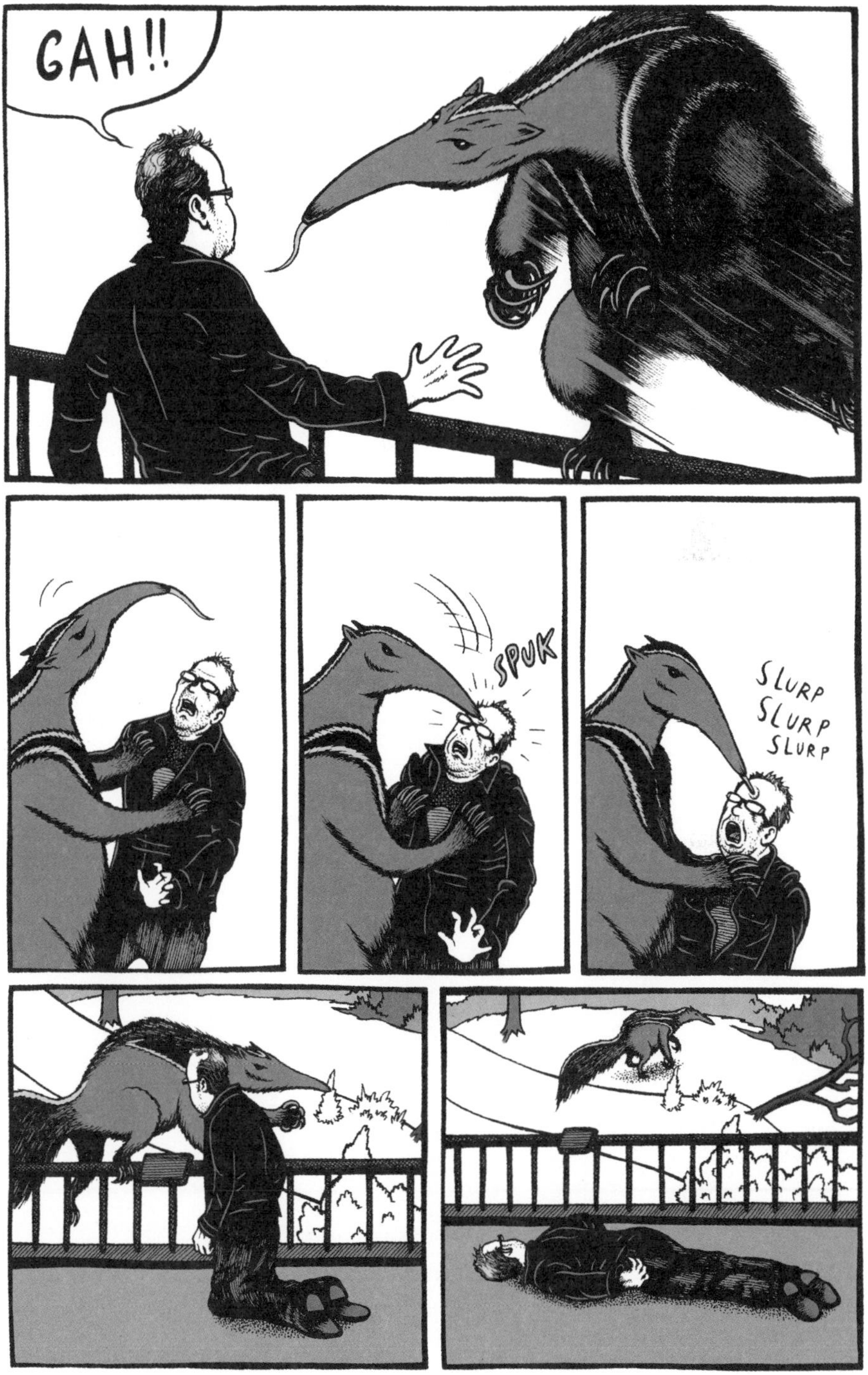
GAH!!
SPUK
SLURP
SLURP
SLURP

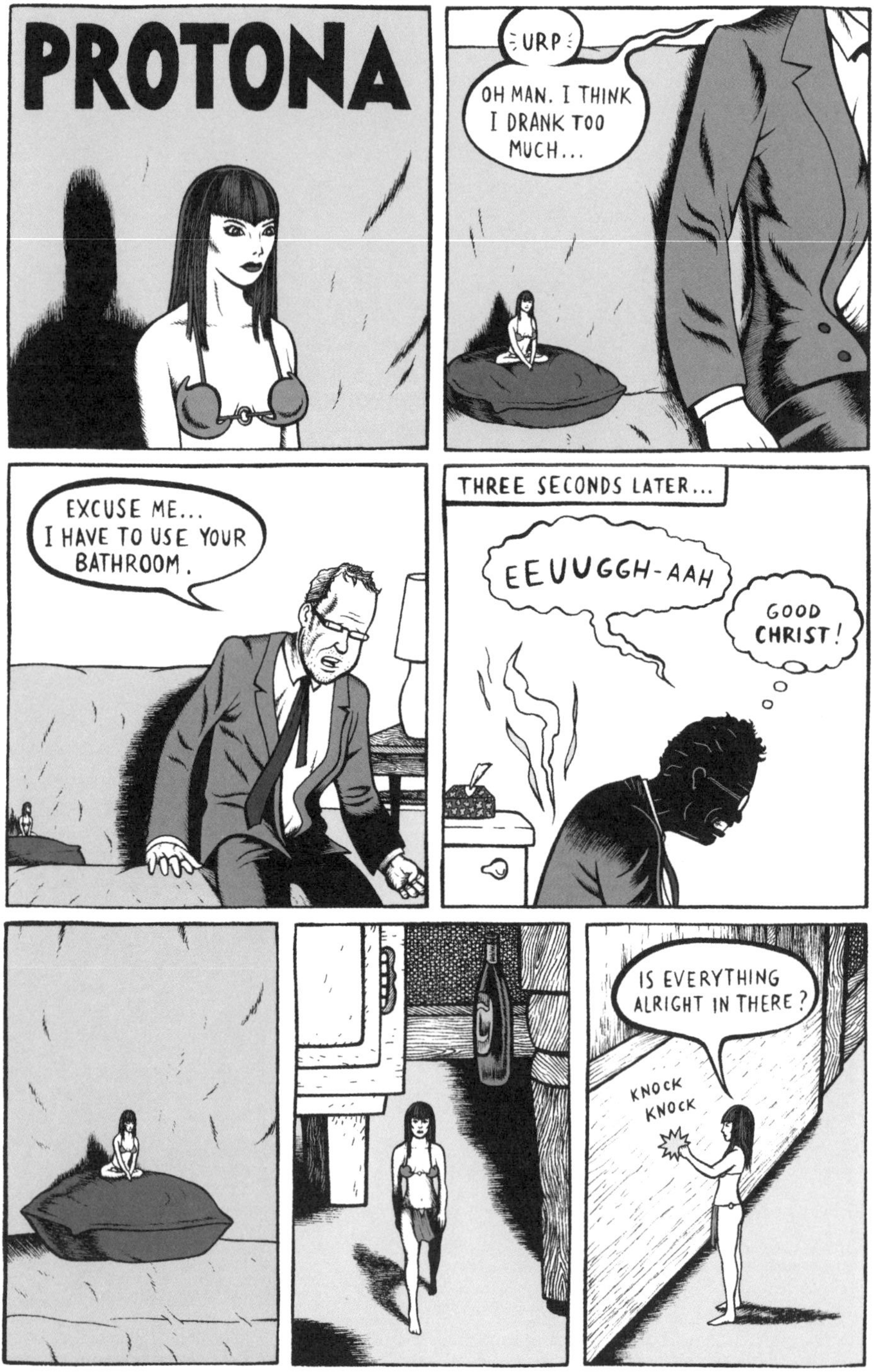
PROTONA
URP
OH MAN. I THINK I DRANK TOO MUCH...
EXCUSE ME... I HAVE TO USE YOUR BATHROOM.
THREE SECONDS LATER...
EEUUGGH-AAH
GOOD CHRIST!
IS EVERYTHING ALRIGHT IN THERE?
KNOCK KNOCK

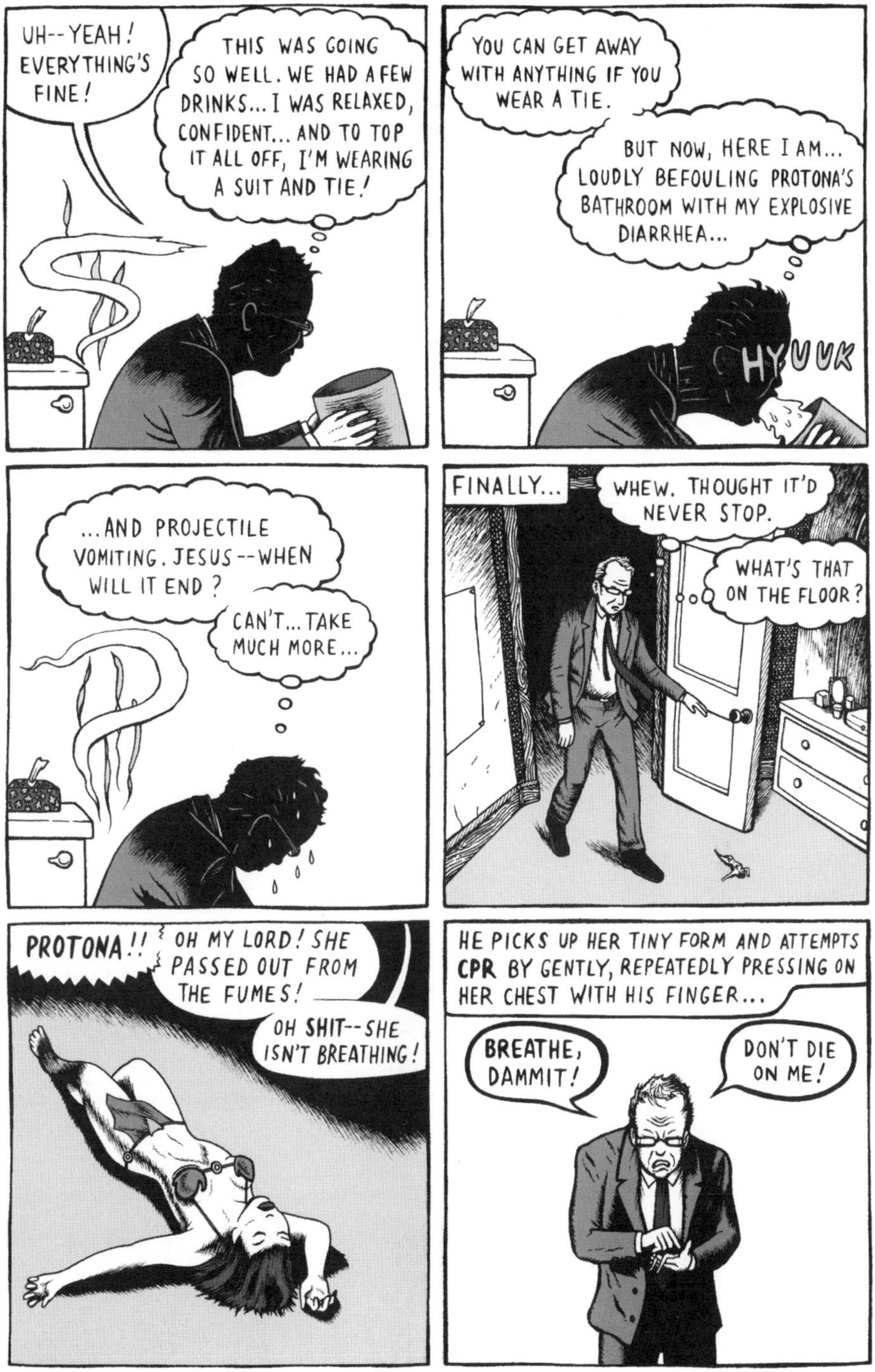
UH--YEAH! EVERYTHING'S FINE!
THIS WAS GOING SO WELL. WE HAD A FEW DRINKS... I WAS RELAXED, CONFIDENT... AND TO TOP IT ALL OFF, I'M WEARING A SUIT AND TIE!
YOU CAN GET AWAY WITH ANYTHING IF YOU WEAR A TIE.
BUT NOW, HERE I AM... LOUDLY BEFOULING PROTONA'S BATHROOM WITH MY EXPLOSIVE DIARRHEA...
HYUUK
...AND PROJECTILE VOMITING. JESUS--WHEN WILL IT END?
CAN'T... TAKE MUCH MORE...
FINALLY...
WHEW. THOUGHT IT'D NEVER STOP.
WHAT'S THAT ON THE FLOOR?
PROTONA!!
OH MY LORD! SHE PASSED OUT FROM THE FUMES!
OH SHIT--SHE ISN'T BREATHING!
HE PICKS UP HER TINY FORM AND ATTEMPTS CPR BY GENTLY, REPEATEDLY PRESSING ON HER CHEST WITH HIS FINGER...
BREATHE, DAMMIT!
DON'T DIE ON ME!

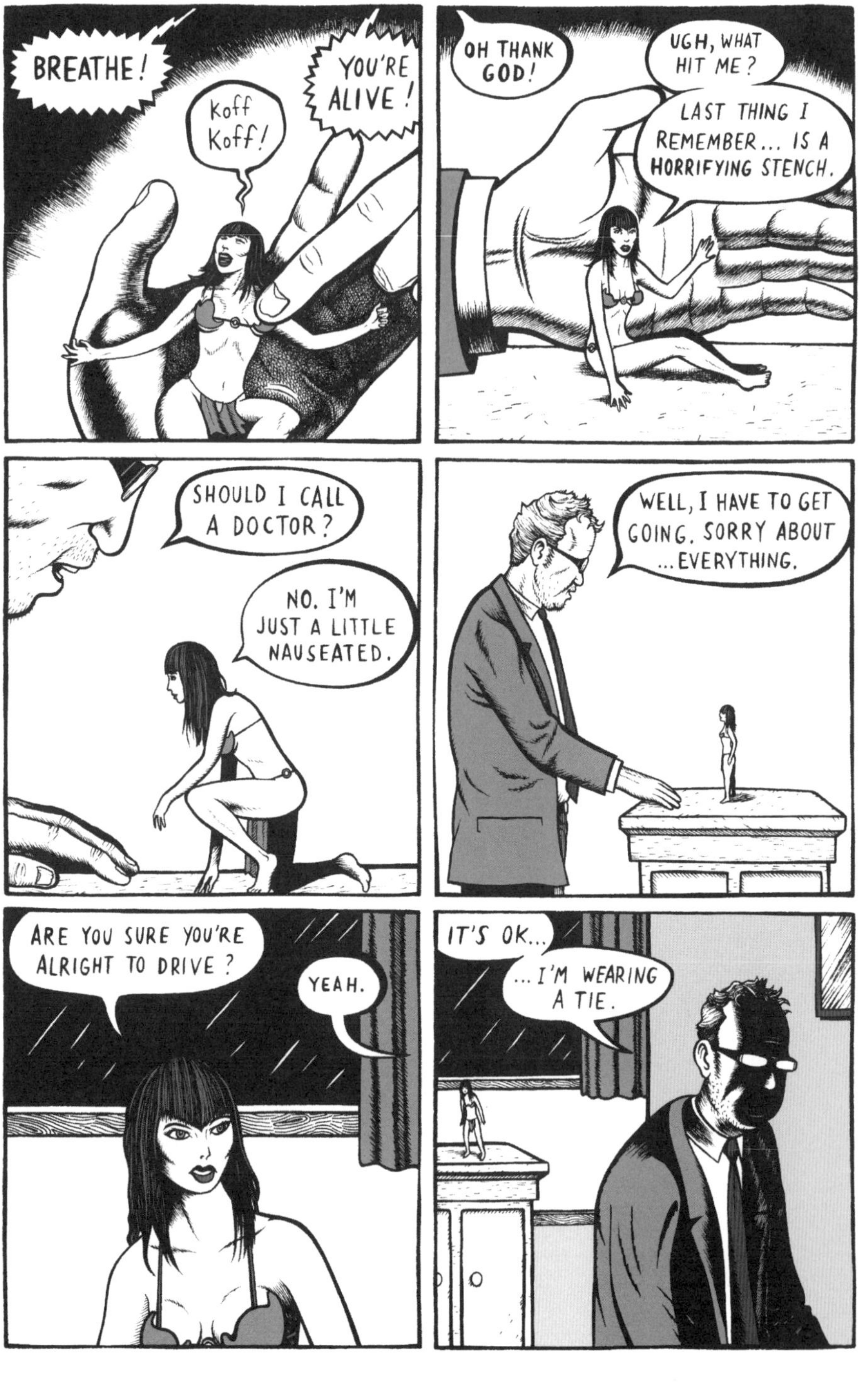
BREATHE!
Koff Koff!
YOU'RE ALIVE!
OH THANK GOD!
UGH, WHAT HIT ME?
LAST THING I REMEMBER... IS A HORRIFYING STENCH.
SHOULD I CALL A DOCTOR?
NO. I'M JUST A LITTLE NAUSEATED.
WELL, I HAVE TO GET GOING. SORRY ABOUT ...EVERYTHING.
ARE YOU SURE YOU'RE ALRIGHT TO DRIVE?
YEAH.
IT'S OK...
...I'M WEARING A TIE.

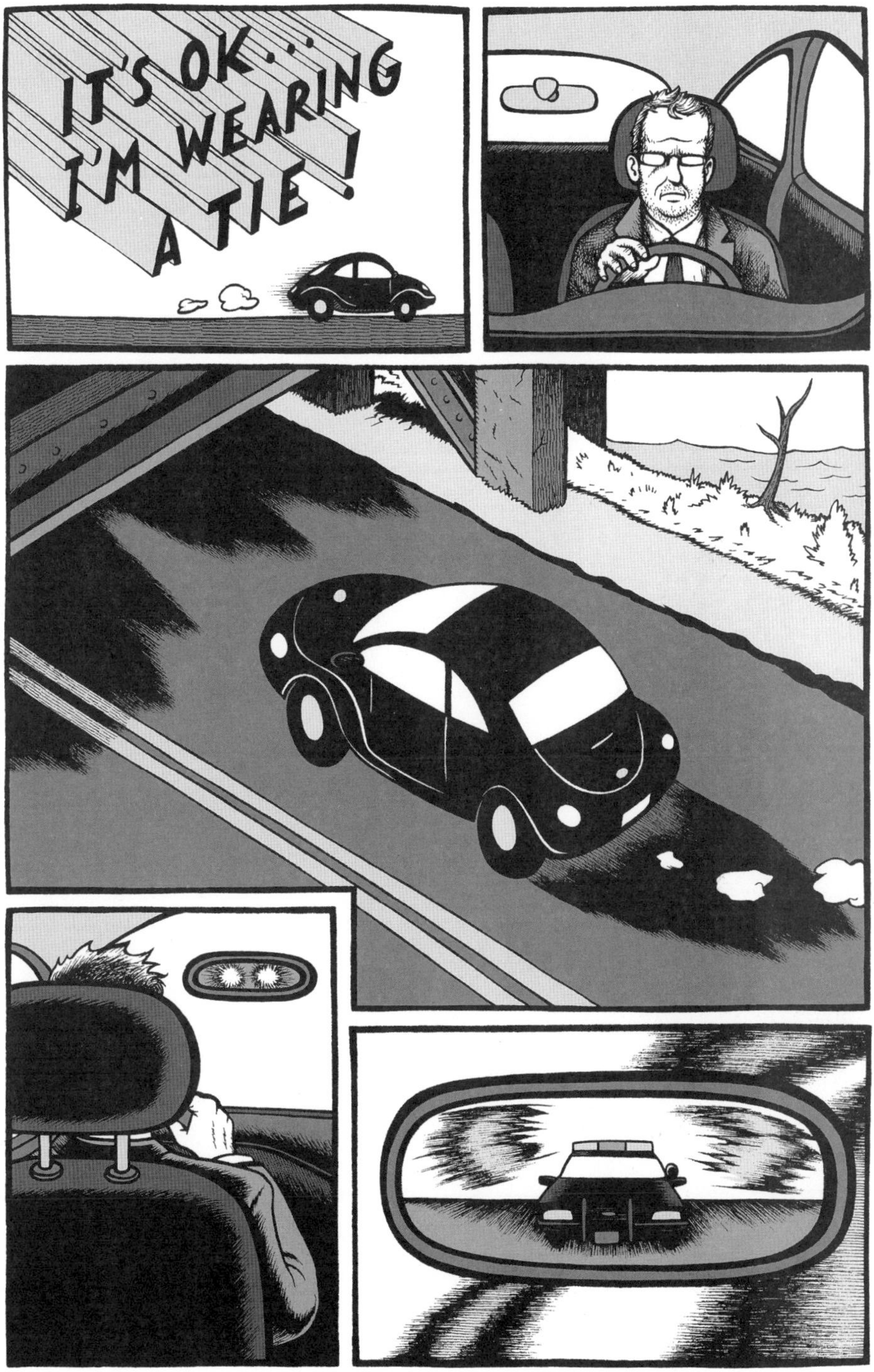
IT'S OK... I'M WEARING A TIE!

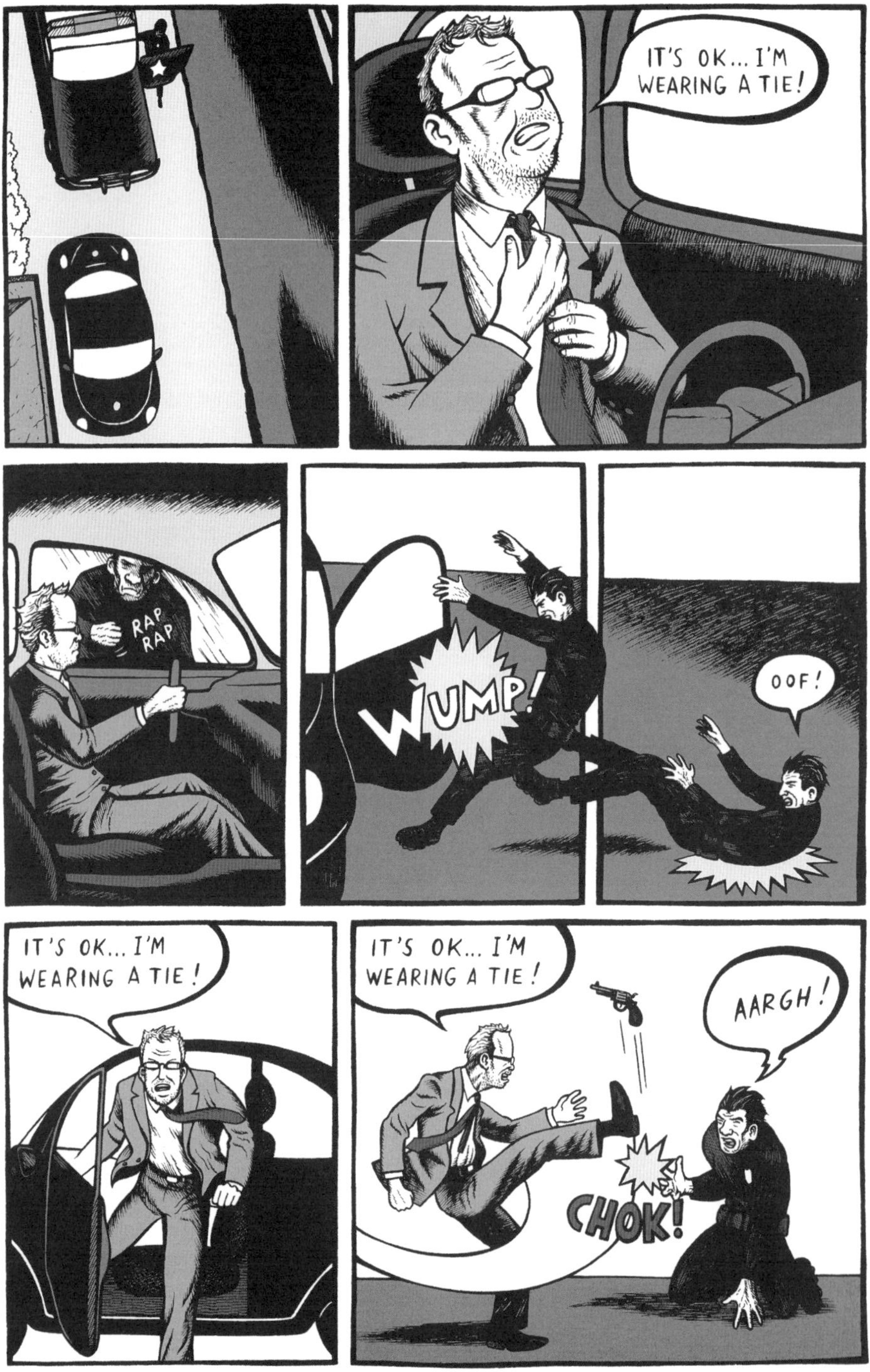
IT'S OK... I'M WEARING A TIE!
RAP RAP
WUMP!
OOF!
IT'S OK... I'M WEARING A TIE!
IT'S OK... I'M WEARING A TIE!
AARGH!
CHOK!

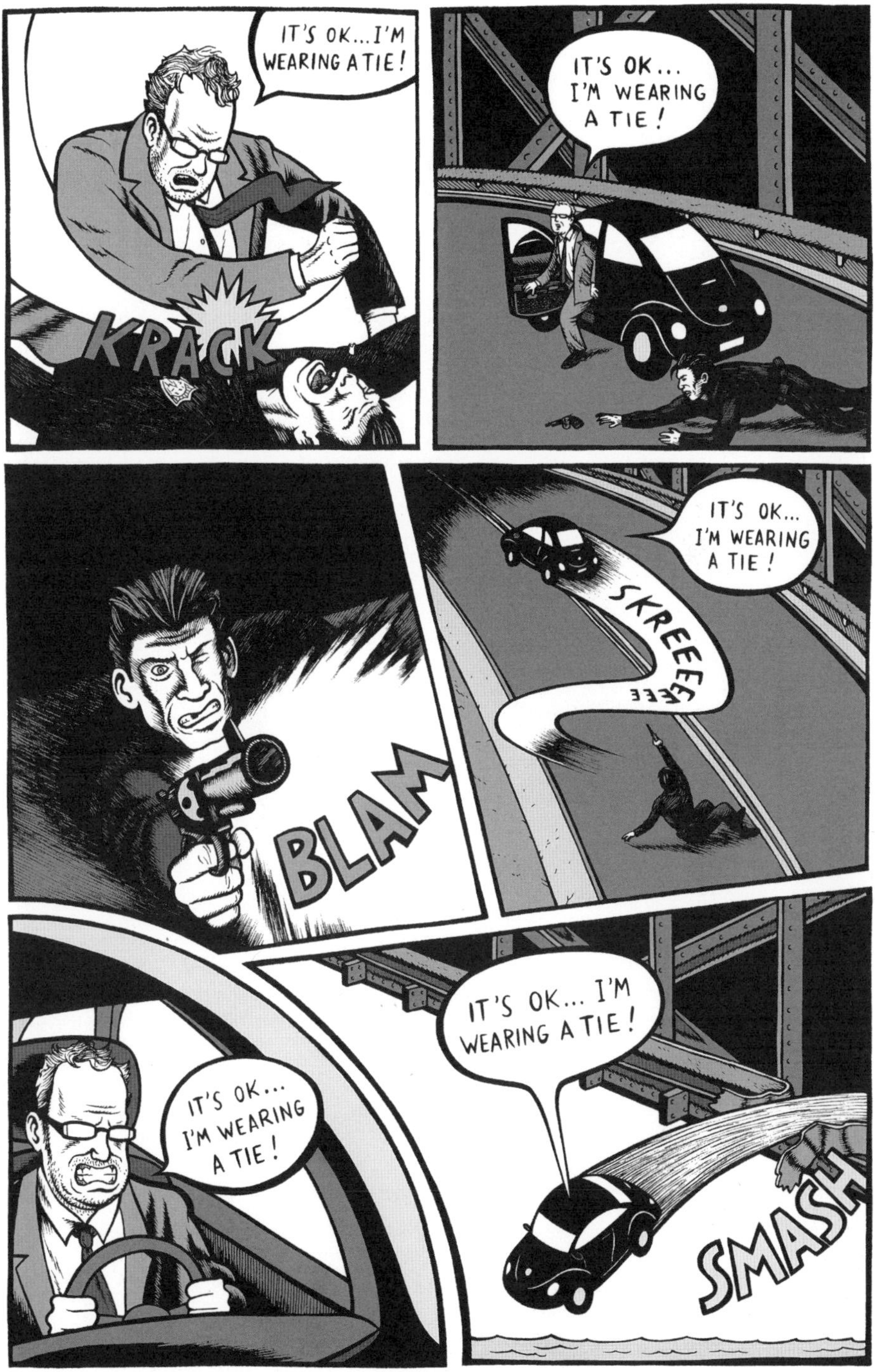
IT'S OK...I'M WEARING A TIE!
KRACK
IT'S OK... I'M WEARING A TIE!
BLAM
IT'S OK... I'M WEARING A TIE!
SKREEEEEEEE
IT'S OK... I'M WEARING A TIE!
IT'S OK... I'M WEARING A TIE!
SMASH

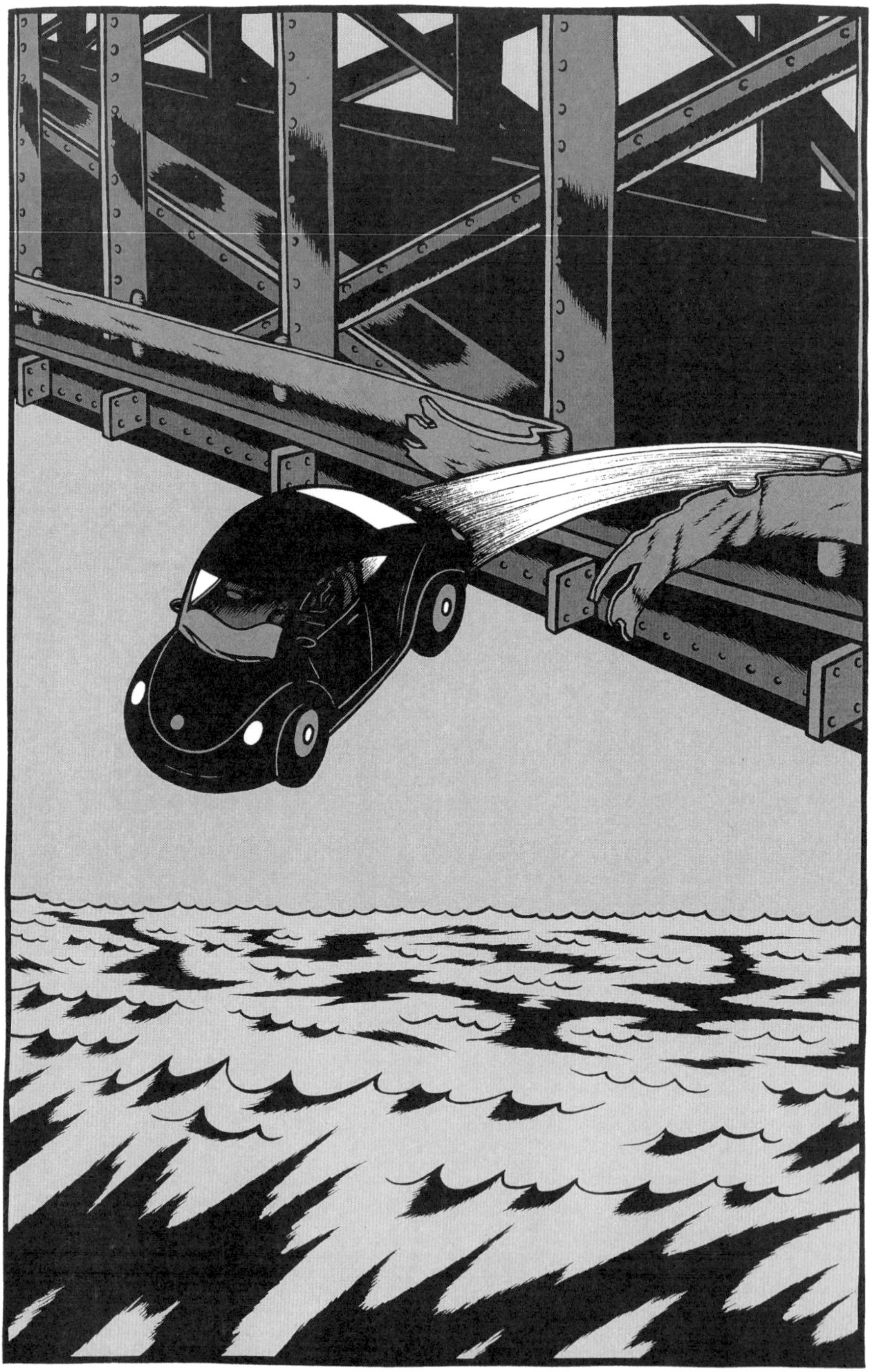

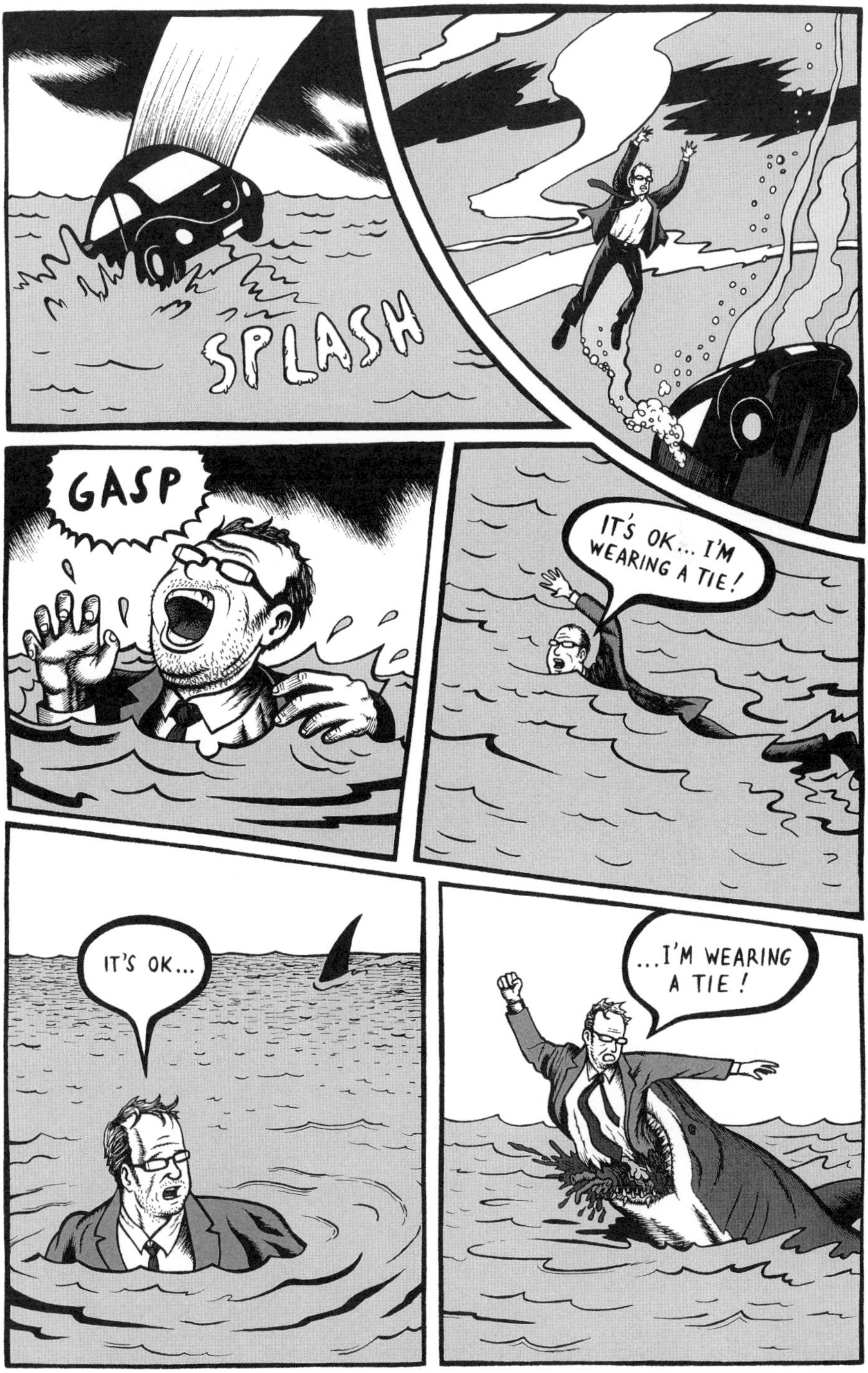
SPLASH
GASP
IT'S OK... I'M WEARING A TIE!
IT'S OK...
...I'M WEARING A TIE!

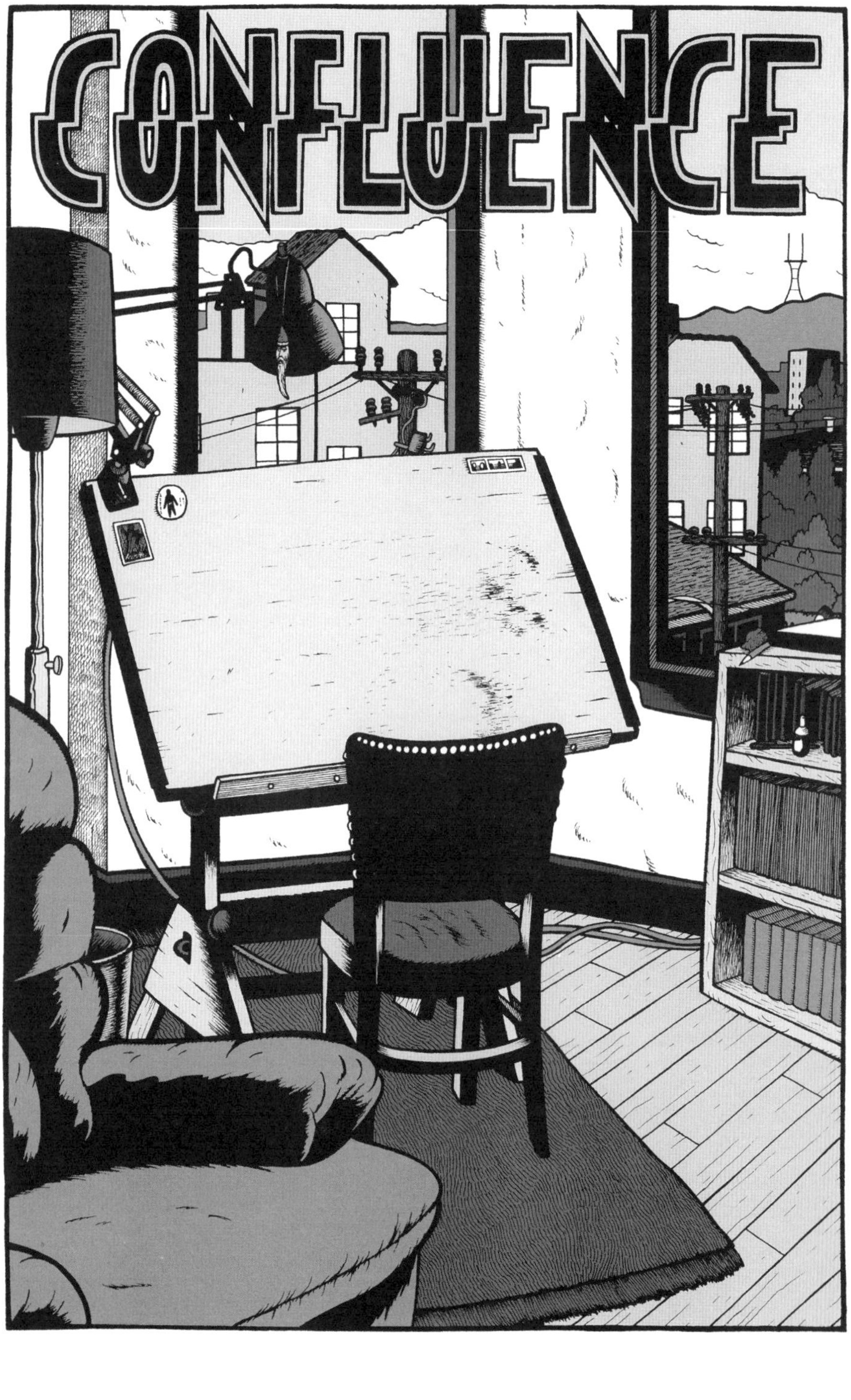
CONFLUENCE

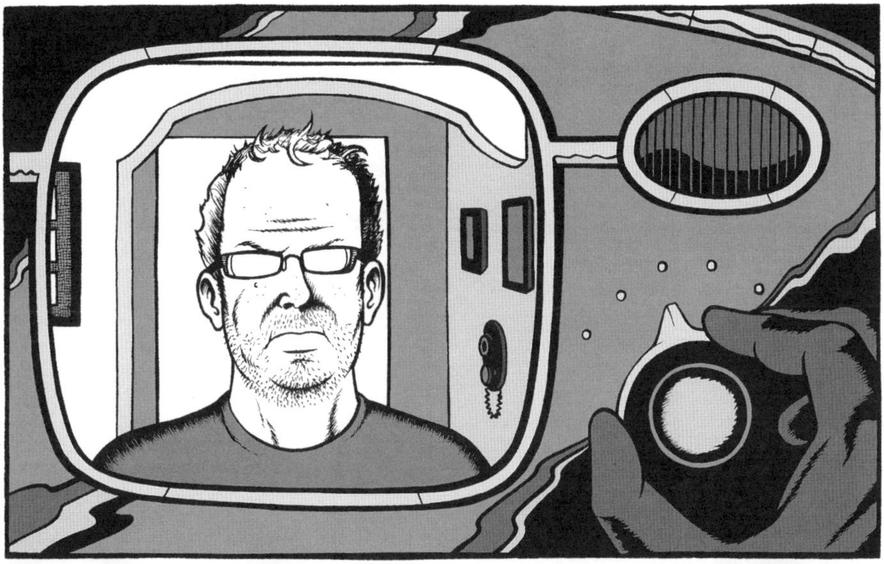

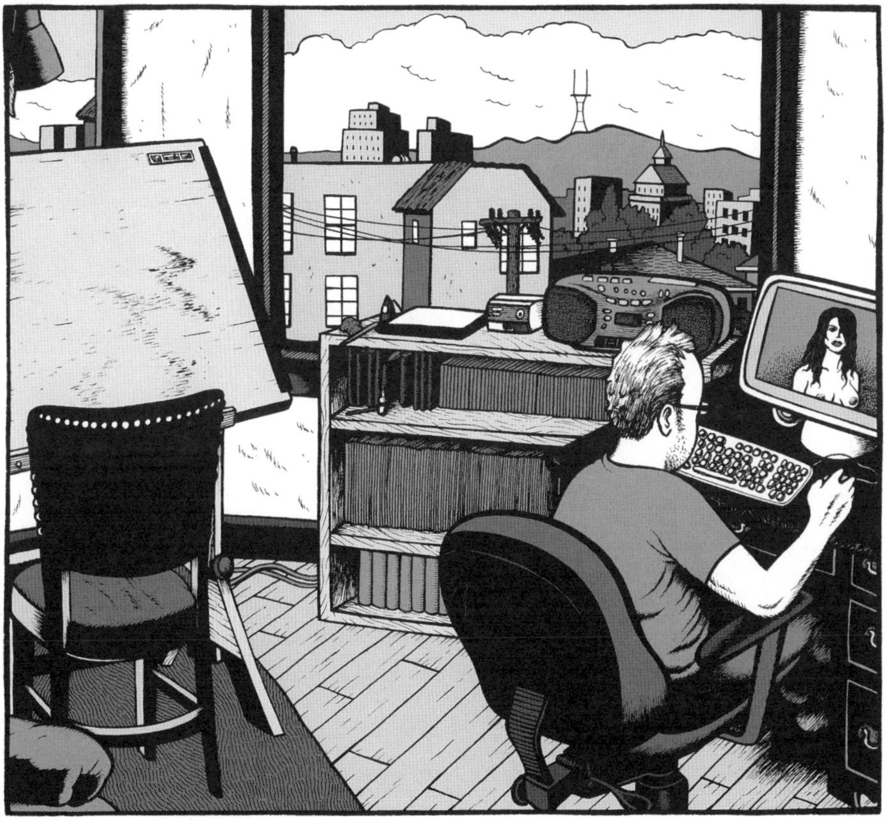

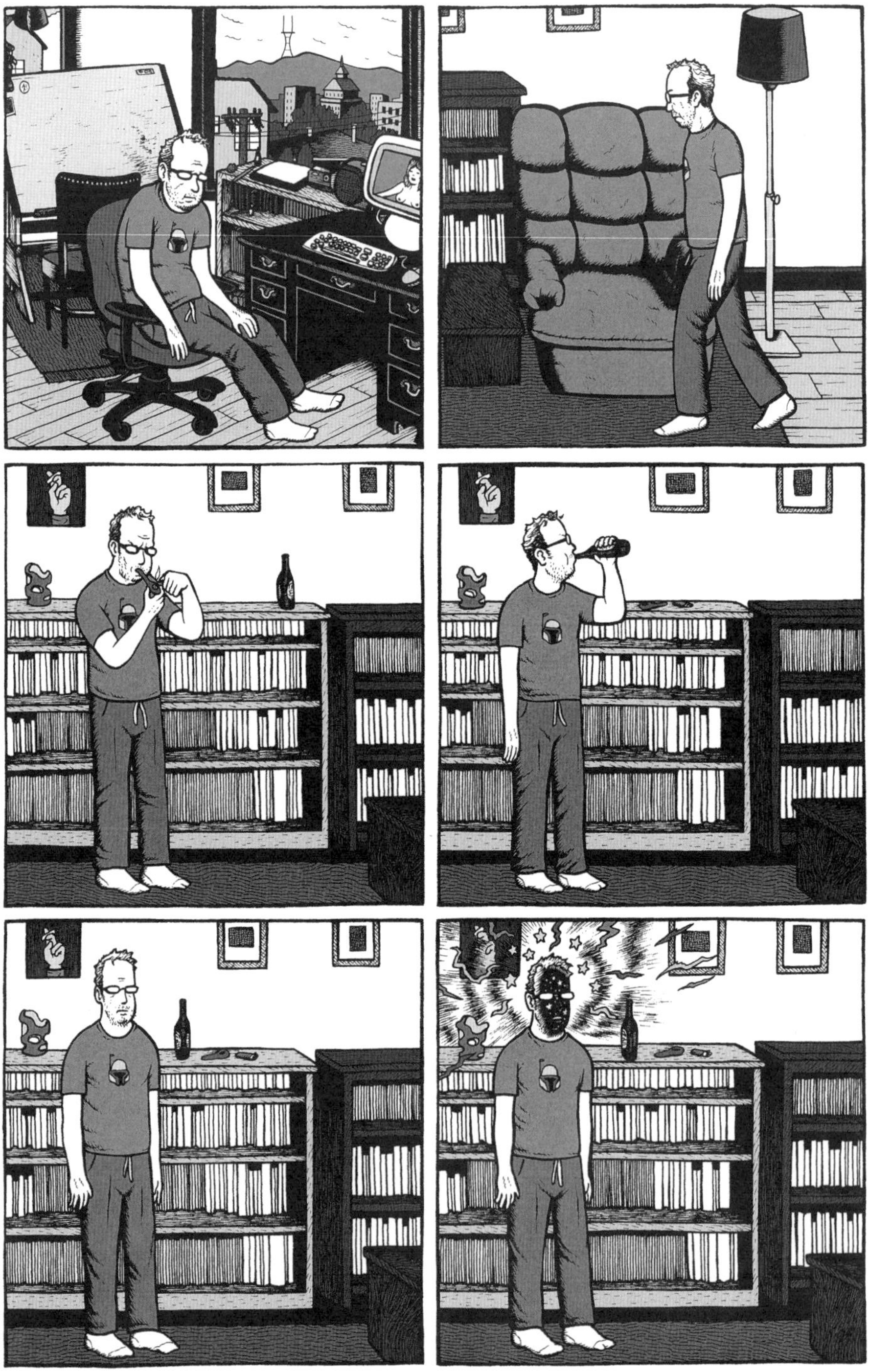

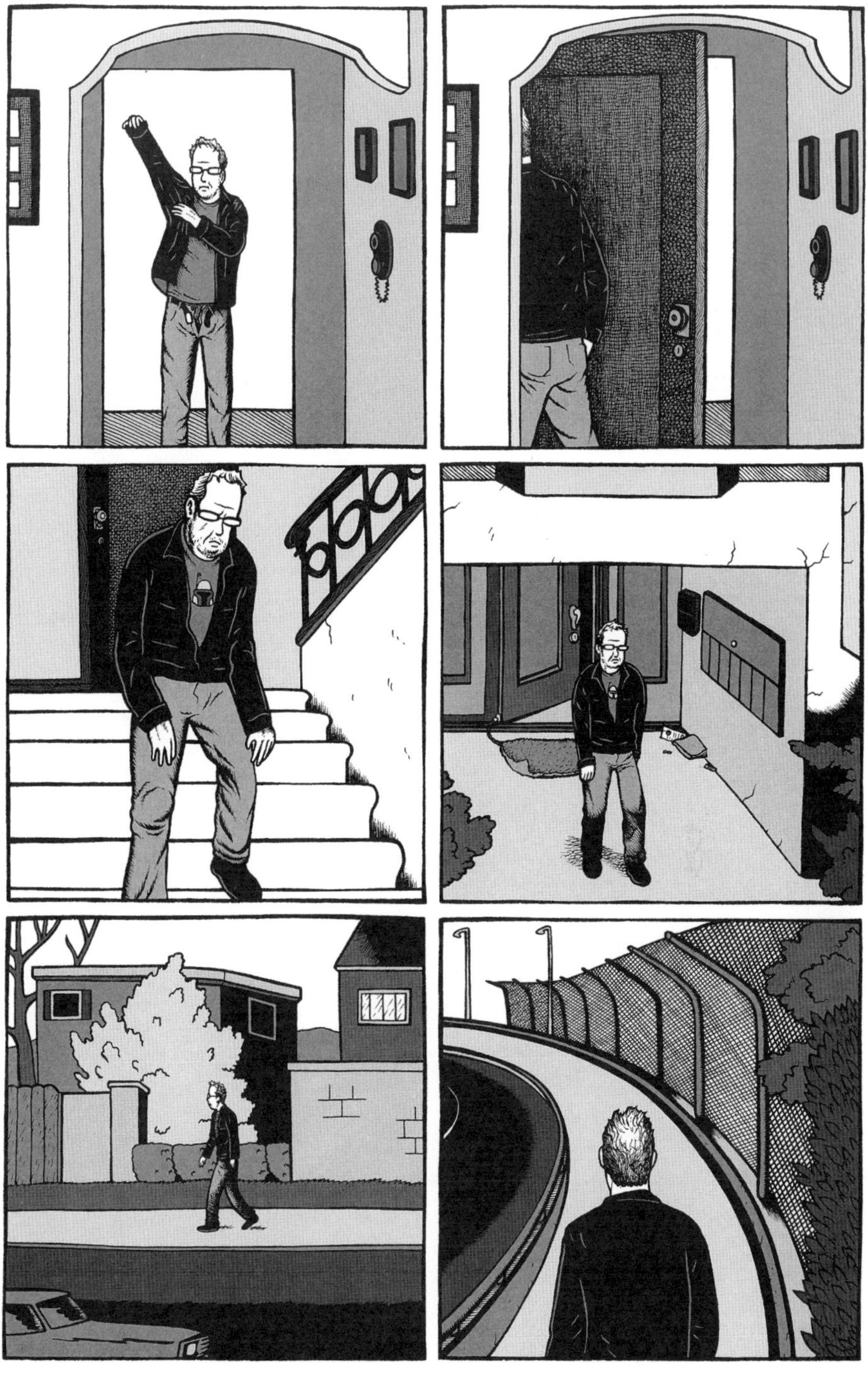

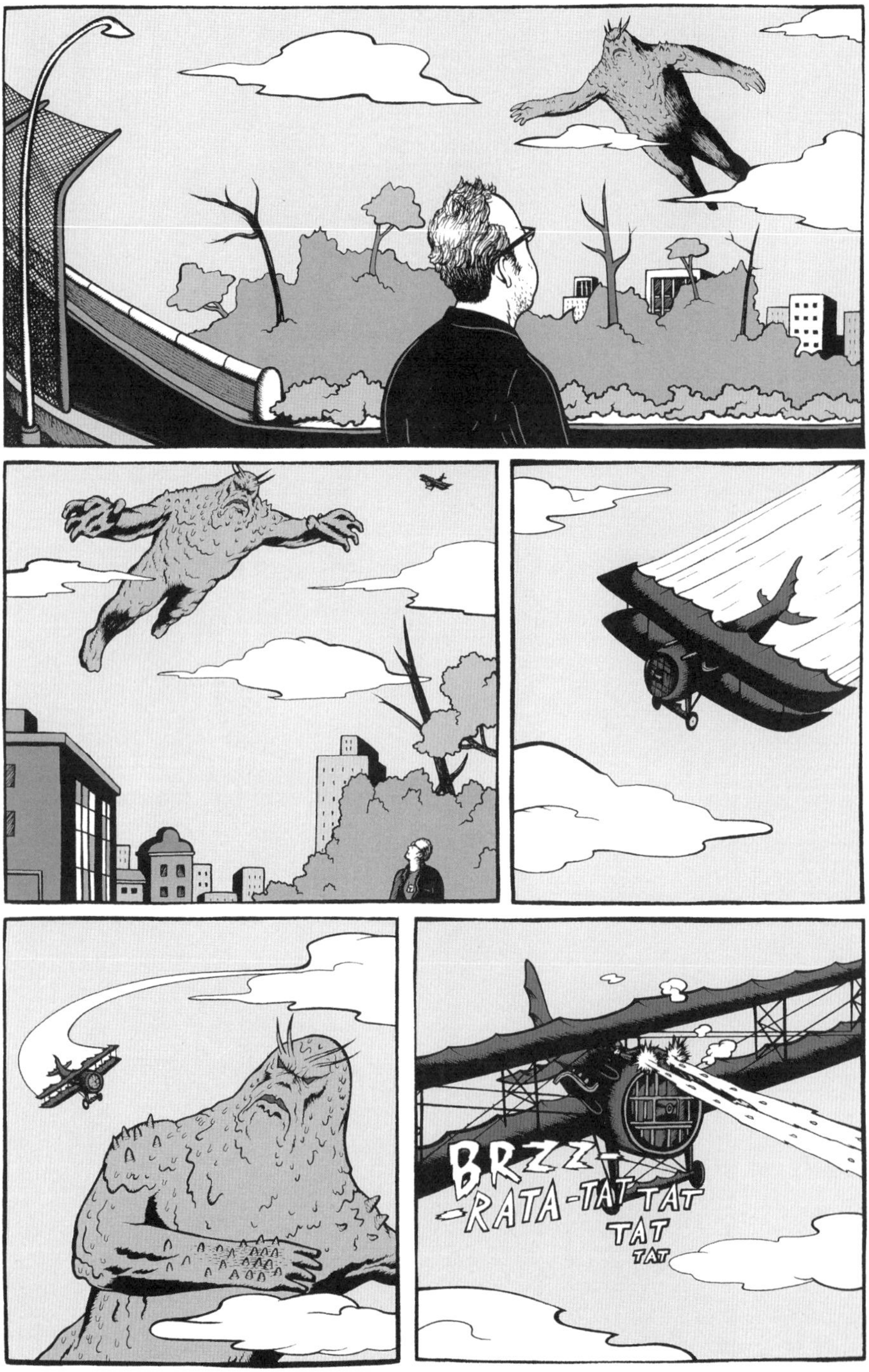
BRZZ-
-RATA-TAT TAT
TAT
TAT

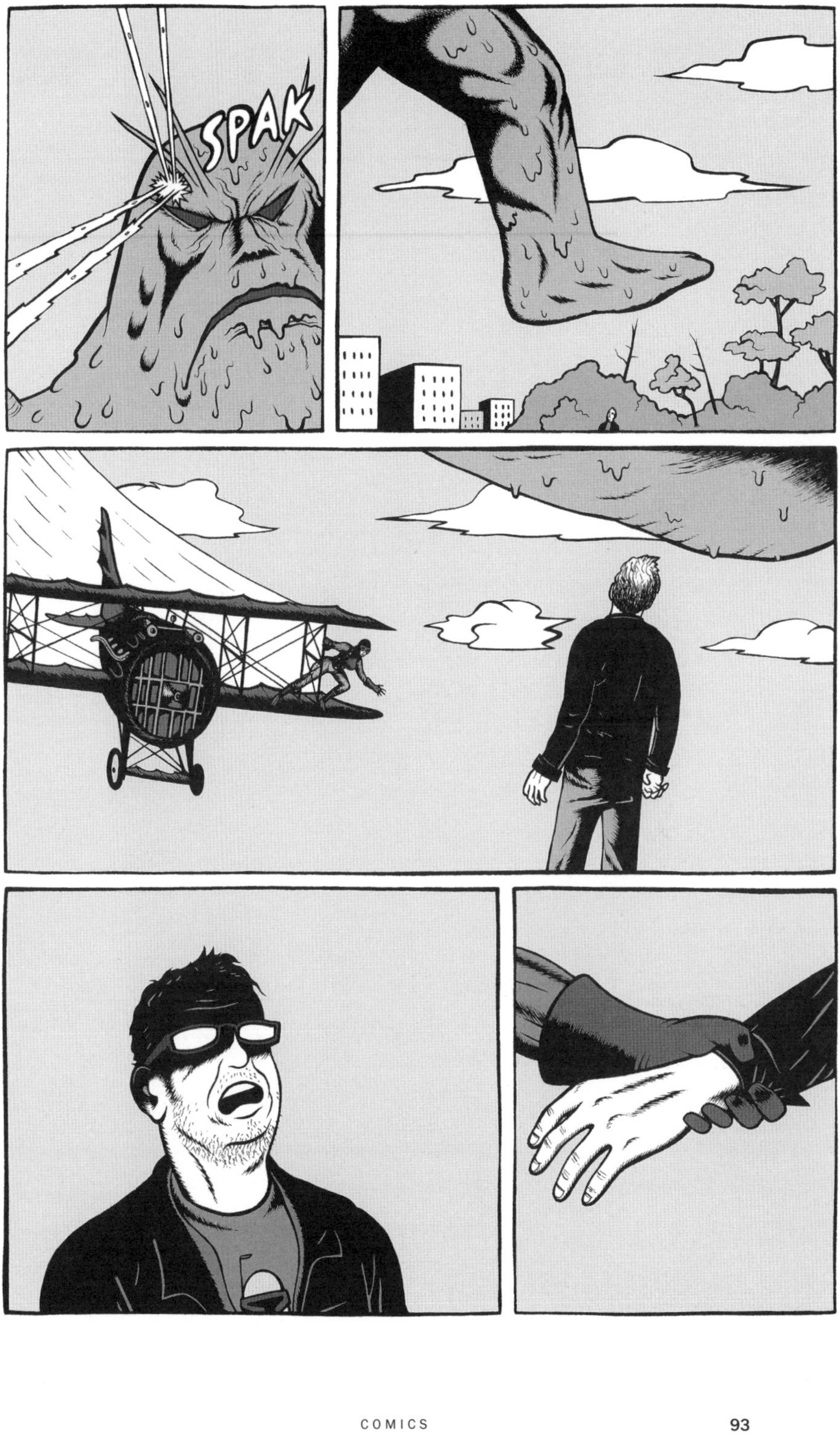
SPAK

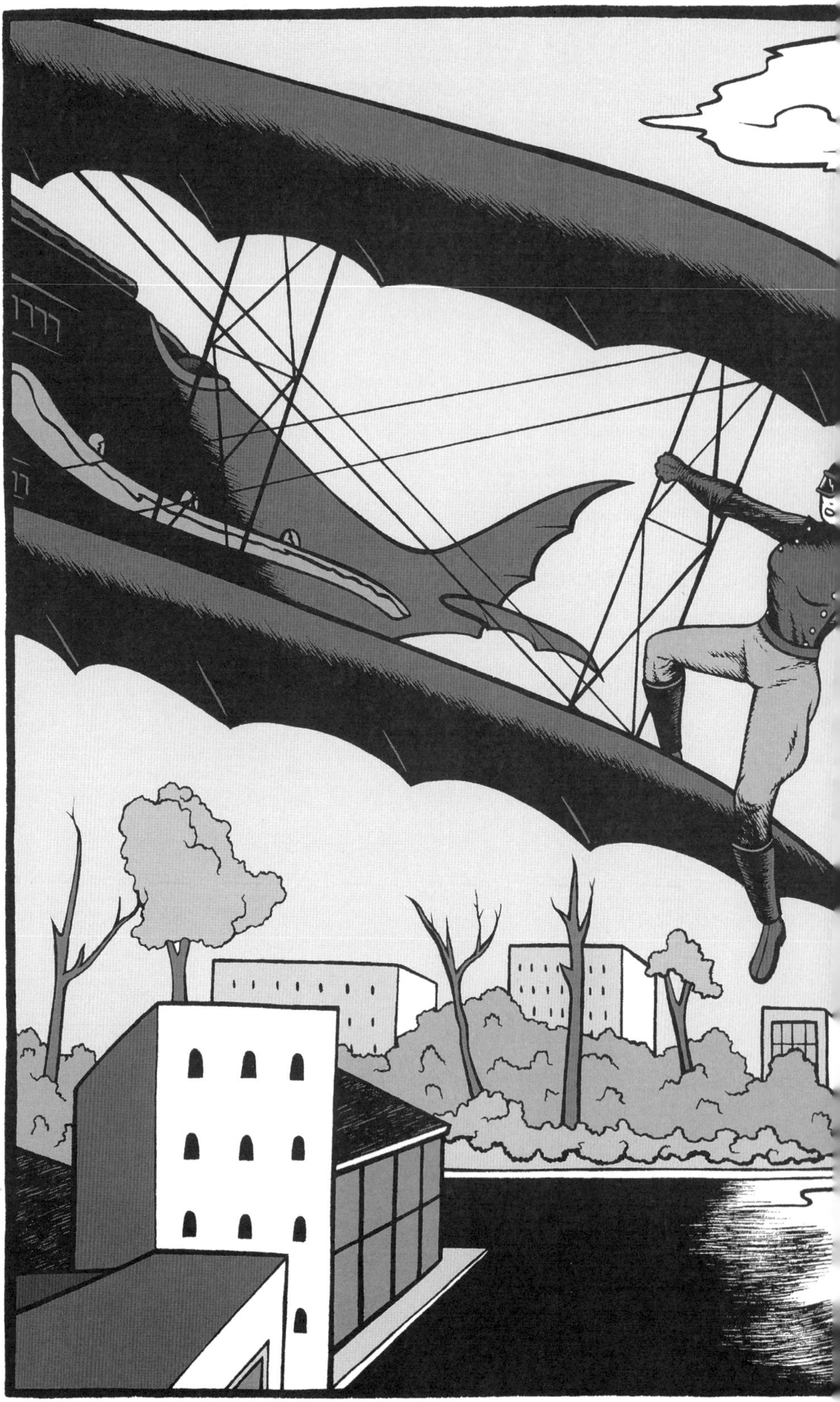

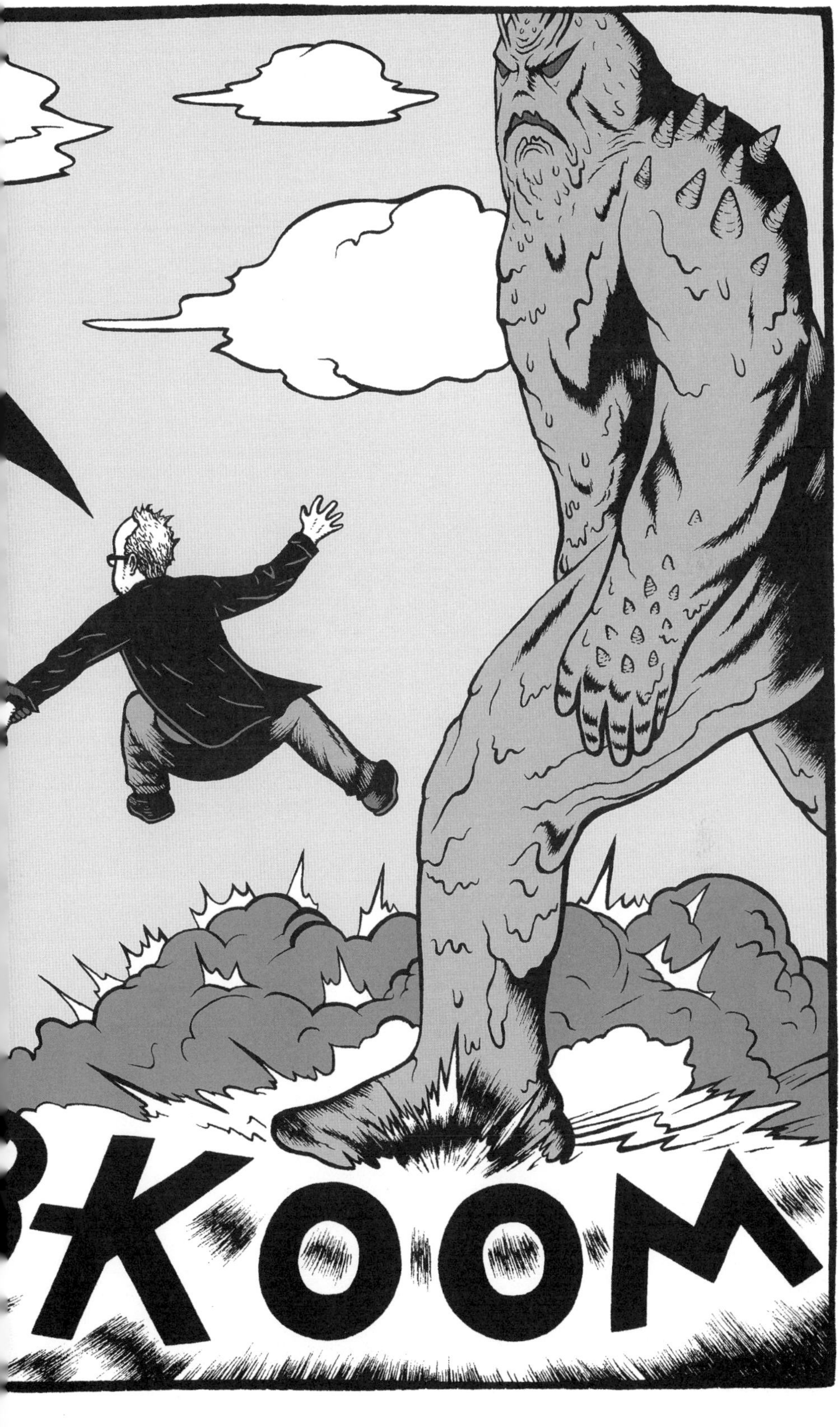
-KOOM

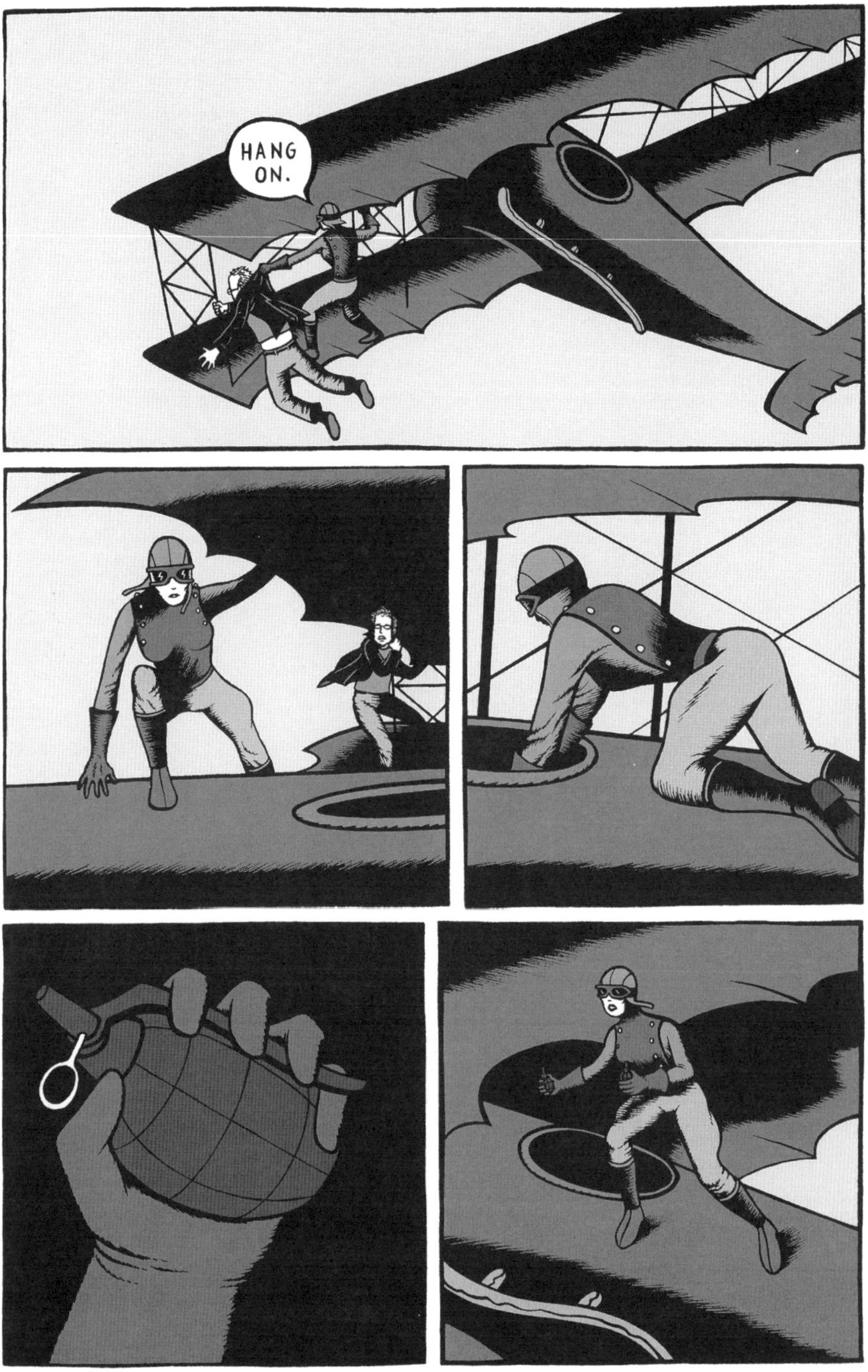
HANG ON.

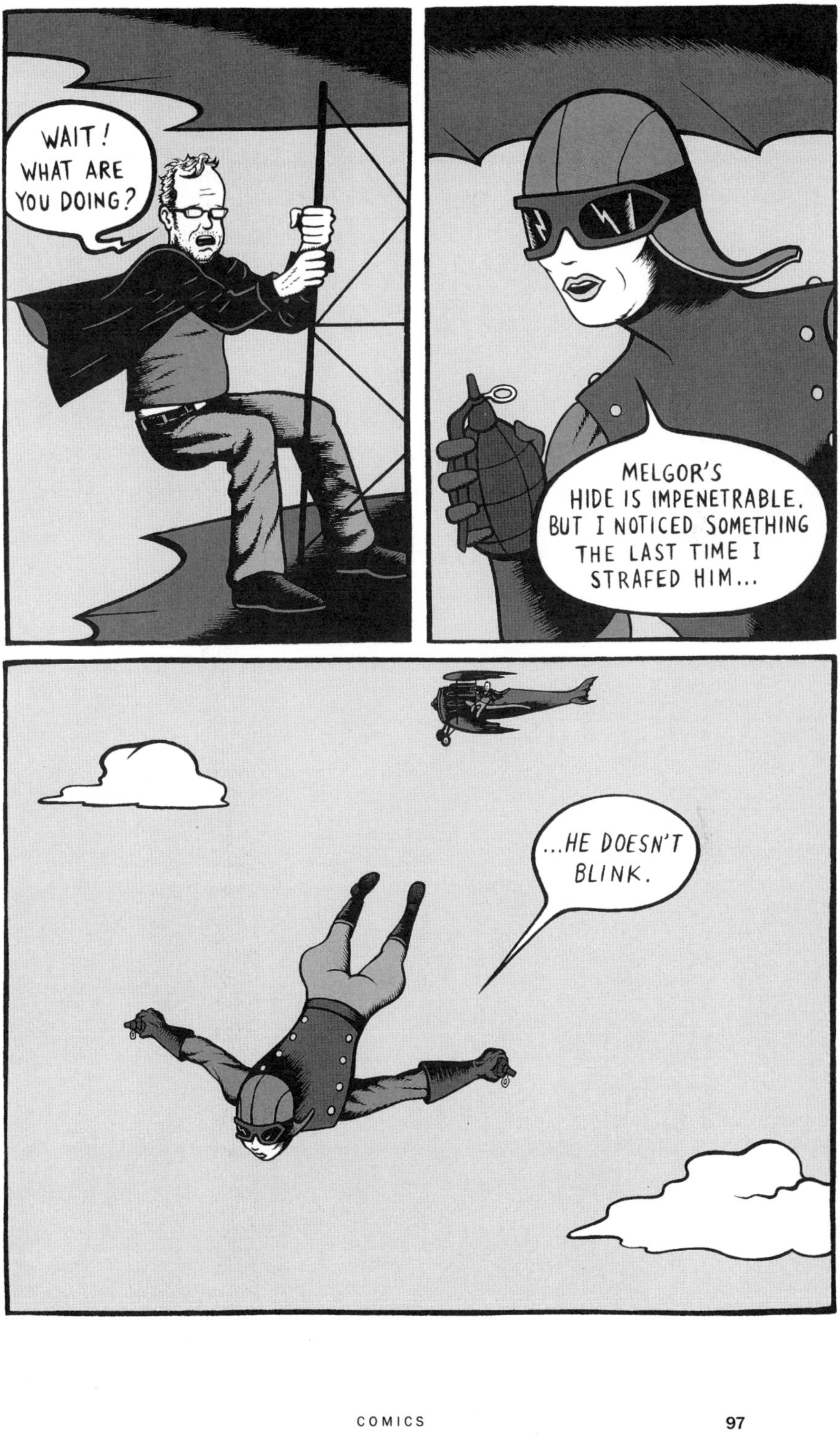
WAIT! WHAT ARE YOU DOING?
MELGOR'S HIDE IS IMPENETRABLE. BUT I NOTICED SOMETHING THE LAST TIME I STRAFED HIM...
...HE DOESN'T BLINK.

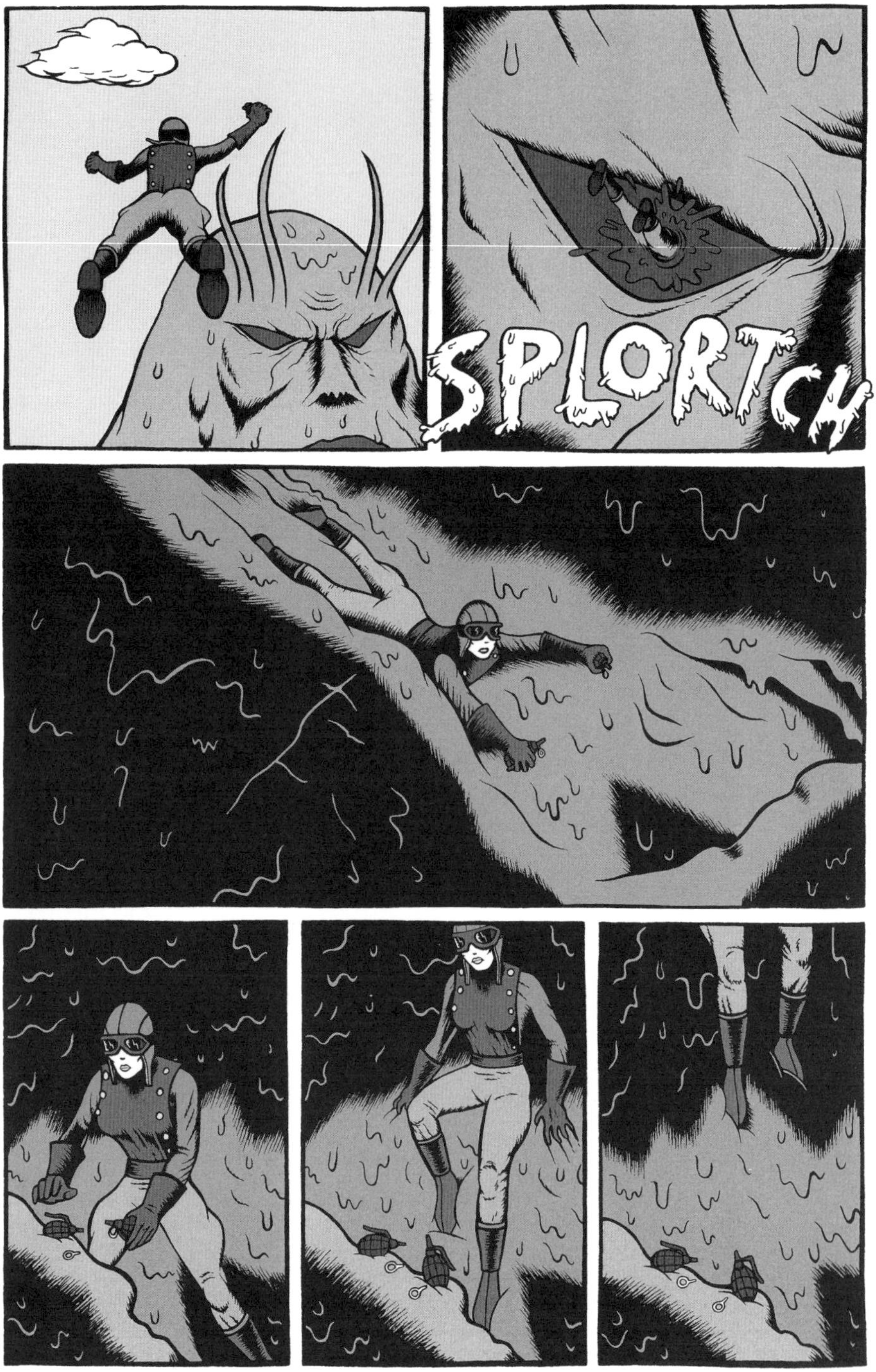
SPLORTCH

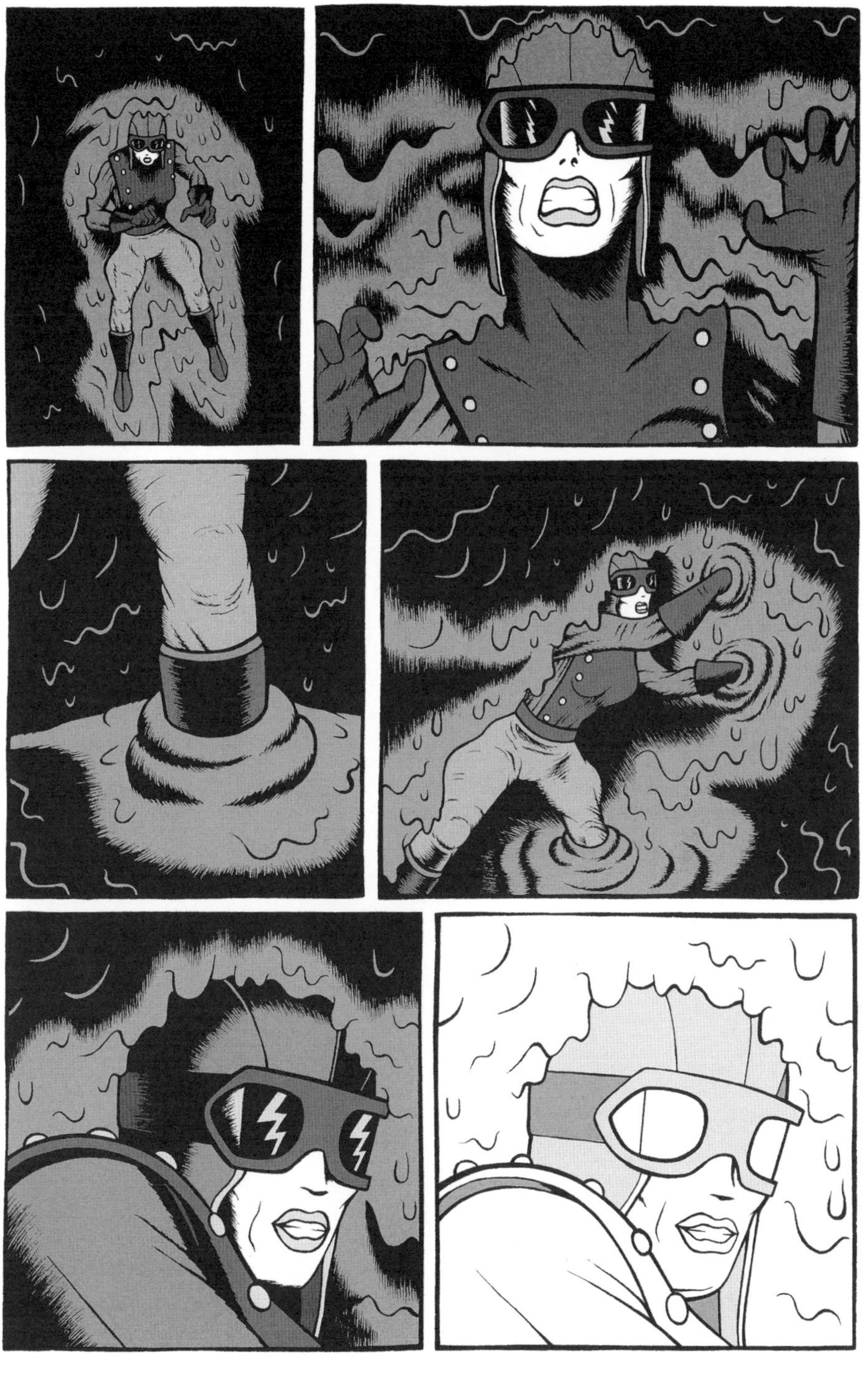

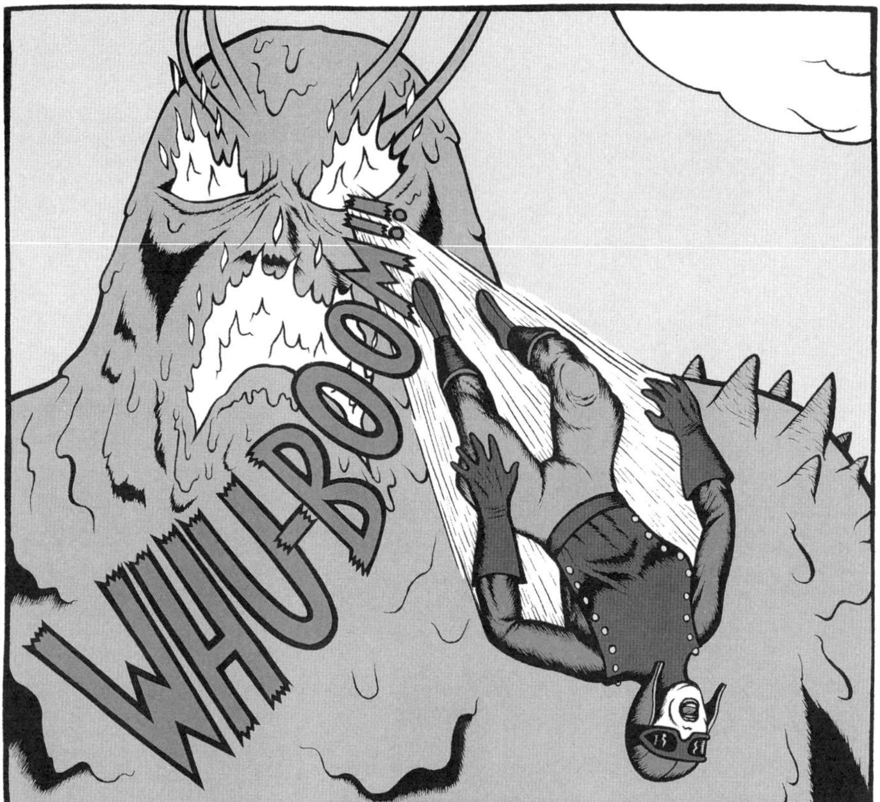
WHU-BOOM!!

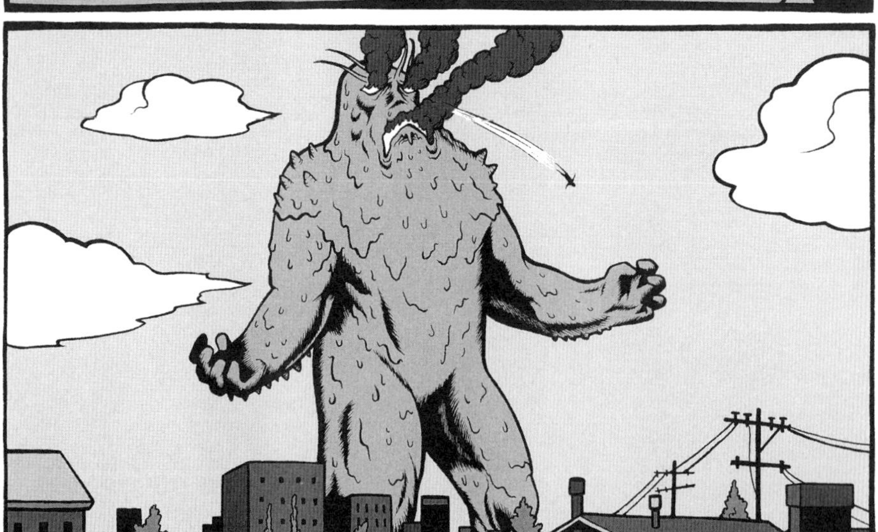

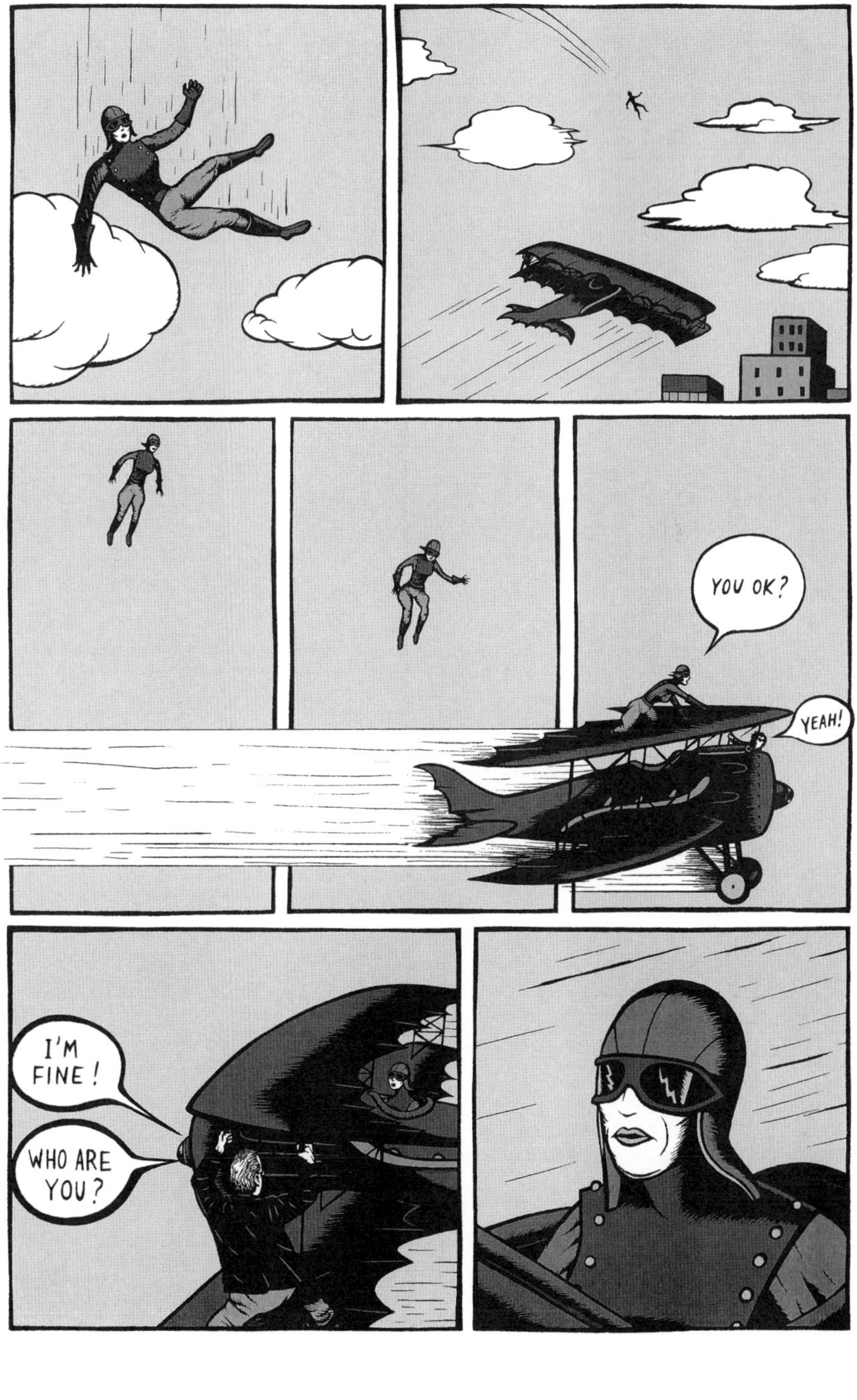
YOU OK?
YEAH!
I'M FINE!
WHO ARE YOU?

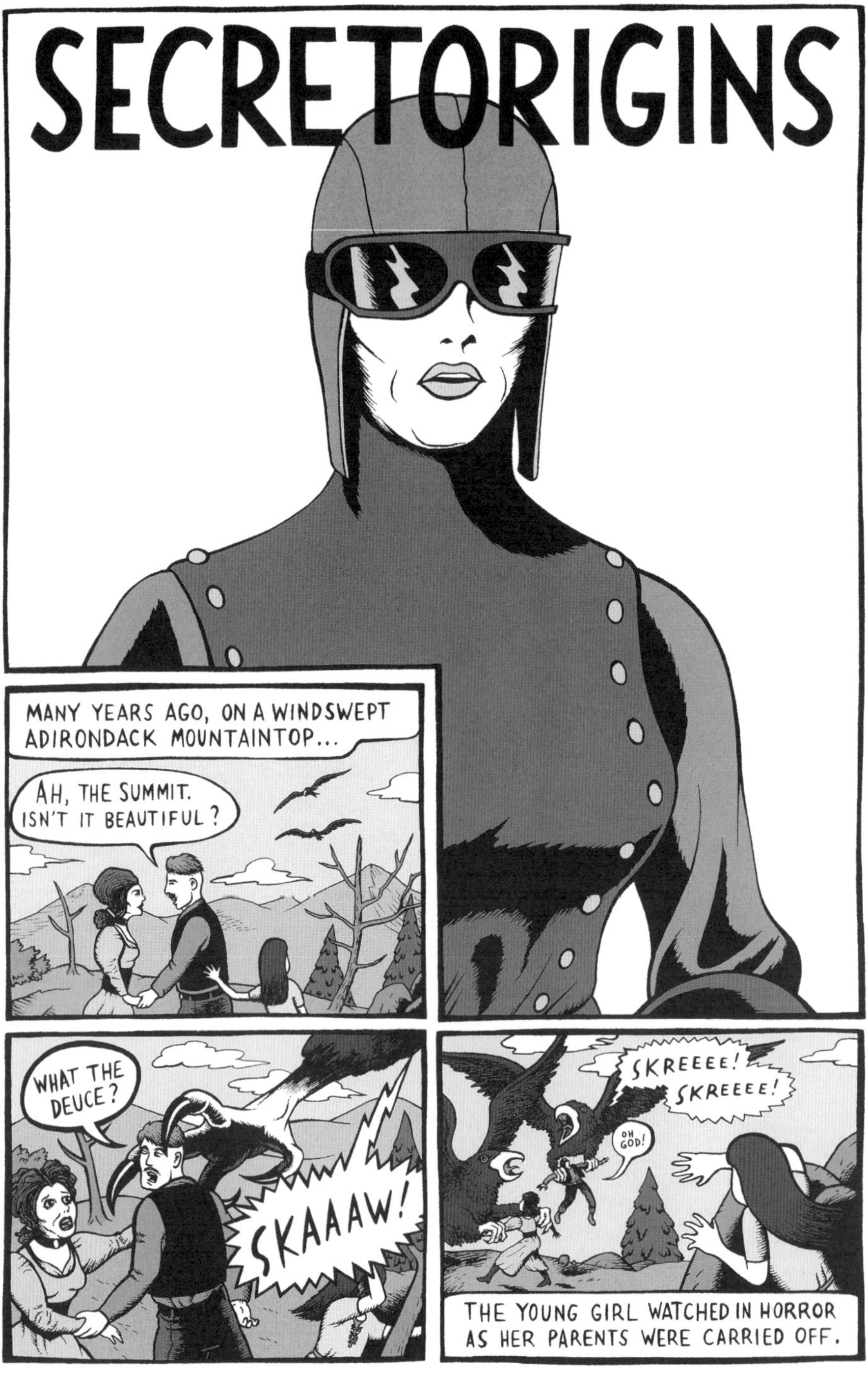
SECRETORIGINS
MANY YEARS AGO, ON A WINDSWEPT ADIRONDACK MOUNTAINTOP...
AH, THE SUMMIT. ISN'T IT BEAUTIFUL?
WHAT THE DEUCE?
SKAAAW!
SKREEEE! SKREEEE!
OH GOD!
THE YOUNG GIRL WATCHED IN HORROR AS HER PARENTS WERE CARRIED OFF.

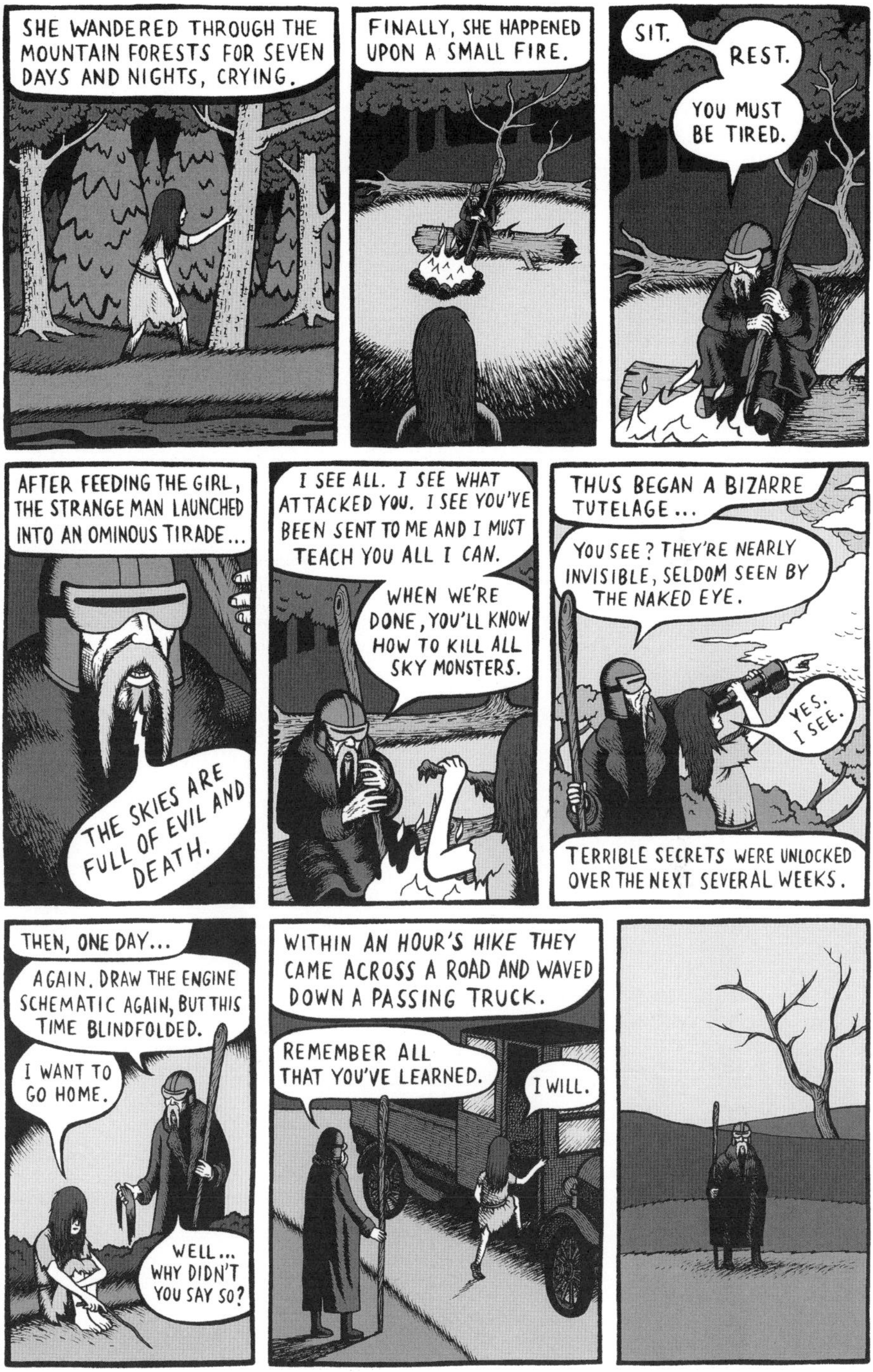
SHE WANDERED THROUGH THE MOUNTAIN FORESTS FOR SEVEN DAYS AND NIGHTS, CRYING.
FINALLY, SHE HAPPENED UPON A SMALL FIRE.
SIT.
REST.
YOU MUST BE TIRED.
AFTER FEEDING THE GIRL, THE STRANGE MAN LAUNCHED INTO AN OMINOUS TIRADE...
THE SKIES ARE FULL OF EVIL AND DEATH.
I SEE ALL. I SEE WHAT ATTACKED YOU. I SEE YOU'VE BEEN SENT TO ME AND I MUST TEACH YOU ALL I CAN.
WHEN WE'RE DONE, YOU'LL KNOW HOW TO KILL ALL SKY MONSTERS.
THUS BEGAN A BIZARRE TUTELAGE...
YOU SEE? THEY'RE NEARLY INVISIBLE, SELDOM SEEN BY THE NAKED EYE.
YES. I SEE.
TERRIBLE SECRETS WERE UNLOCKED OVER THE NEXT SEVERAL WEEKS.
THEN, ONE DAY...
AGAIN. DRAW THE ENGINE SCHEMATIC AGAIN, BUT THIS TIME BLINDFOLDED.
I WANT TO GO HOME.
WELL... WHY DIDN'T YOU SAY SO?
WITHIN AN HOUR'S HIKE THEY CAME ACROSS A ROAD AND WAVED DOWN A PASSING TRUCK.
REMEMBER ALL THAT YOU'VE LEARNED.
I WILL.

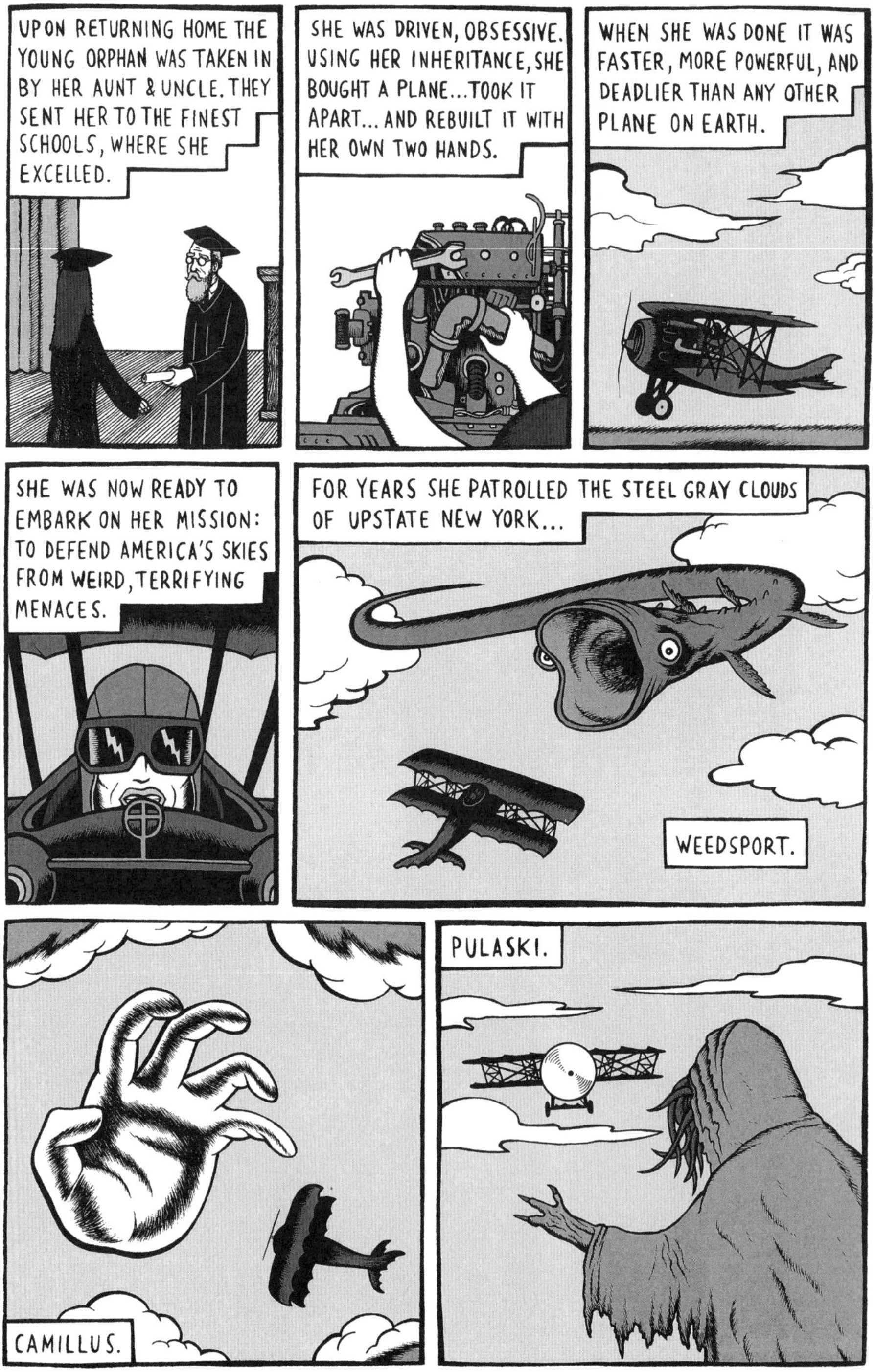
UPON RETURNING HOME THE YOUNG ORPHAN WAS TAKEN IN BY HER AUNT & UNCLE. THEY SENT HER TO THE FINEST SCHOOLS, WHERE SHE EXCELLED.
SHE WAS DRIVEN, OBSESSIVE. USING HER INHERITANCE, SHE BOUGHT A PLANE...TOOK IT APART... AND REBUILT IT WITH HER OWN TWO HANDS.
WHEN SHE WAS DONE IT WAS FASTER, MORE POWERFUL, AND DEADLIER THAN ANY OTHER PLANE ON EARTH.
SHE WAS NOW READY TO EMBARK ON HER MISSION: TO DEFEND AMERICA'S SKIES FROM WEIRD, TERRIFYING MENACES.
FOR YEARS SHE PATROLLED THE STEEL GRAY CLOUDS OF UPSTATE NEW YORK...
WEEDSPORT.
CAMILLUS.
PULASKI.

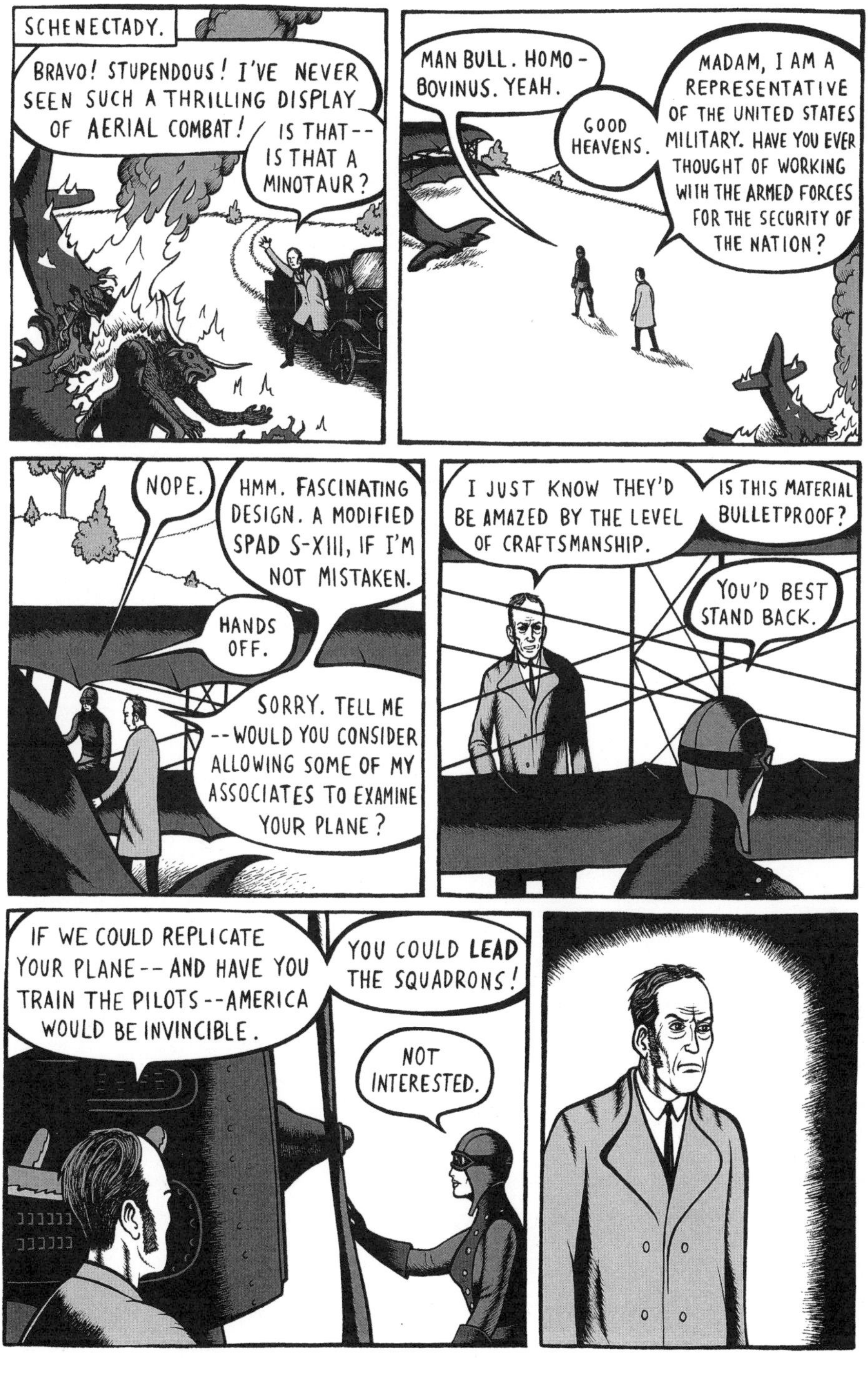
SCHENECTADY.
BRAVO! STUPENDOUS! I'VE NEVER SEEN SUCH A THRILLING DISPLAY OF AERIAL COMBAT!
IS THAT-- IS THAT A MINOTAUR?
MAN BULL. HOMO-BOVINUS. YEAH.
GOOD HEAVENS.
MADAM, I AM A REPRESENTATIVE OF THE UNITED STATES MILITARY. HAVE YOU EVER THOUGHT OF WORKING WITH THE ARMED FORCES FOR THE SECURITY OF THE NATION?
HMM. FASCINATING DESIGN. A MODIFIED SPAD S-XIII, IF I'M NOT MISTAKEN.
NOPE.
HANDS OFF.
SORRY. TELL ME --WOULD YOU CONSIDER ALLOWING SOME OF MY ASSOCIATES TO EXAMINE YOUR PLANE?
I JUST KNOW THEY'D BE AMAZED BY THE LEVEL OF CRAFTSMANSHIP.
IS THIS MATERIAL BULLETPROOF?
YOU'D BEST STAND BACK.
IF WE COULD REPLICATE YOUR PLANE--AND HAVE YOU TRAIN THE PILOTS--AMERICA WOULD BE INVINCIBLE.
YOU COULD **LEAD** THE SQUADRONS!
NOT INTERESTED.

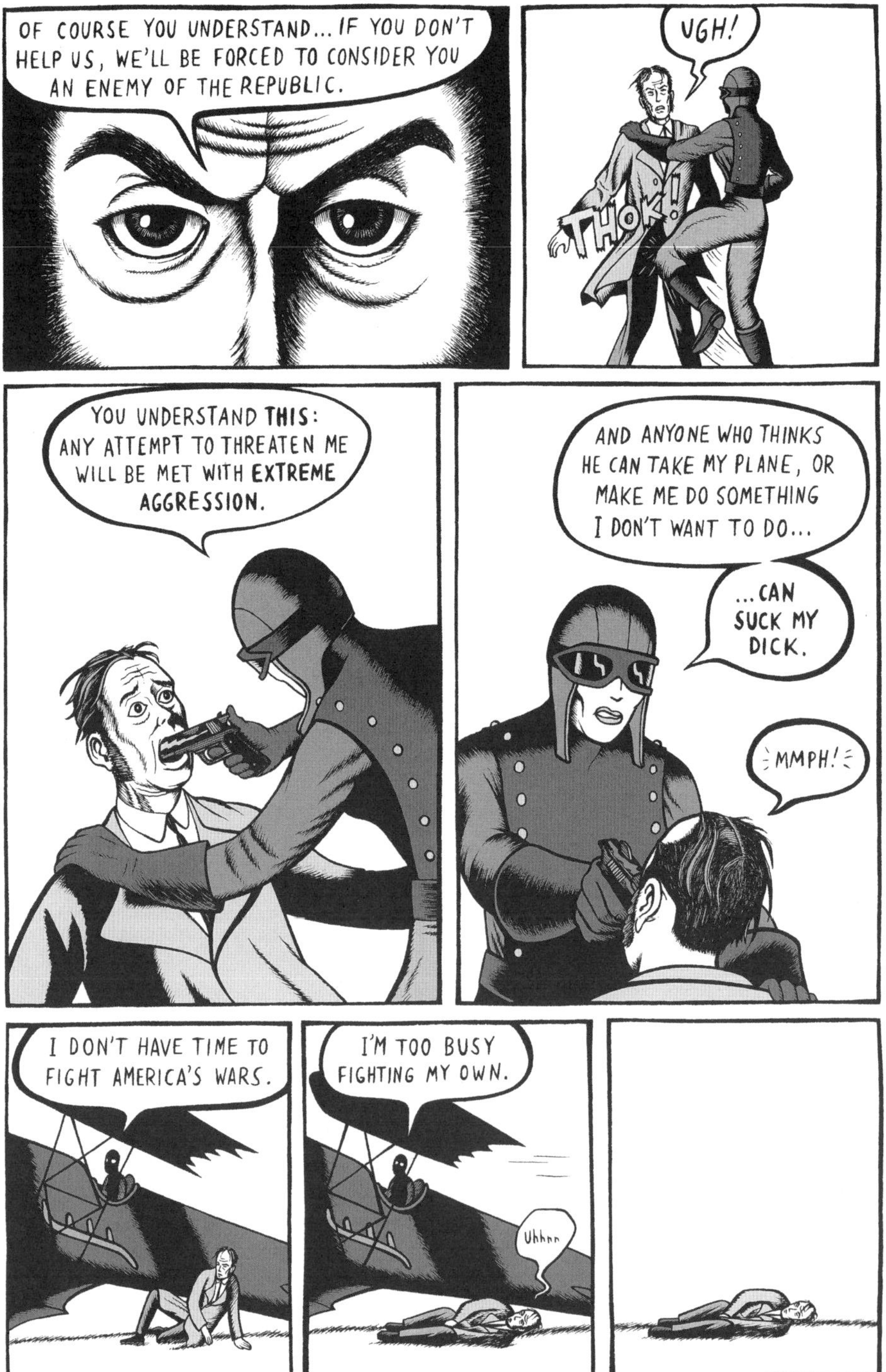
OF COURSE YOU UNDERSTAND... IF YOU DON'T HELP US, WE'LL BE FORCED TO CONSIDER YOU AN ENEMY OF THE REPUBLIC.
UGH!
THOK!
YOU UNDERSTAND THIS: ANY ATTEMPT TO THREATEN ME WILL BE MET WITH EXTREME AGGRESSION.
AND ANYONE WHO THINKS HE CAN TAKE MY PLANE, OR MAKE ME DO SOMETHING I DON'T WANT TO DO...
...CAN SUCK MY DICK.
MMPH!
I DON'T HAVE TIME TO FIGHT AMERICA'S WARS.
I'M TOO BUSY FIGHTING MY OWN.
Uhhnn

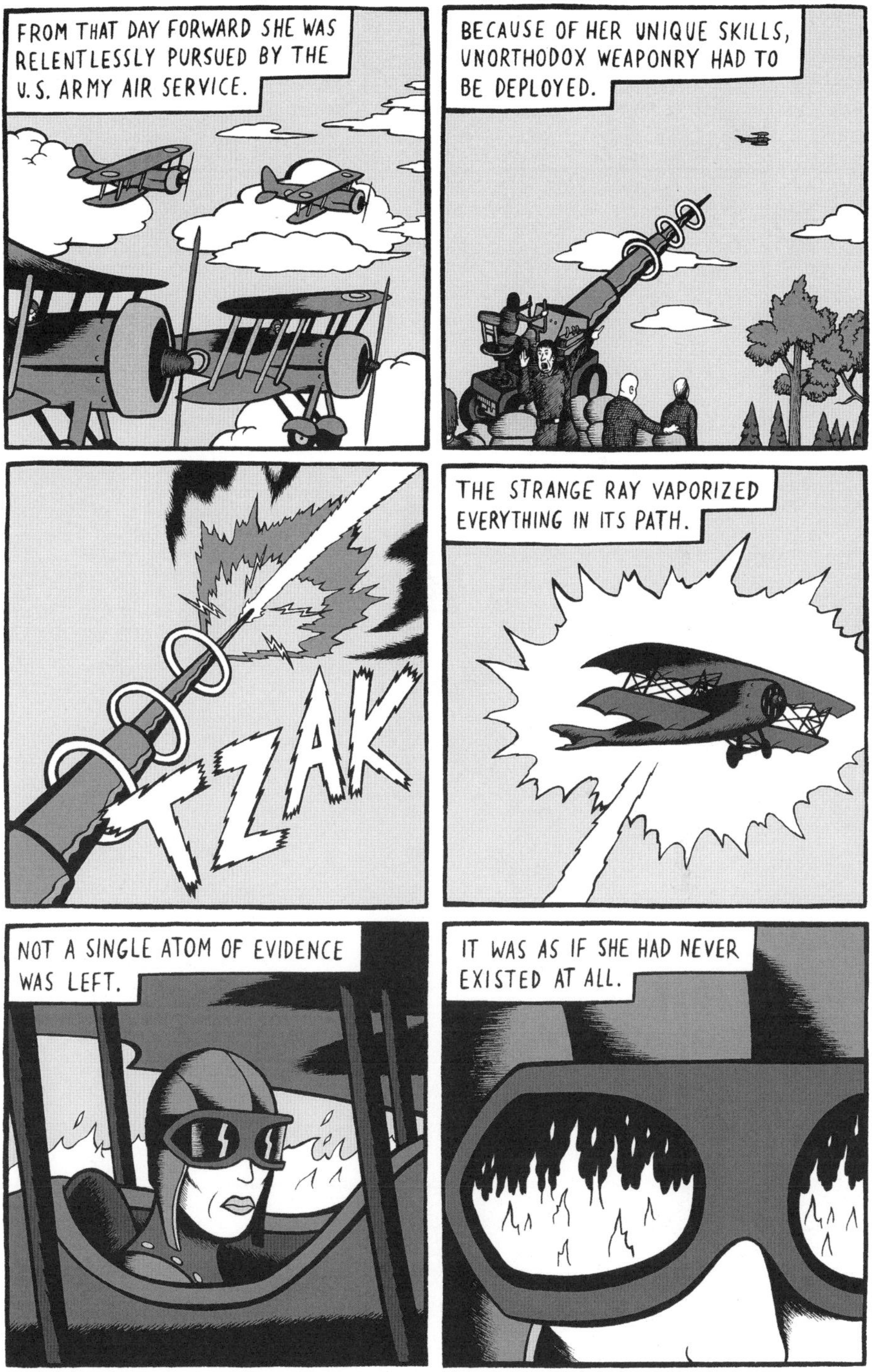
FROM THAT DAY FORWARD SHE WAS RELENTLESSLY PURSUED BY THE U.S. ARMY AIR SERVICE.
BECAUSE OF HER UNIQUE SKILLS, UNORTHODOX WEAPONRY HAD TO BE DEPLOYED.
TZAK
THE STRANGE RAY VAPORIZED EVERYTHING IN ITS PATH.
NOT A SINGLE ATOM OF EVIDENCE WAS LEFT.
IT WAS AS IF SHE HAD NEVER EXISTED AT ALL.

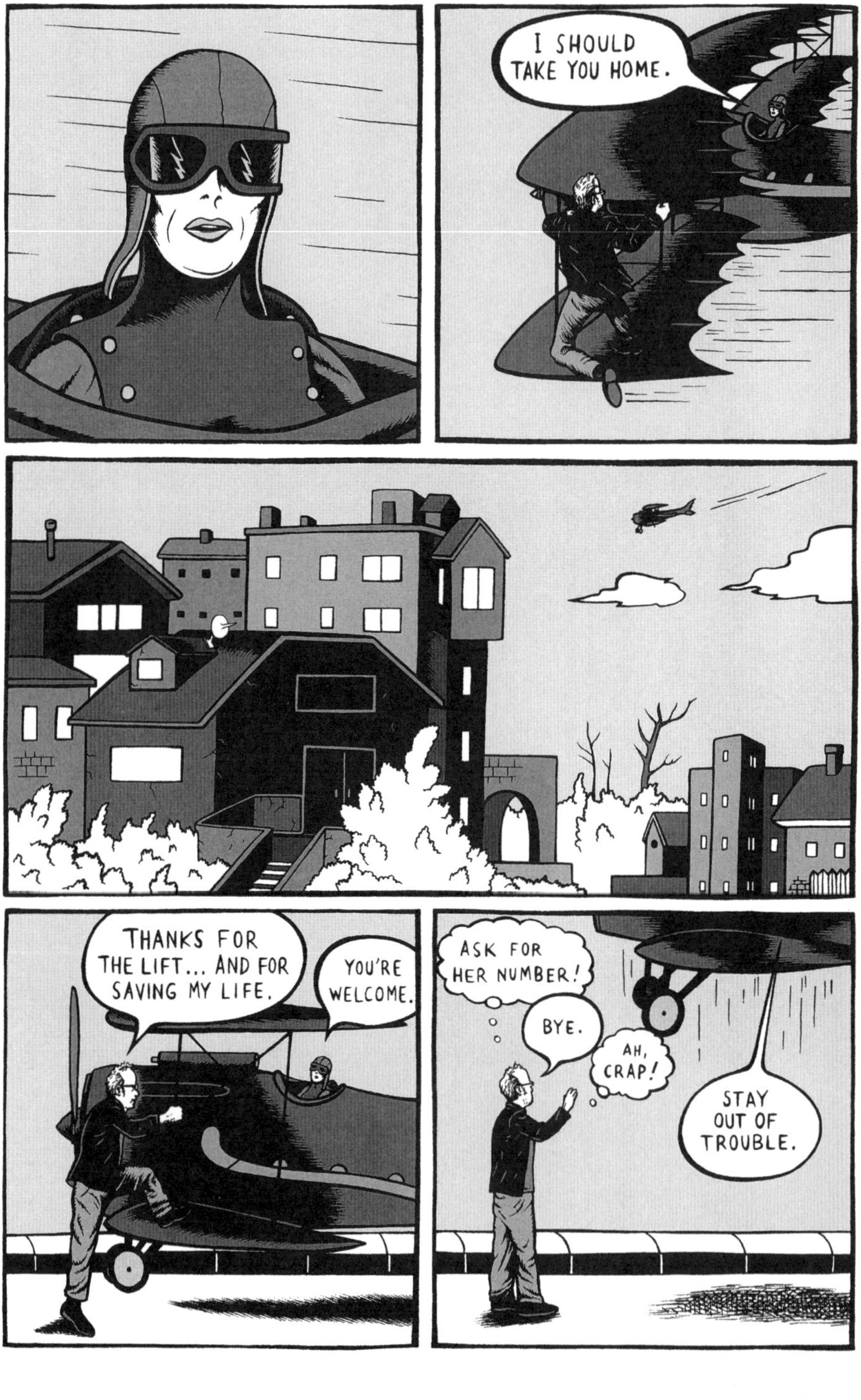
I SHOULD TAKE YOU HOME.
THANKS FOR THE LIFT... AND FOR SAVING MY LIFE.
YOU'RE WELCOME.
ASK FOR HER NUMBER!
BYE.
AH, CRAP!
STAY OUT OF TROUBLE.

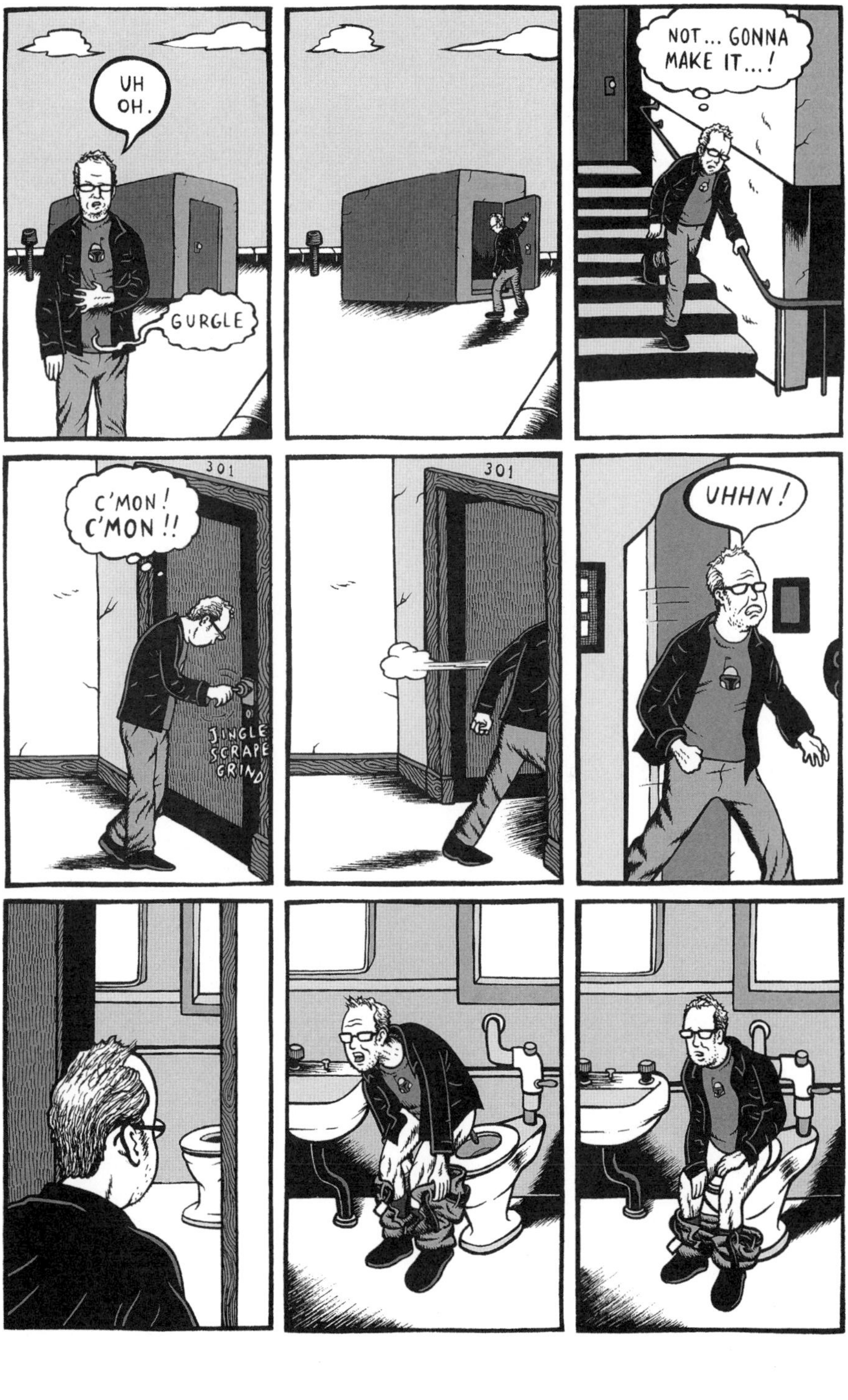
UH OH.
GURGLE
NOT... GONNA MAKE IT...!
C'MON! C'MON!!
JINGLE SCRAPE GRIND
301
301
UHHN!

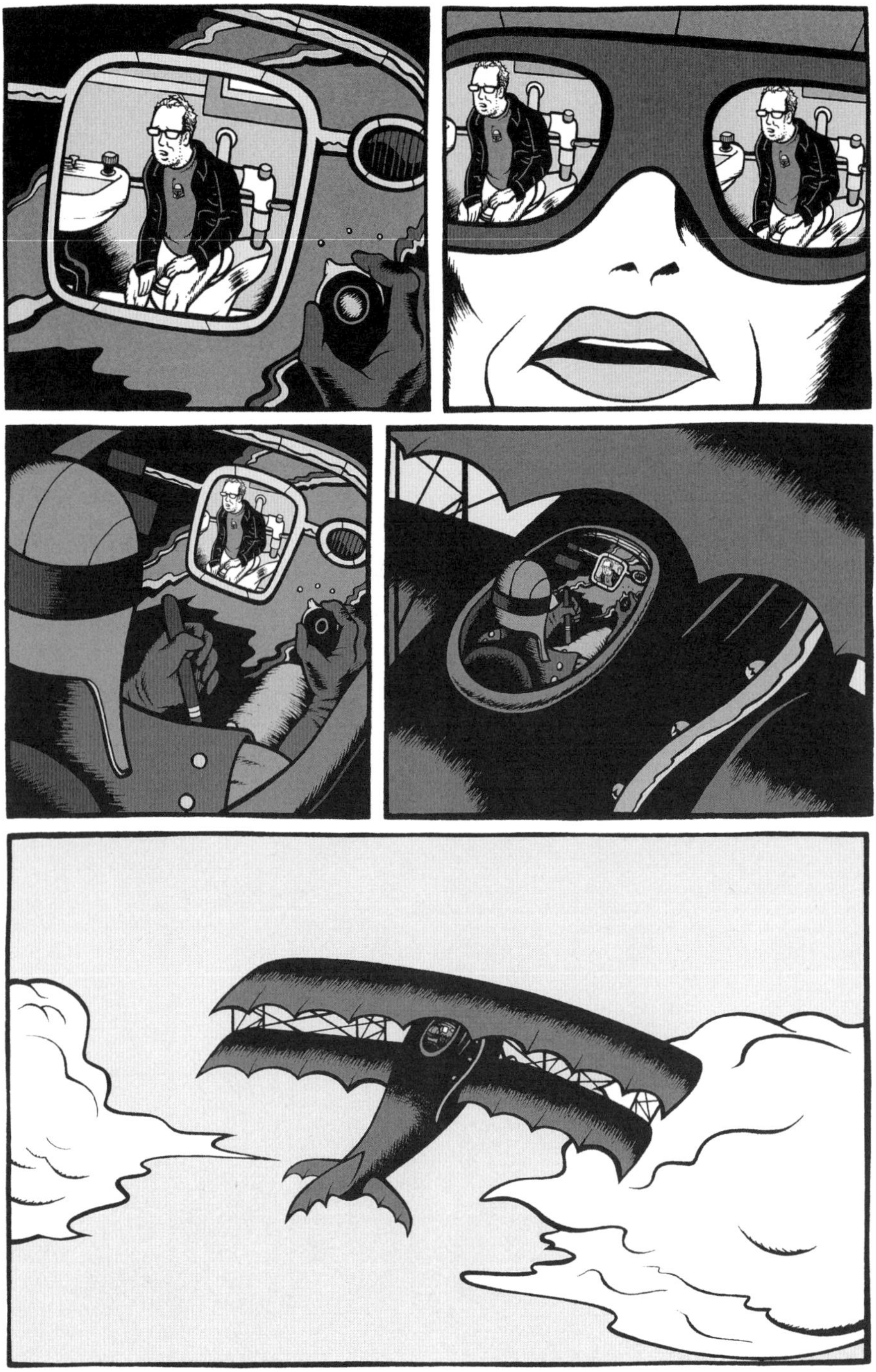

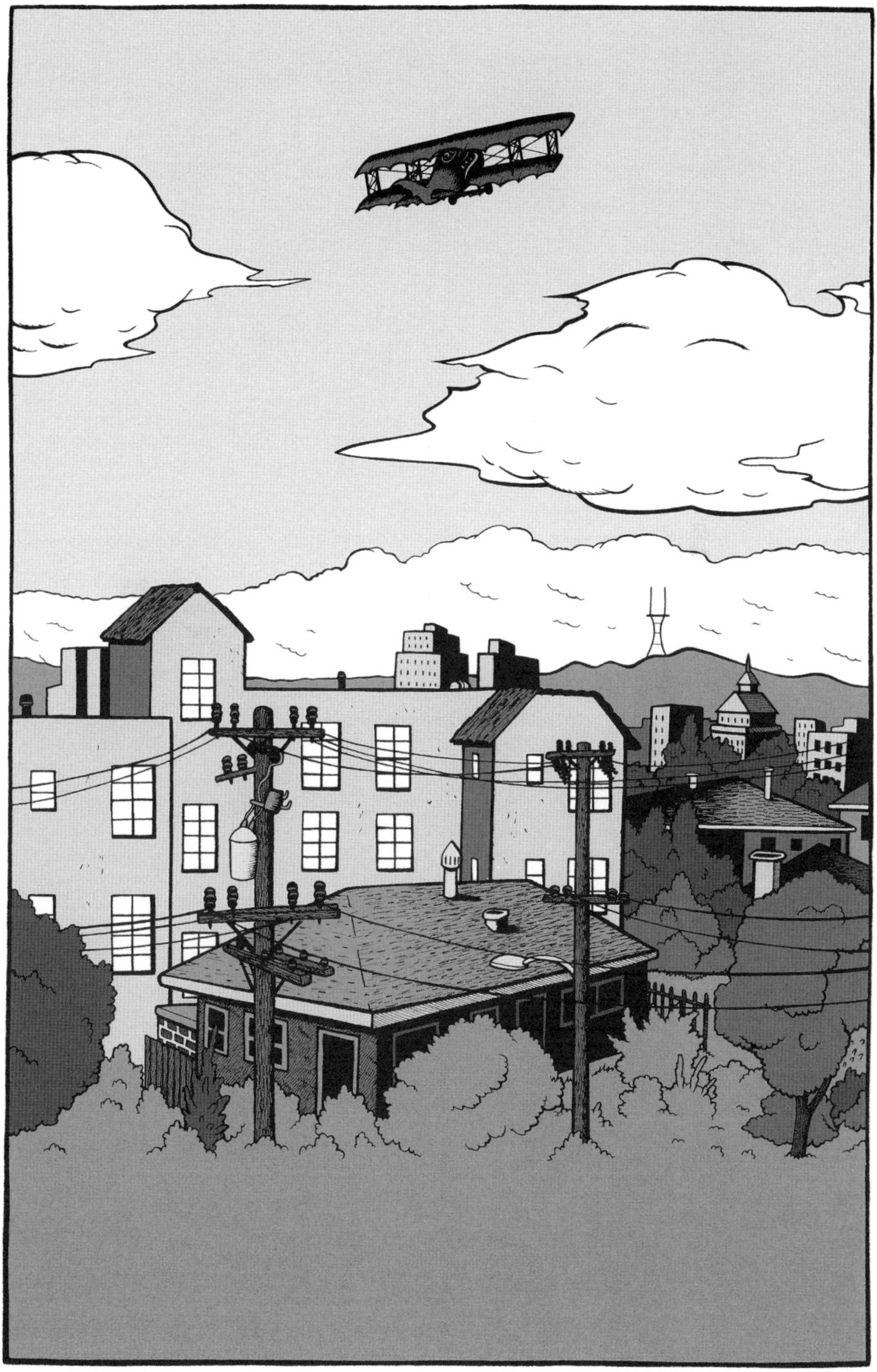

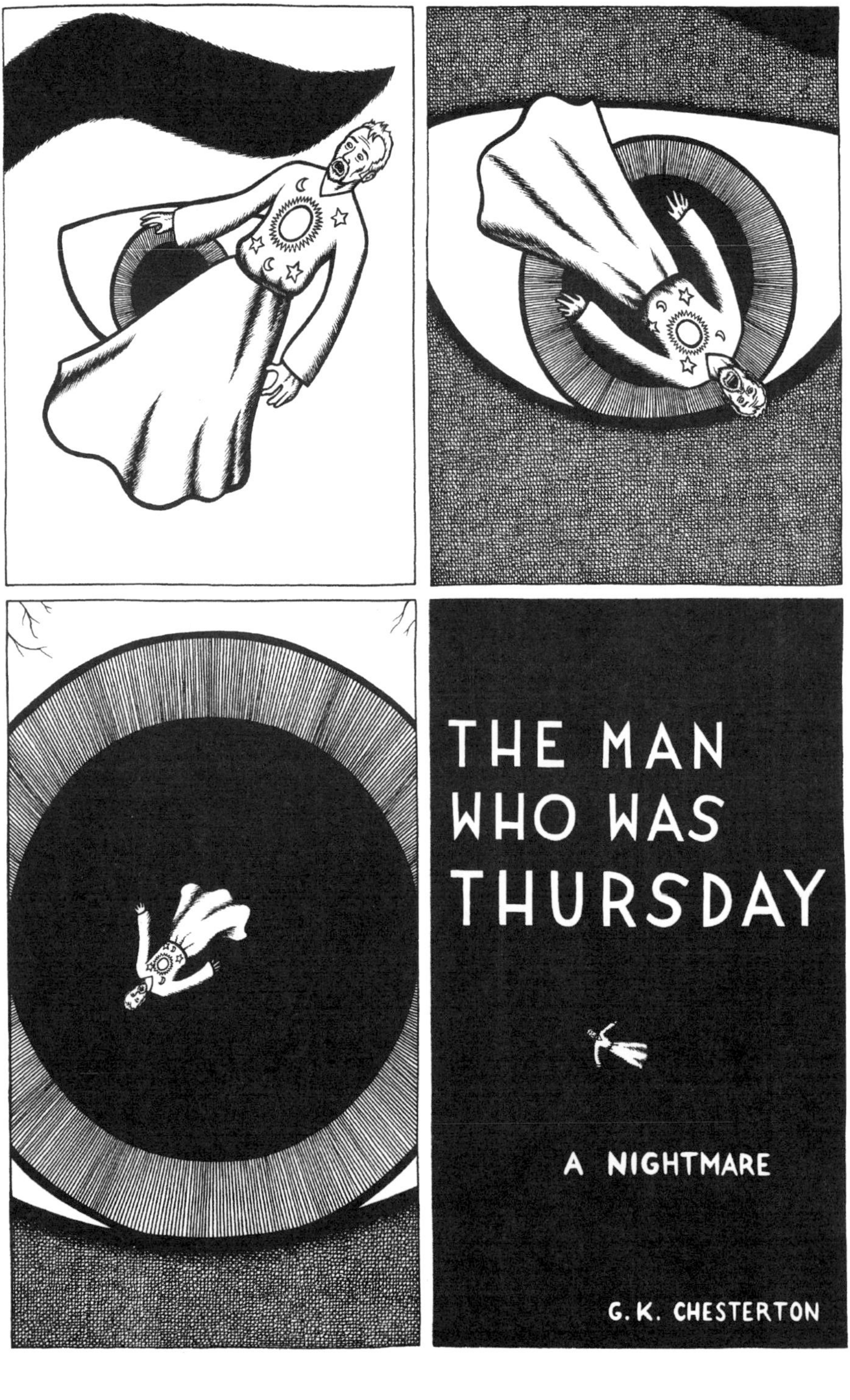
THE MAN WHO WAS THURSDAY
A NIGHTMARE
G.K. CHESTERTON

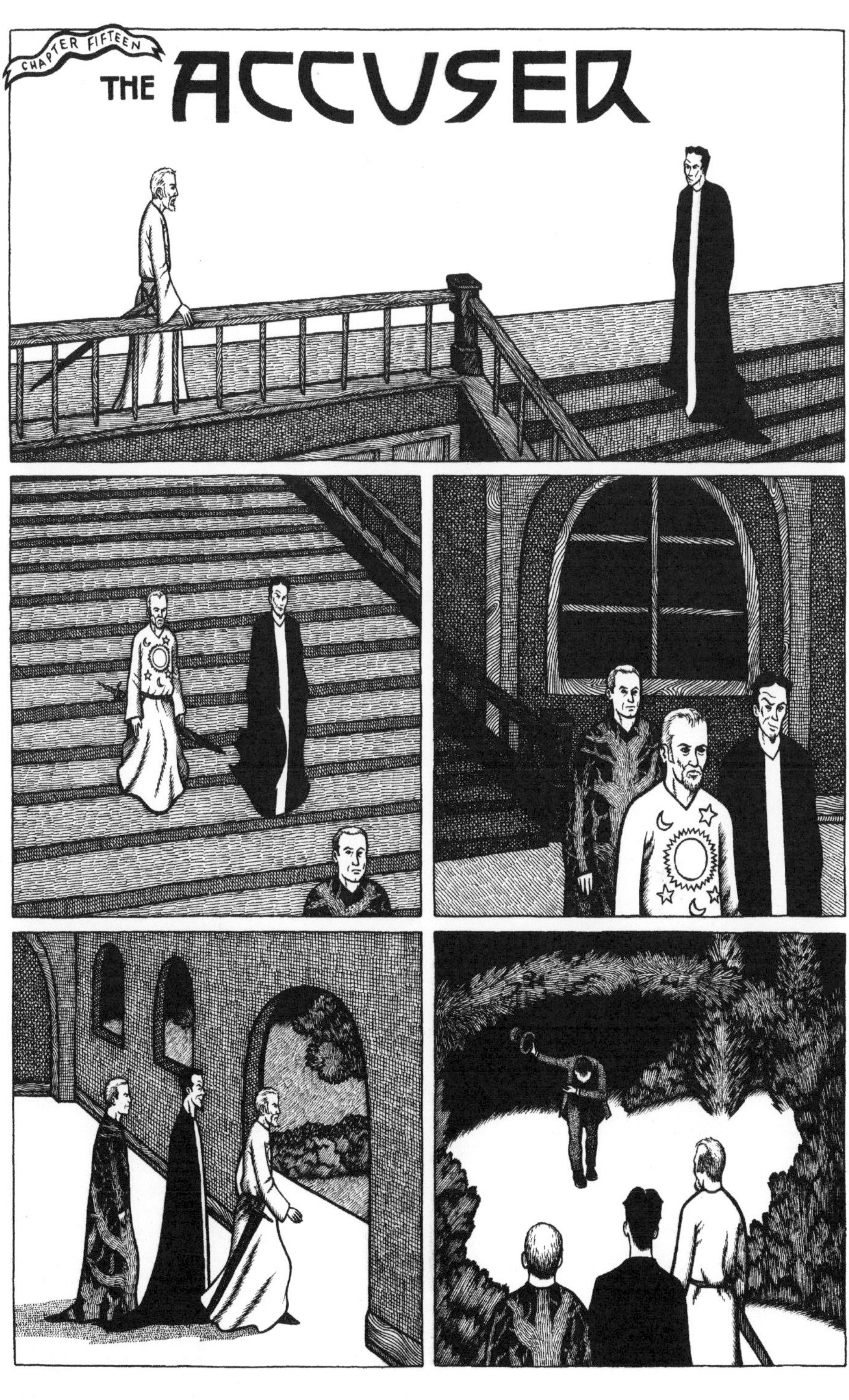
CHAPTER FIFTEEN
THE ACCUSER

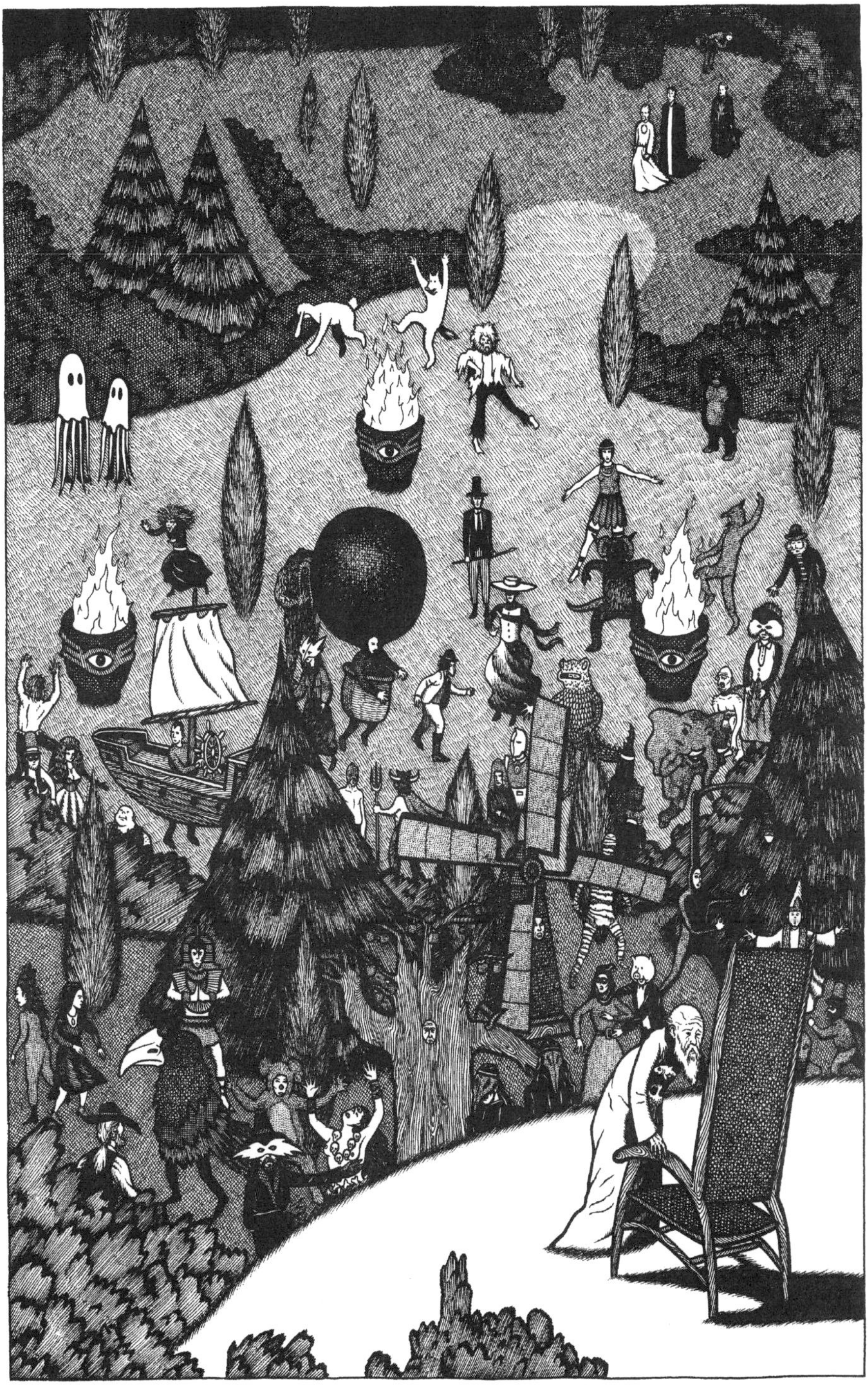

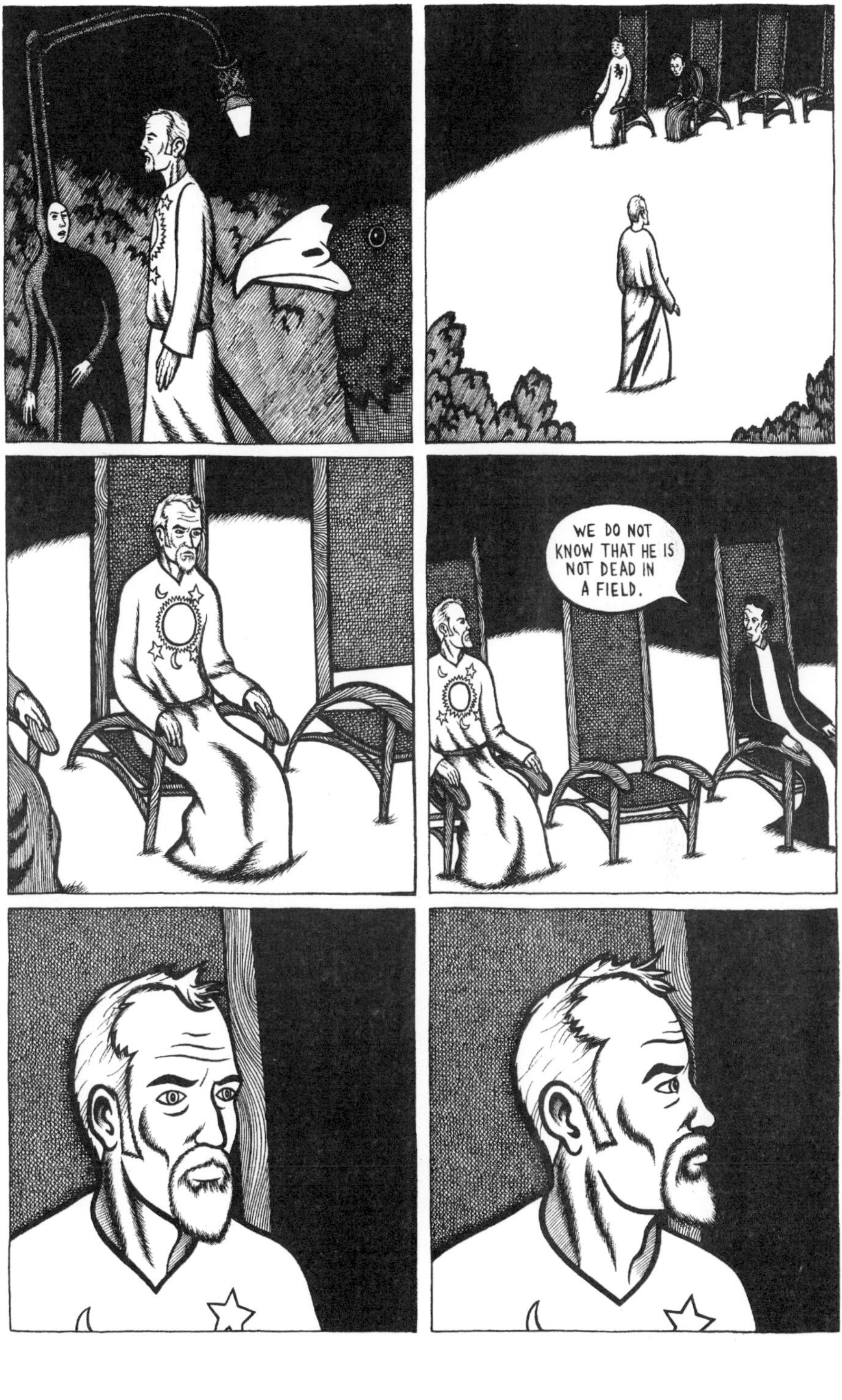
WE DO NOT KNOW THAT HE IS NOT DEAD IN A FIELD.

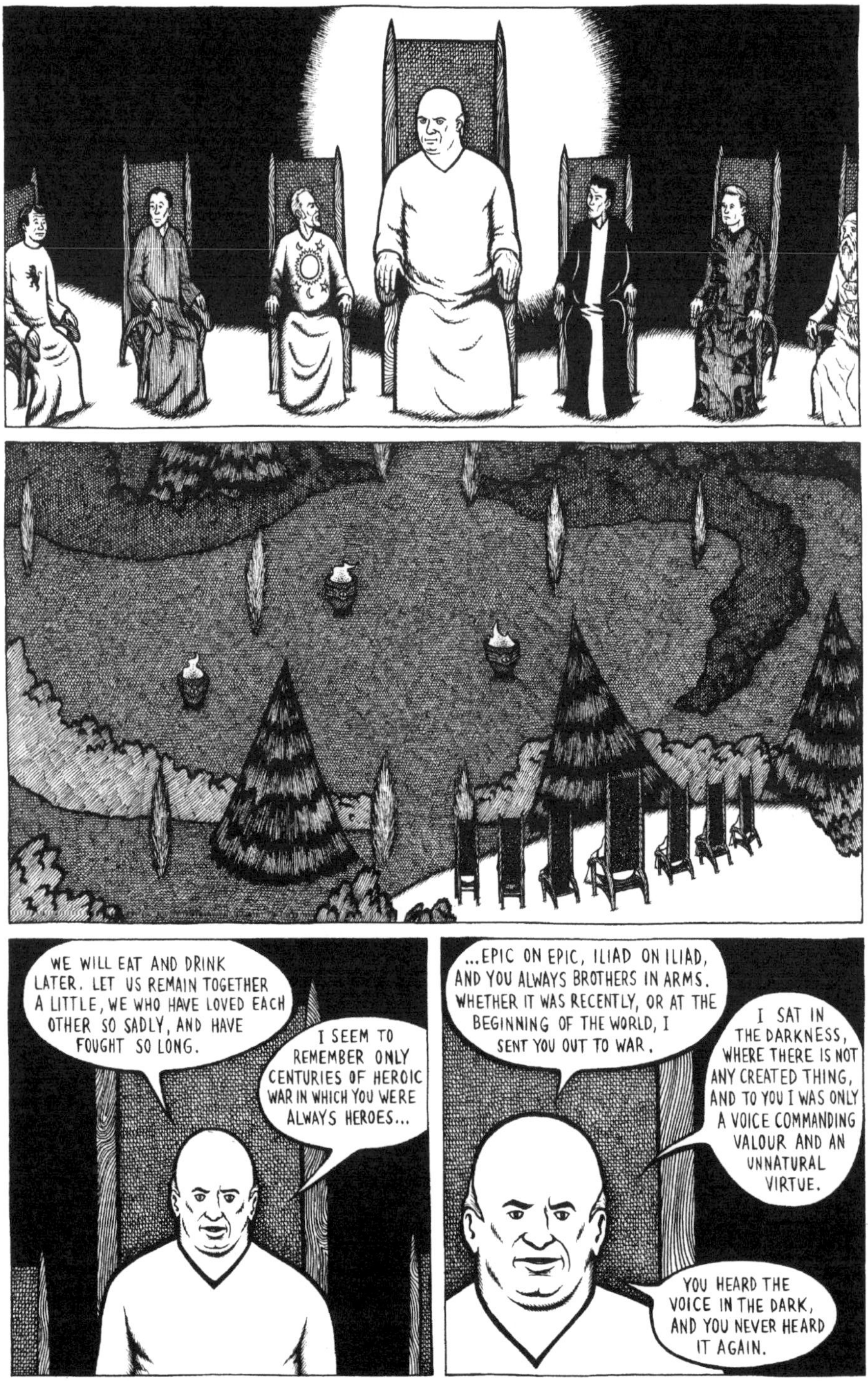
WE WILL EAT AND DRINK LATER. LET US REMAIN TOGETHER A LITTLE, WE WHO HAVE LOVED EACH OTHER SO SADLY, AND HAVE FOUGHT SO LONG.
I SEEM TO REMEMBER ONLY CENTURIES OF HEROIC WAR IN WHICH YOU WERE ALWAYS HEROES...
...EPIC ON EPIC, ILIAD ON ILIAD, AND YOU ALWAYS BROTHERS IN ARMS. WHETHER IT WAS RECENTLY, OR AT THE BEGINNING OF THE WORLD, I SENT YOU OUT TO WAR.
I SAT IN THE DARKNESS, WHERE THERE IS NOT ANY CREATED THING, AND TO YOU I WAS ONLY A VOICE COMMANDING VALOUR AND AN UNNATURAL VIRTUE.
YOU HEARD THE VOICE IN THE DARK, AND YOU NEVER HEARD IT AGAIN.

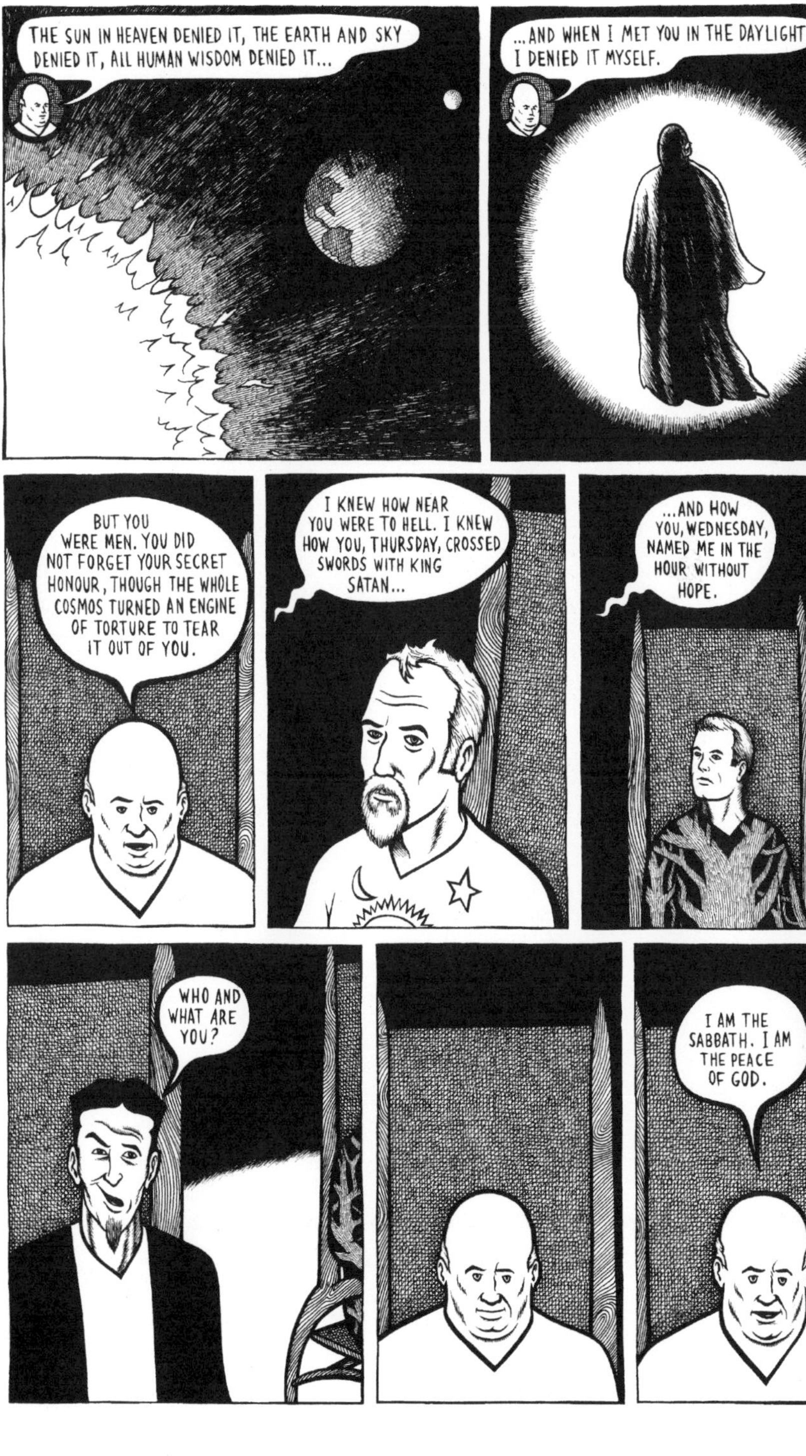
THE SUN IN HEAVEN DENIED IT, THE EARTH AND SKY DENIED IT, ALL HUMAN WISDOM DENIED IT...
...AND WHEN I MET YOU IN THE DAYLIGHT I DENIED IT MYSELF.
BUT YOU WERE MEN. YOU DID NOT FORGET YOUR SECRET HONOUR, THOUGH THE WHOLE COSMOS TURNED AN ENGINE OF TORTURE TO TEAR IT OUT OF YOU.
I KNEW HOW NEAR YOU WERE TO HELL. I KNEW HOW YOU, THURSDAY, CROSSED SWORDS WITH KING SATAN...
...AND HOW YOU, WEDNESDAY, NAMED ME IN THE HOUR WITHOUT HOPE.
WHO AND WHAT ARE YOU?
I AM THE SABBATH. I AM THE PEACE OF GOD.

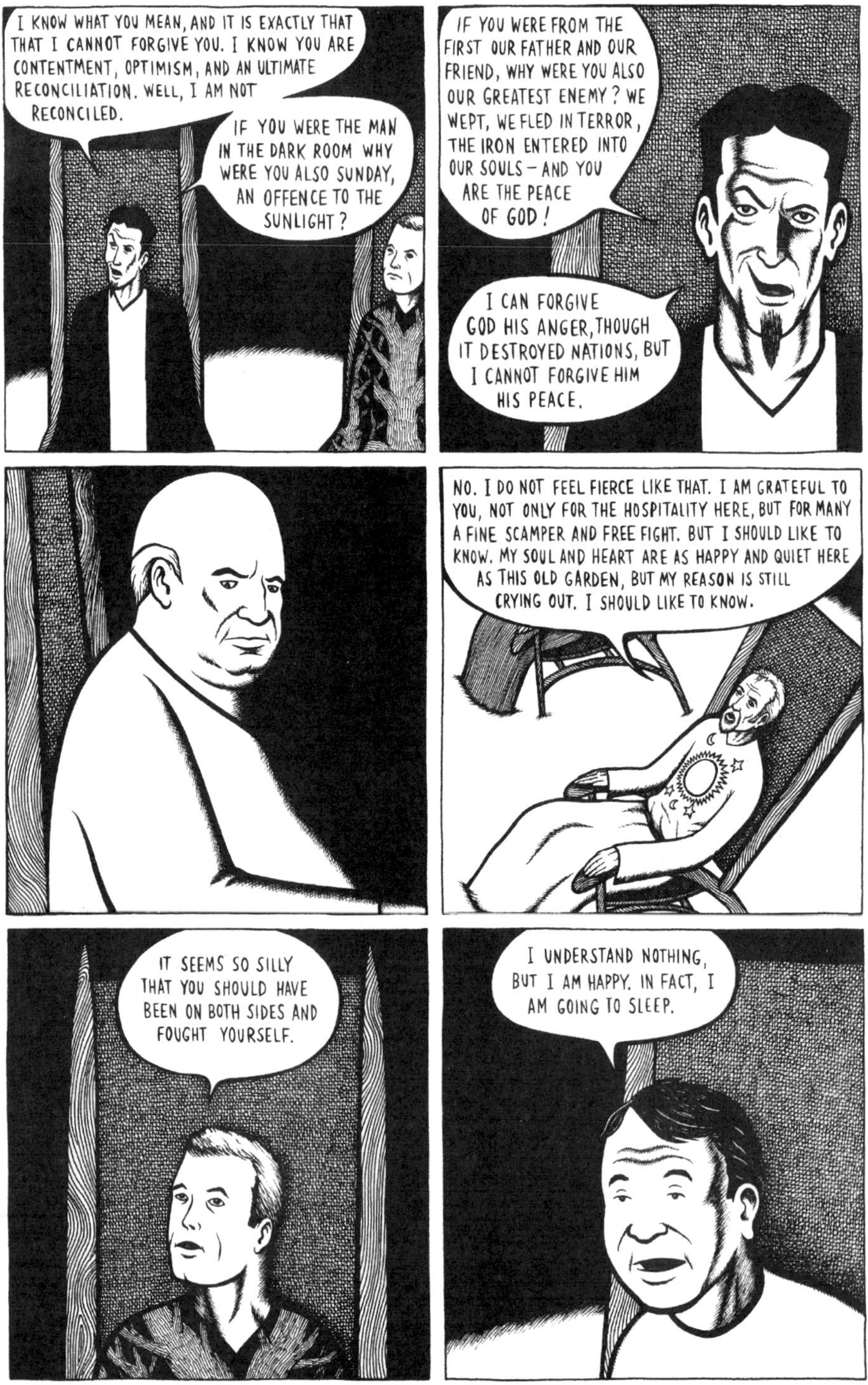
I KNOW WHAT YOU MEAN, AND IT IS EXACTLY THAT THAT I CANNOT FORGIVE YOU. I KNOW YOU ARE CONTENTMENT, OPTIMISM, AND AN ULTIMATE RECONCILIATION. WELL, I AM NOT RECONCILED.
IF YOU WERE THE MAN IN THE DARK ROOM WHY WERE YOU ALSO SUNDAY, AN OFFENCE TO THE SUNLIGHT?
IF YOU WERE FROM THE FIRST OUR FATHER AND OUR FRIEND, WHY WERE YOU ALSO OUR GREATEST ENEMY? WE WEPT, WE FLED IN TERROR, THE IRON ENTERED INTO OUR SOULS – AND YOU ARE THE PEACE OF GOD!
I CAN FORGIVE GOD HIS ANGER, THOUGH IT DESTROYED NATIONS, BUT I CANNOT FORGIVE HIM HIS PEACE.
NO. I DO NOT FEEL FIERCE LIKE THAT. I AM GRATEFUL TO YOU, NOT ONLY FOR THE HOSPITALITY HERE, BUT FOR MANY A FINE SCAMPER AND FREE FIGHT. BUT I SHOULD LIKE TO KNOW. MY SOUL AND HEART ARE AS HAPPY AND QUIET HERE AS THIS OLD GARDEN, BUT MY REASON IS STILL CRYING OUT. I SHOULD LIKE TO KNOW.
IT SEEMS SO SILLY THAT YOU SHOULD HAVE BEEN ON BOTH SIDES AND FOUGHT YOURSELF.
I UNDERSTAND NOTHING, BUT I AM HAPPY. IN FACT, I AM GOING TO SLEEP.

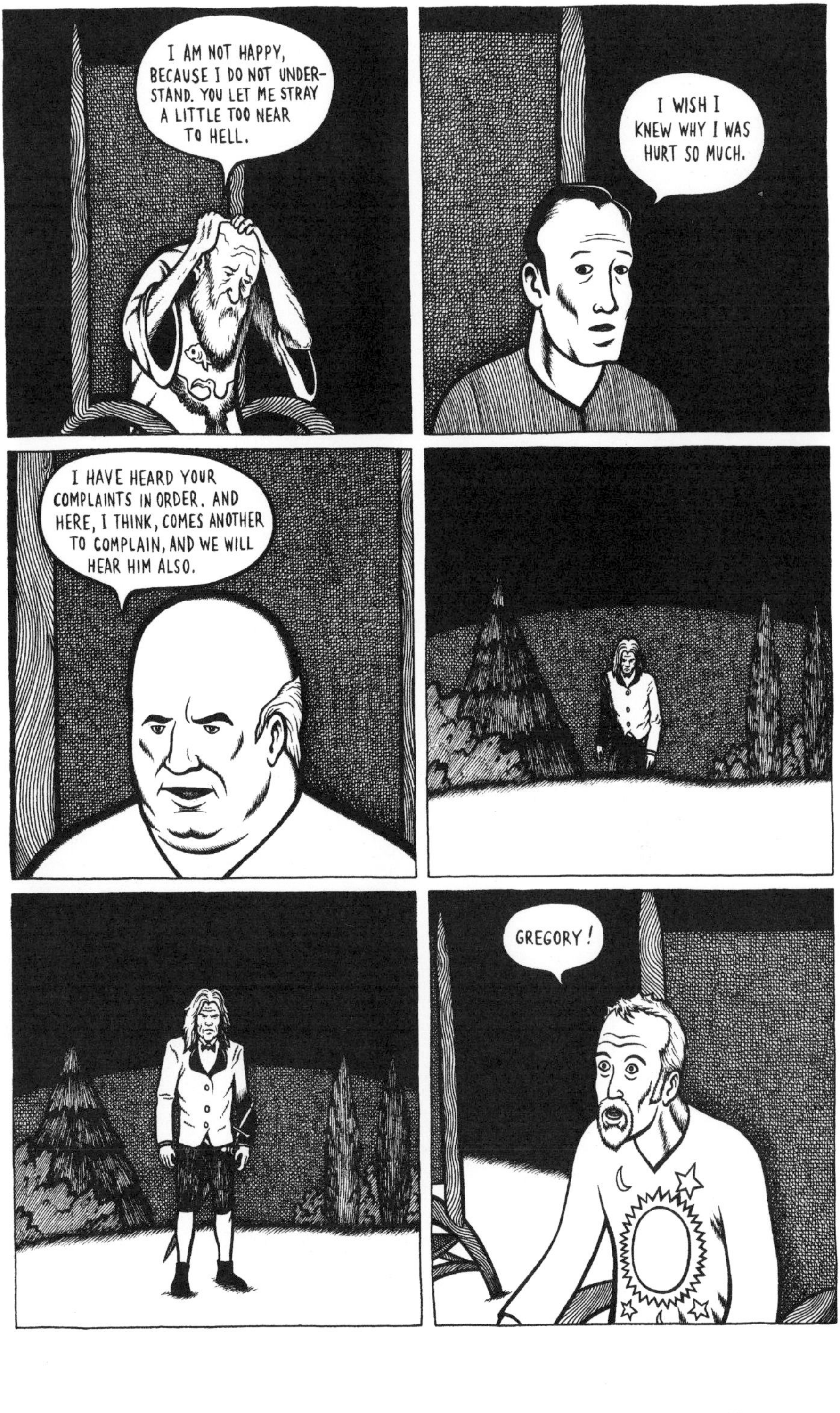
I AM NOT HAPPY, BECAUSE I DO NOT UNDER-STAND. YOU LET ME STRAY A LITTLE TOO NEAR TO HELL.
I WISH I KNEW WHY I WAS HURT SO MUCH.
I HAVE HEARD YOUR COMPLAINTS IN ORDER. AND HERE, I THINK, COMES ANOTHER TO COMPLAIN, AND WE WILL HEAR HIM ALSO.
GREGORY!

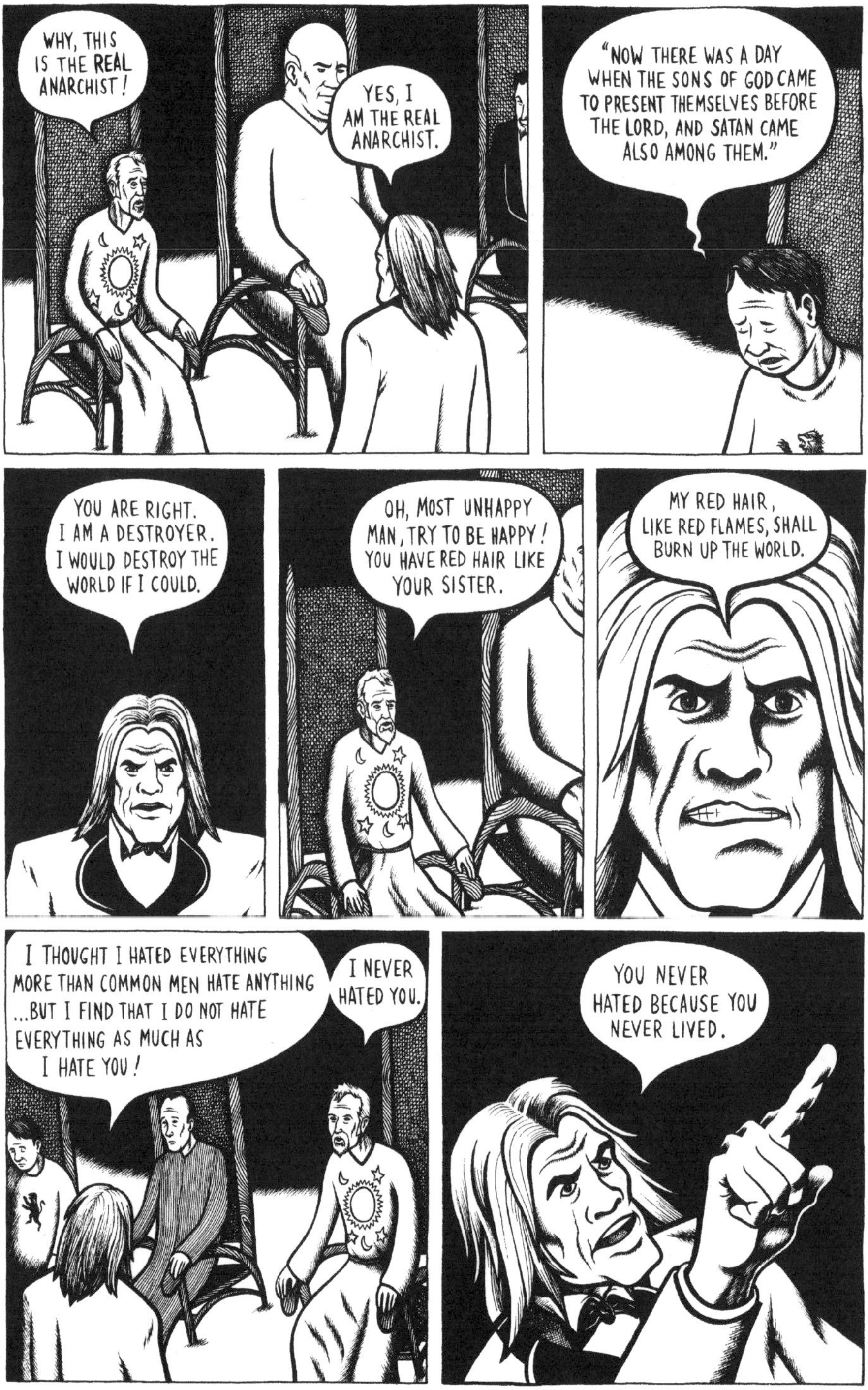
WHY, THIS IS THE REAL ANARCHIST!
YES, I AM THE REAL ANARCHIST.
"NOW THERE WAS A DAY WHEN THE SONS OF GOD CAME TO PRESENT THEMSELVES BEFORE THE LORD, AND SATAN CAME ALSO AMONG THEM."
YOU ARE RIGHT. I AM A DESTROYER. I WOULD DESTROY THE WORLD IF I COULD.
OH, MOST UNHAPPY MAN, TRY TO BE HAPPY! YOU HAVE RED HAIR LIKE YOUR SISTER.
MY RED HAIR, LIKE RED FLAMES, SHALL BURN UP THE WORLD.
I THOUGHT I HATED EVERYTHING MORE THAN COMMON MEN HATE ANYTHING ...BUT I FIND THAT I DO NOT HATE EVERYTHING AS MUCH AS I HATE YOU!
I NEVER HATED YOU.
YOU NEVER HATED BECAUSE YOU NEVER LIVED.

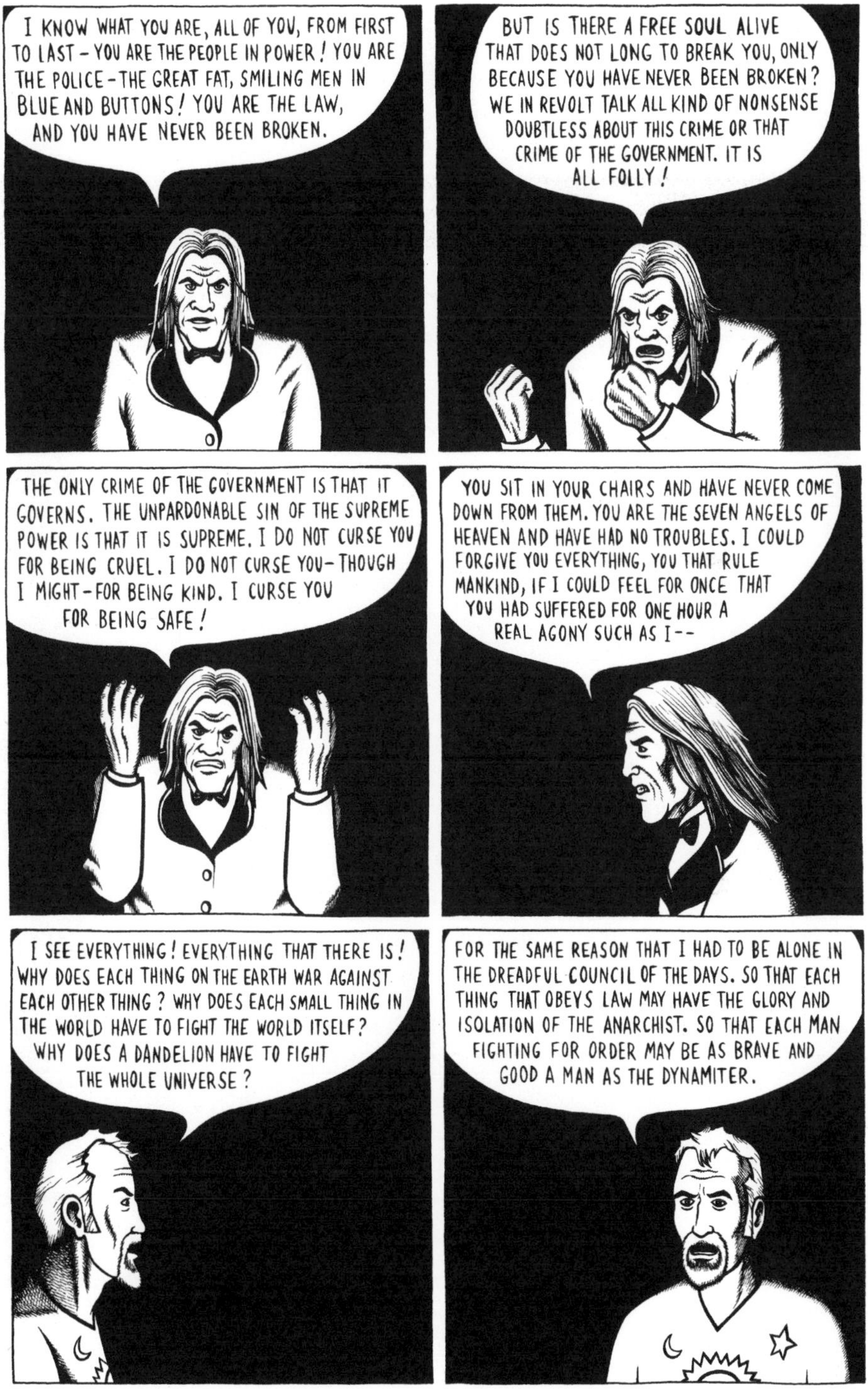
I KNOW WHAT YOU ARE, ALL OF YOU, FROM FIRST TO LAST - YOU ARE THE PEOPLE IN POWER! YOU ARE THE POLICE - THE GREAT FAT, SMILING MEN IN BLUE AND BUTTONS! YOU ARE THE LAW, AND YOU HAVE NEVER BEEN BROKEN.
BUT IS THERE A FREE SOUL ALIVE THAT DOES NOT LONG TO BREAK YOU, ONLY BECAUSE YOU HAVE NEVER BEEN BROKEN? WE IN REVOLT TALK ALL KIND OF NONSENSE DOUBTLESS ABOUT THIS CRIME OR THAT CRIME OF THE GOVERNMENT. IT IS ALL FOLLY!
THE ONLY CRIME OF THE GOVERNMENT IS THAT IT GOVERNS. THE UNPARDONABLE SIN OF THE SUPREME POWER IS THAT IT IS SUPREME. I DO NOT CURSE YOU FOR BEING CRUEL. I DO NOT CURSE YOU - THOUGH I MIGHT - FOR BEING KIND. I CURSE YOU FOR BEING SAFE!
YOU SIT IN YOUR CHAIRS AND HAVE NEVER COME DOWN FROM THEM. YOU ARE THE SEVEN ANGELS OF HEAVEN AND HAVE HAD NO TROUBLES. I COULD FORGIVE YOU EVERYTHING, YOU THAT RULE MANKIND, IF I COULD FEEL FOR ONCE THAT YOU HAD SUFFERED FOR ONE HOUR A REAL AGONY SUCH AS I--
I SEE EVERYTHING! EVERYTHING THAT THERE IS! WHY DOES EACH THING ON THE EARTH WAR AGAINST EACH OTHER THING? WHY DOES EACH SMALL THING IN THE WORLD HAVE TO FIGHT THE WORLD ITSELF? WHY DOES A DANDELION HAVE TO FIGHT THE WHOLE UNIVERSE?
FOR THE SAME REASON THAT I HAD TO BE ALONE IN THE DREADFUL COUNCIL OF THE DAYS. SO THAT EACH THING THAT OBEYS LAW MAY HAVE THE GLORY AND ISOLATION OF THE ANARCHIST. SO THAT EACH MAN FIGHTING FOR ORDER MAY BE AS BRAVE AND GOOD A MAN AS THE DYNAMITER.

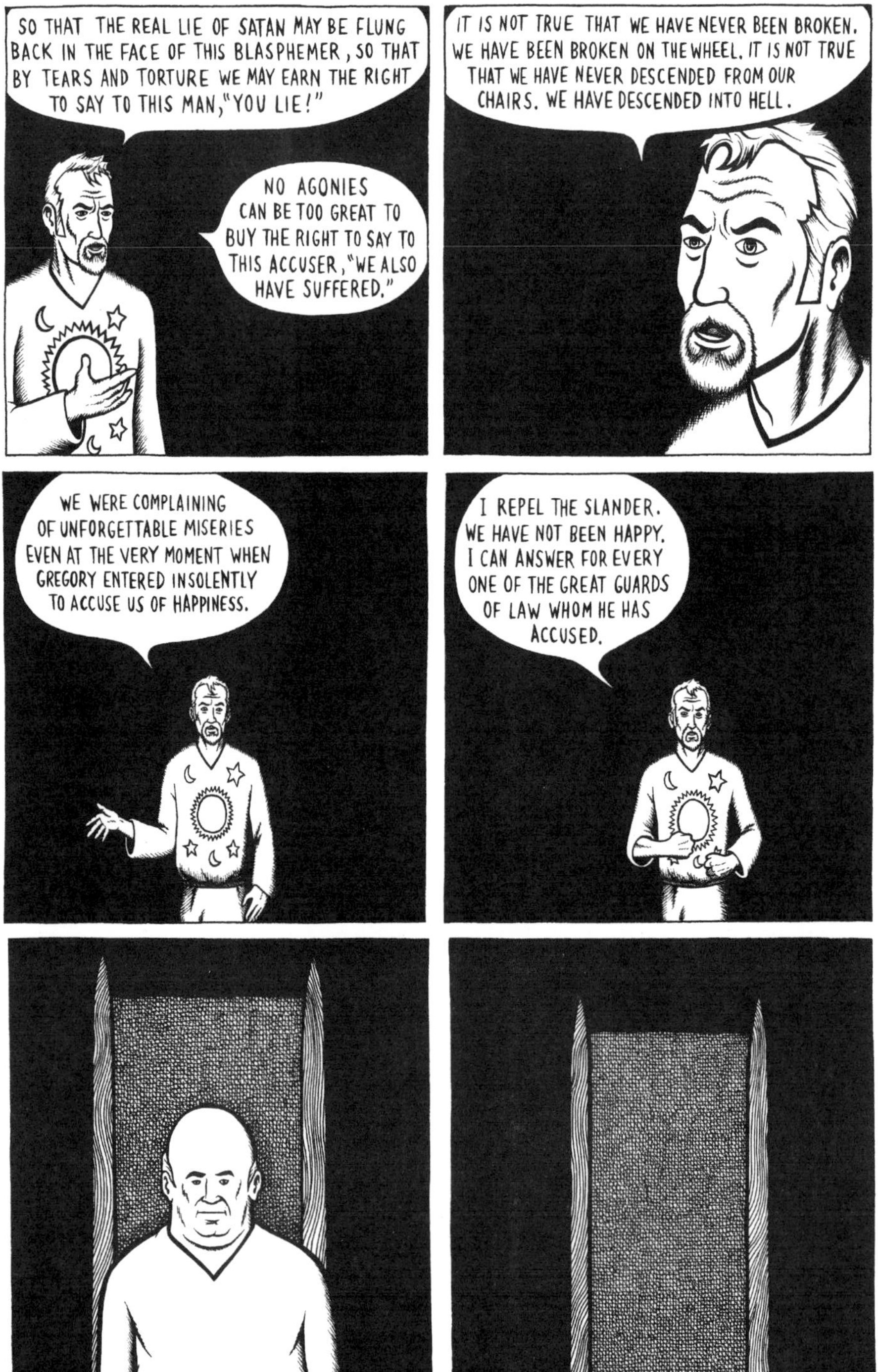
SO THAT THE REAL LIE OF SATAN MAY BE FLUNG BACK IN THE FACE OF THIS BLASPHEMER, SO THAT BY TEARS AND TORTURE WE MAY EARN THE RIGHT TO SAY TO THIS MAN, "YOU LIE!"
NO AGONIES CAN BE TOO GREAT TO BUY THE RIGHT TO SAY TO THIS ACCUSER, "WE ALSO HAVE SUFFERED."
IT IS NOT TRUE THAT WE HAVE NEVER BEEN BROKEN. WE HAVE BEEN BROKEN ON THE WHEEL. IT IS NOT TRUE THAT WE HAVE NEVER DESCENDED FROM OUR CHAIRS. WE HAVE DESCENDED INTO HELL.
WE WERE COMPLAINING OF UNFORGETTABLE MISERIES EVEN AT THE VERY MOMENT WHEN GREGORY ENTERED INSOLENTLY TO ACCUSE US OF HAPPINESS.
I REPEL THE SLANDER. WE HAVE NOT BEEN HAPPY. I CAN ANSWER FOR EVERY ONE OF THE GREAT GUARDS OF LAW WHOM HE HAS ACCUSED.

HAVE YOU EVER SUFFERED?

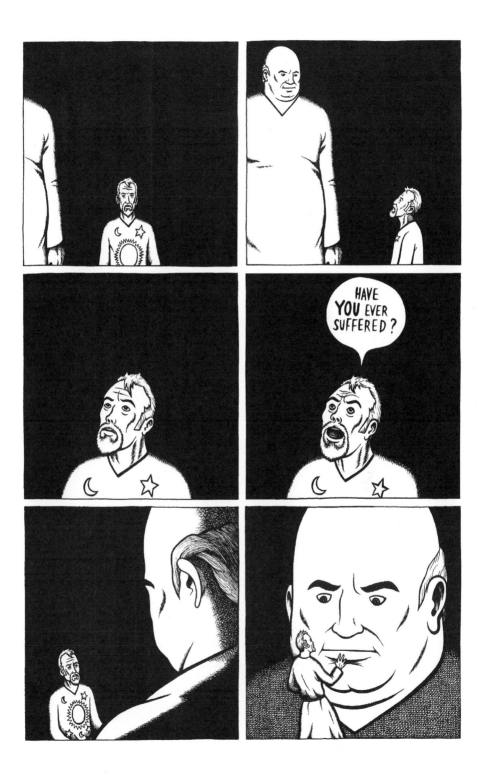

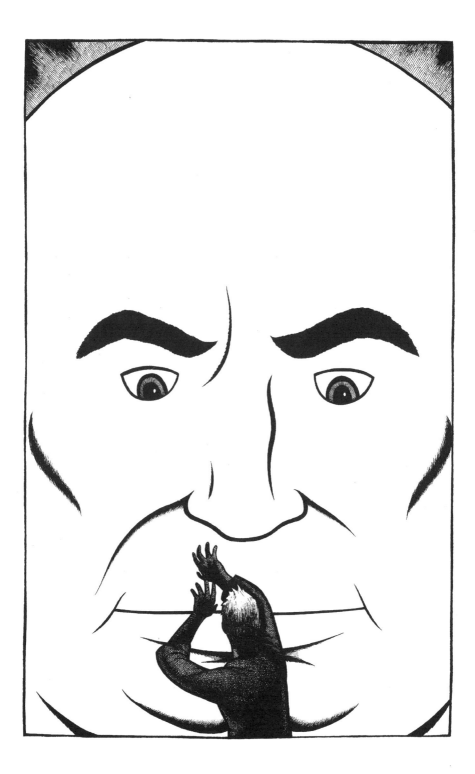

COMPULSIVE

CAN YE DRINK OF THE CUP THAT I DRINK OF?

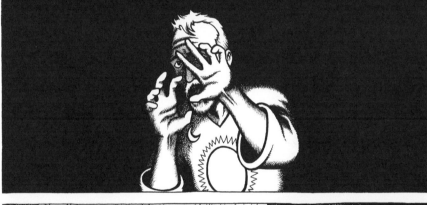

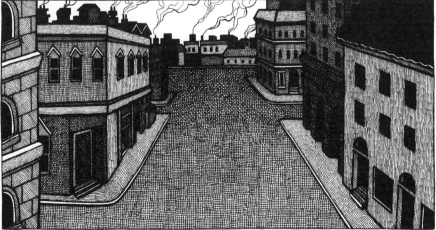

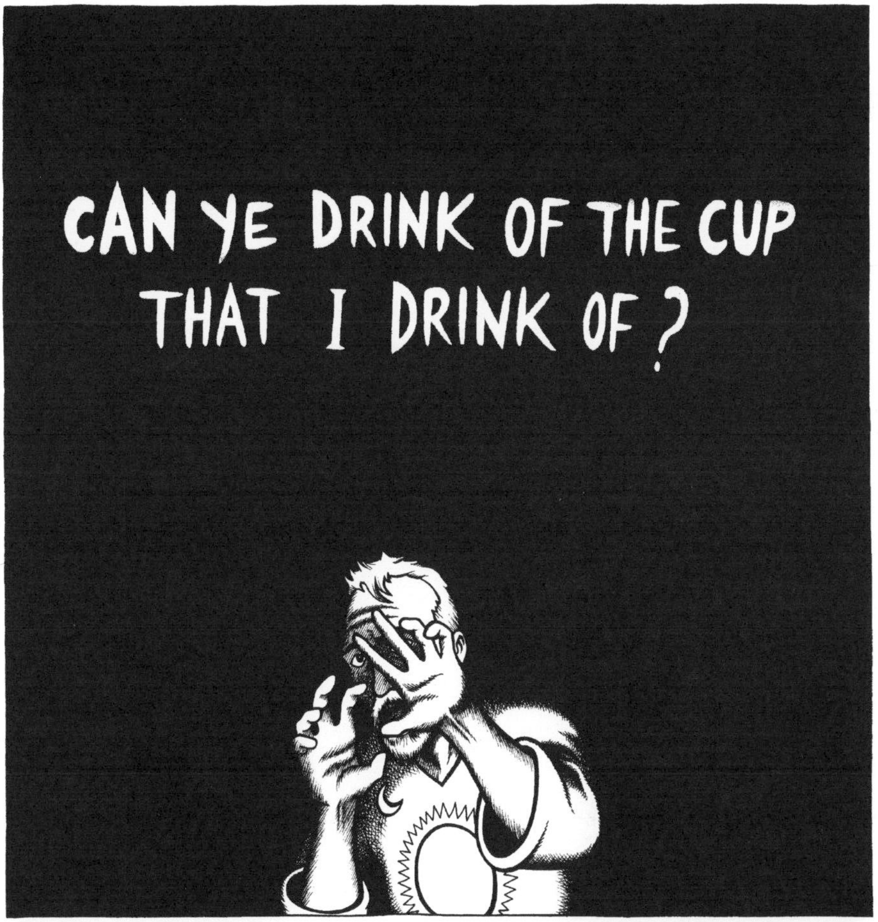

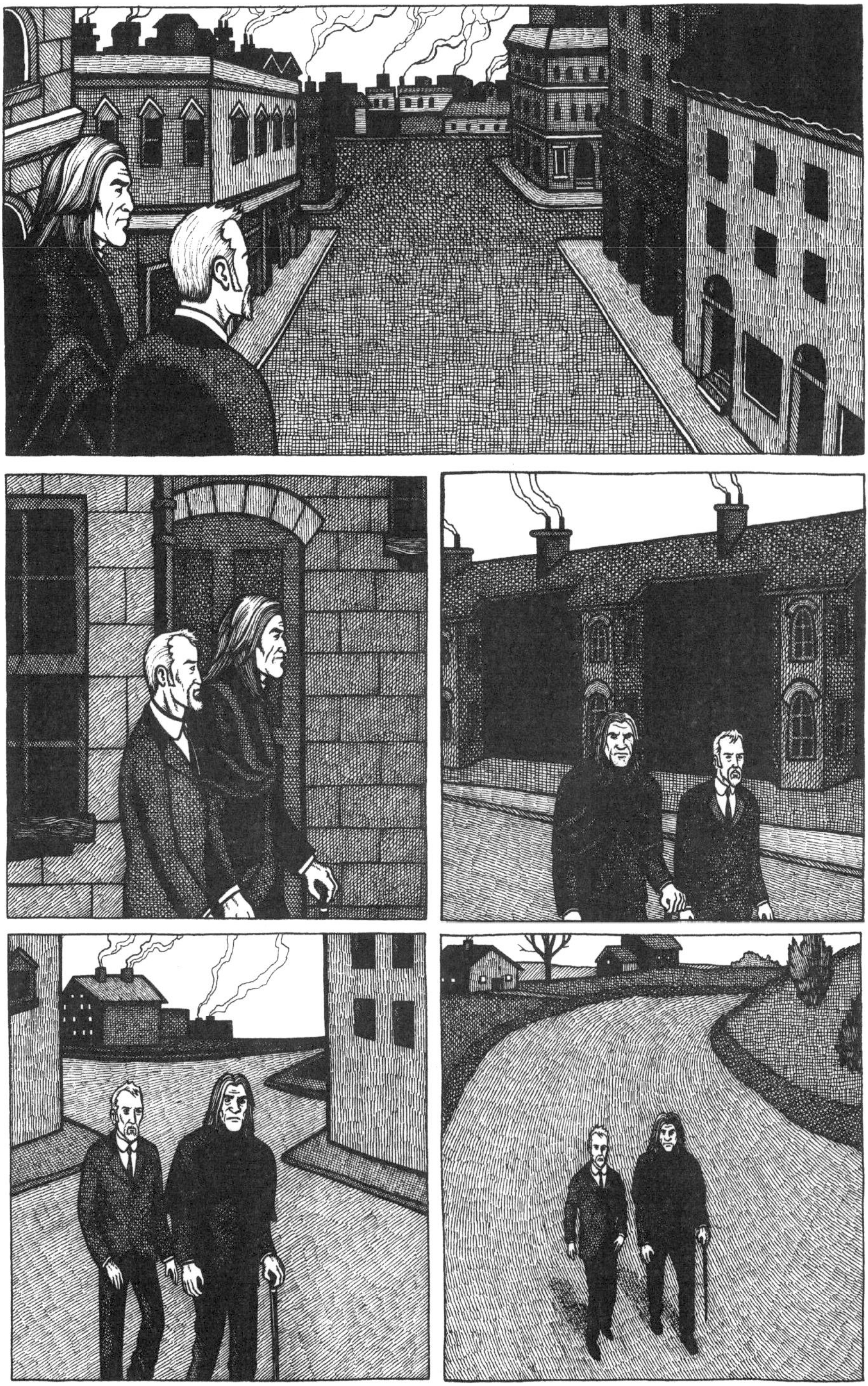

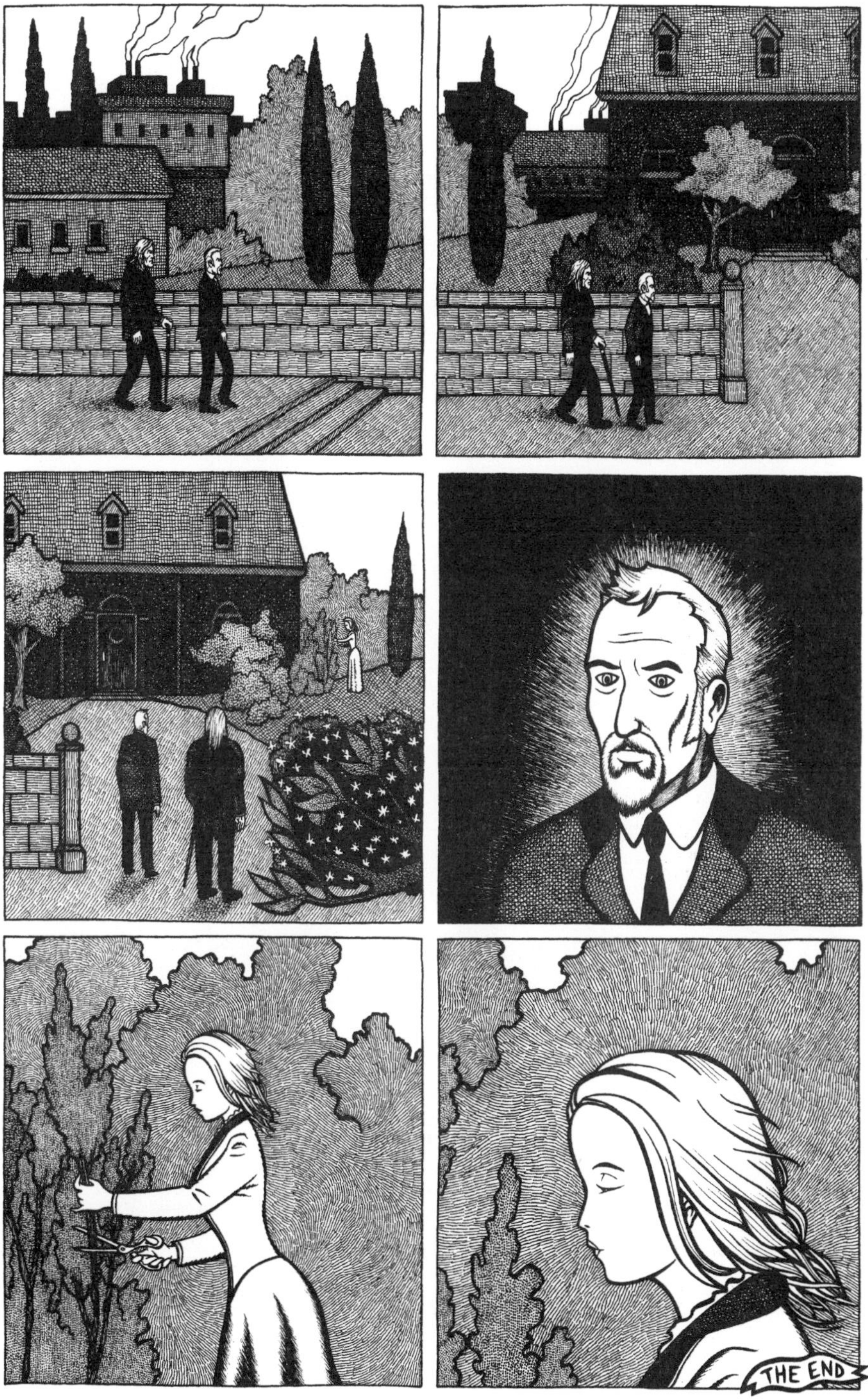
THE END

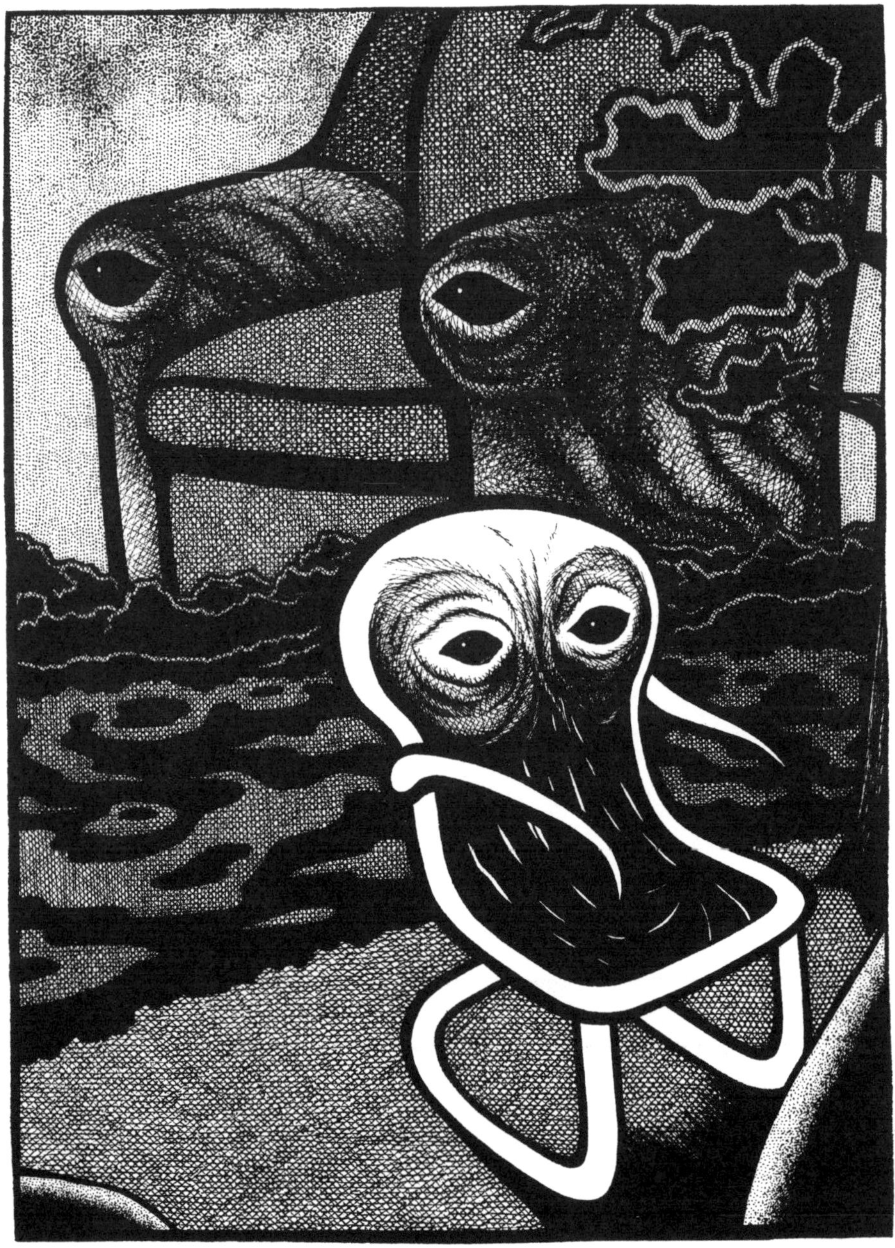

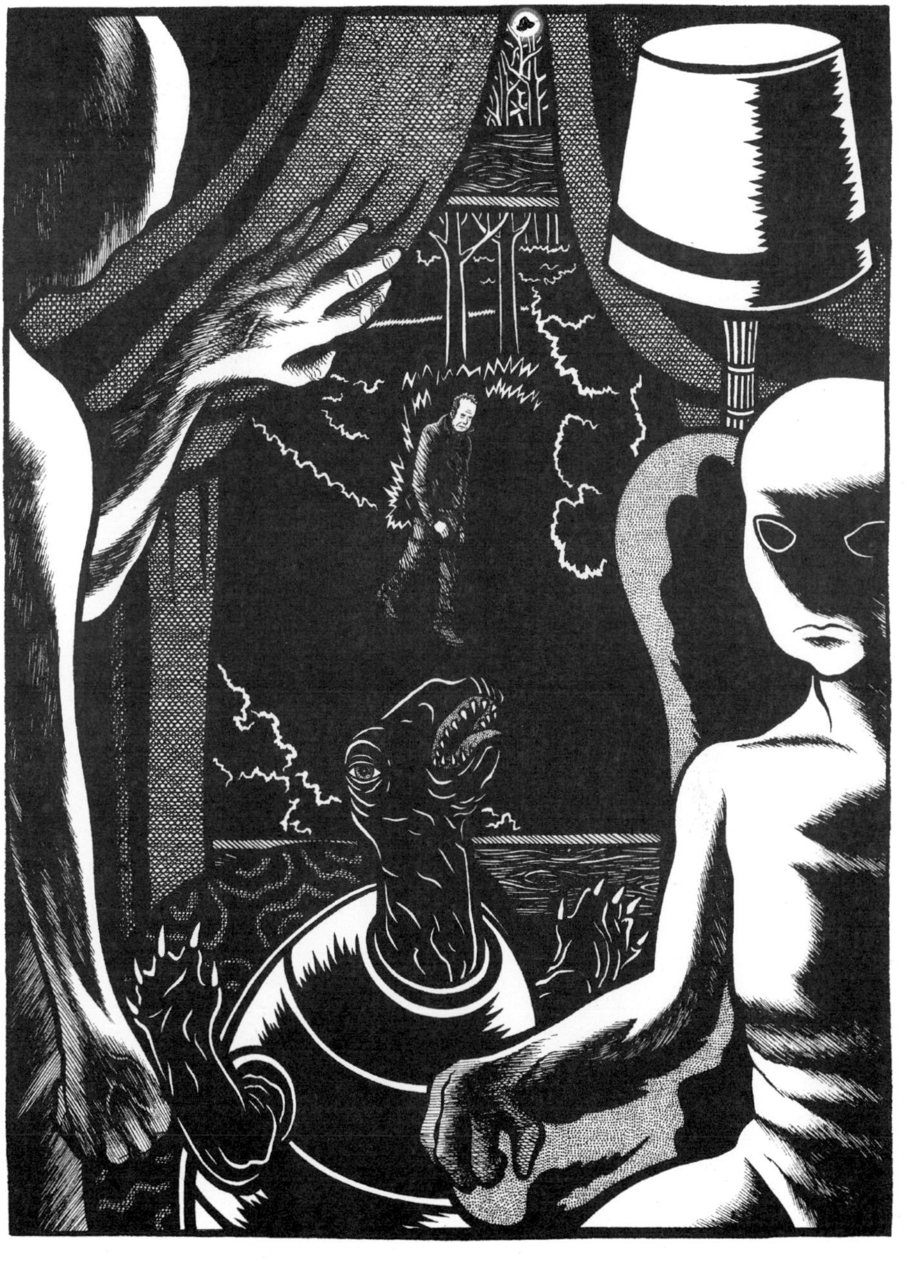

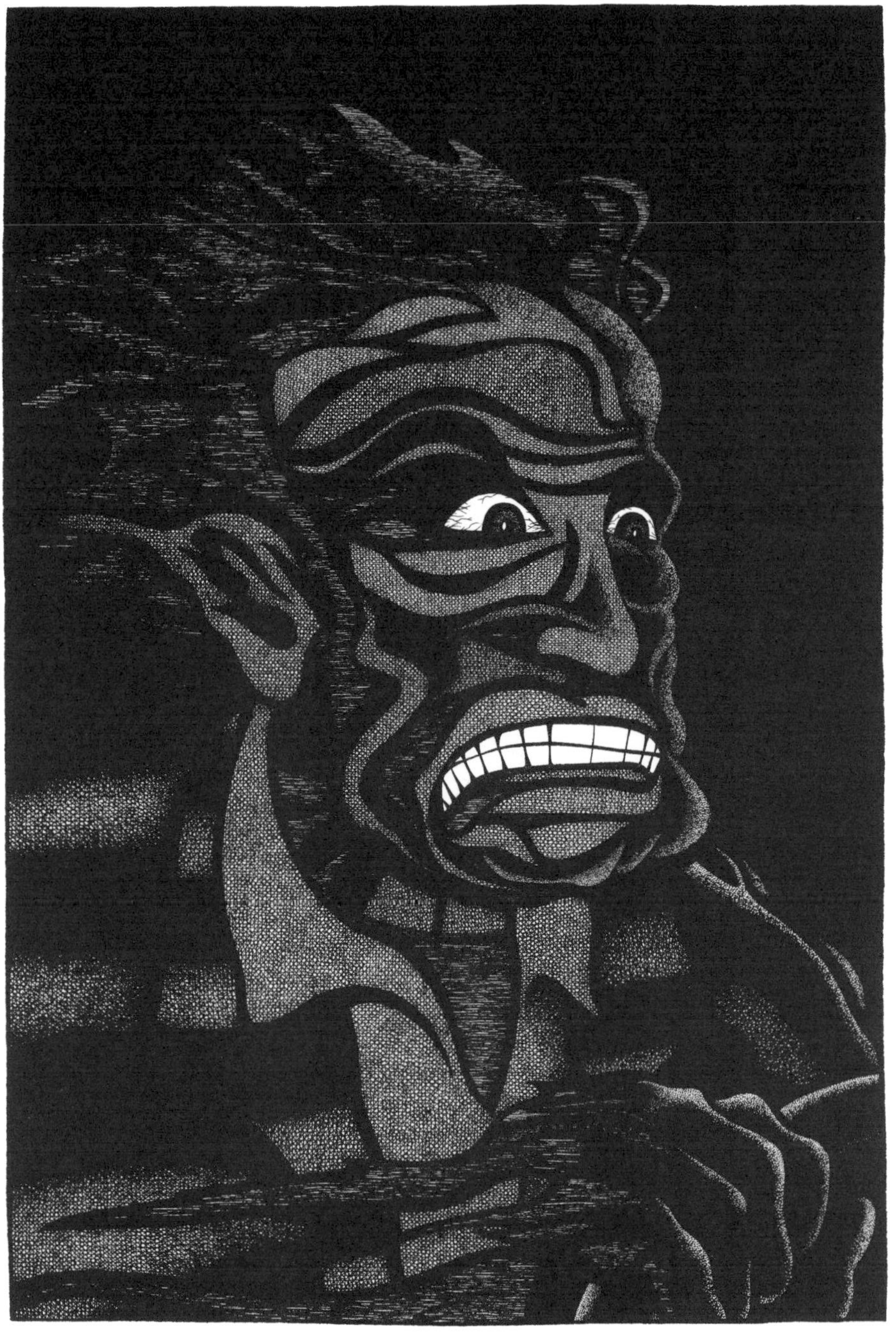

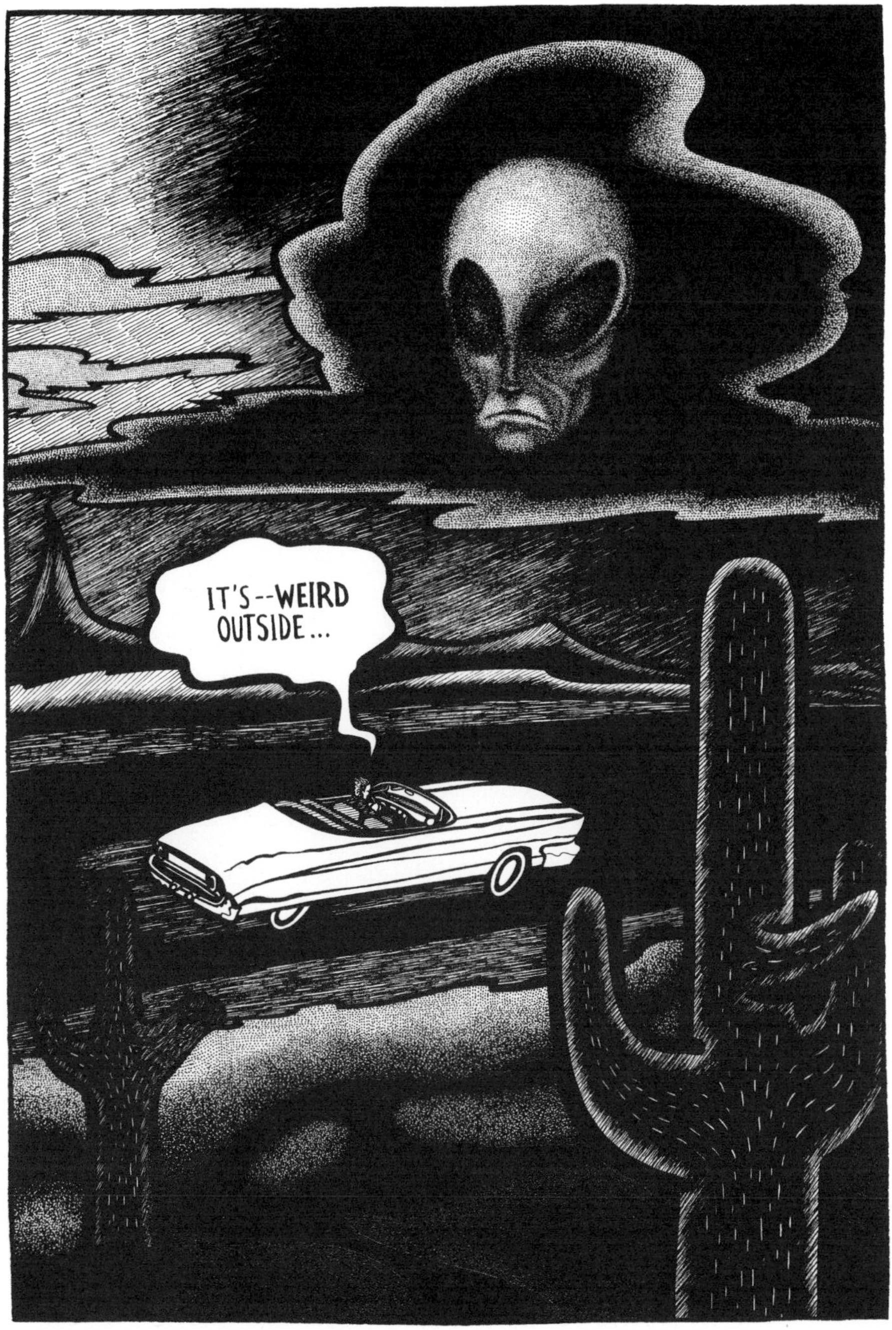
IT'S--WEIRD OUTSIDE...

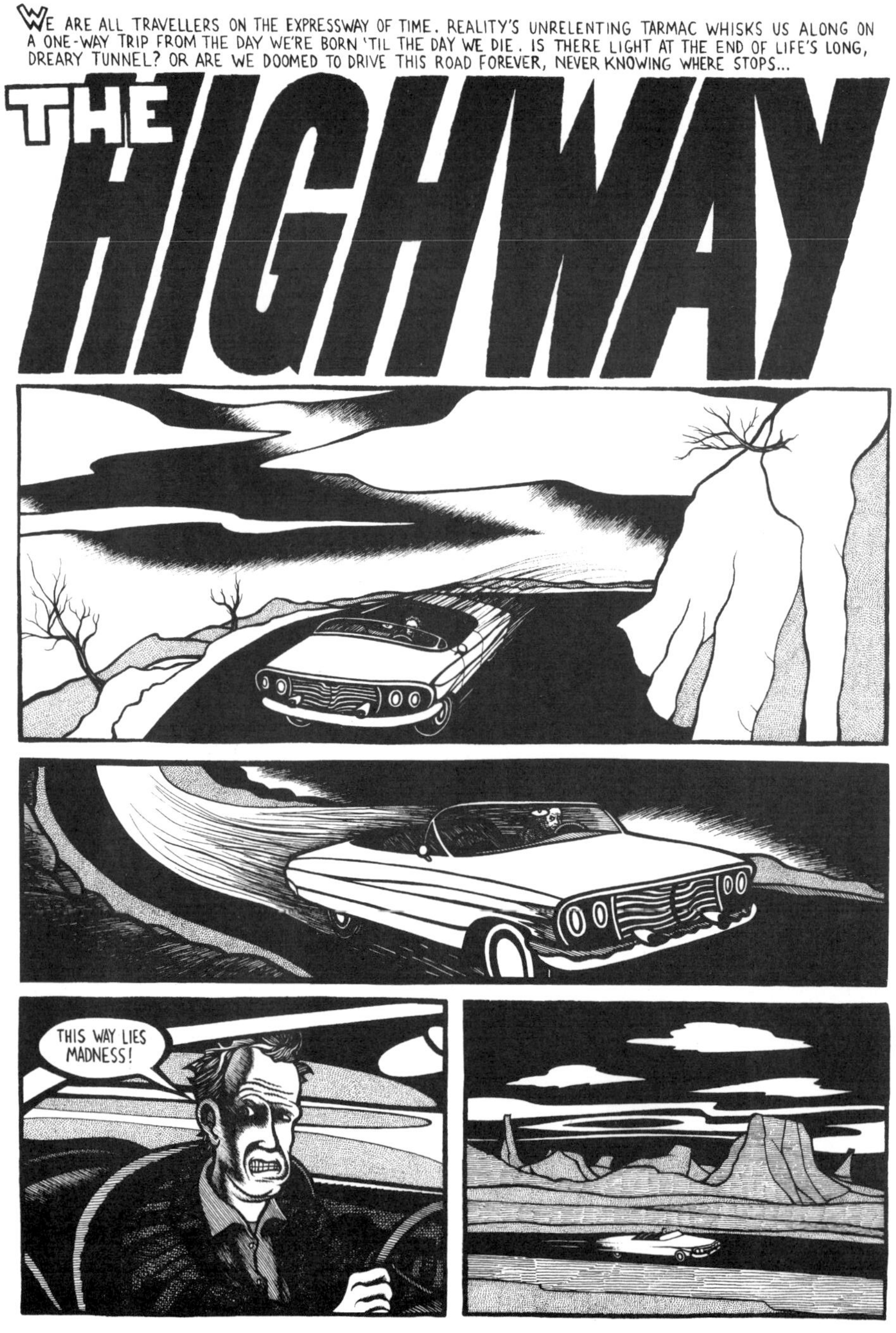
WE ARE ALL TRAVELLERS ON THE EXPRESSWAY OF TIME. REALITY'S UNRELENTING TARMAC WHISKS US ALONG ON A ONE-WAY TRIP FROM THE DAY WE'RE BORN 'TIL THE DAY WE DIE. IS THERE LIGHT AT THE END OF LIFE'S LONG, DREARY TUNNEL? OR ARE WE DOOMED TO DRIVE THIS ROAD FOREVER, NEVER KNOWING WHERE STOPS...
THE HIGHWAY
THIS WAY LIES MADNESS!

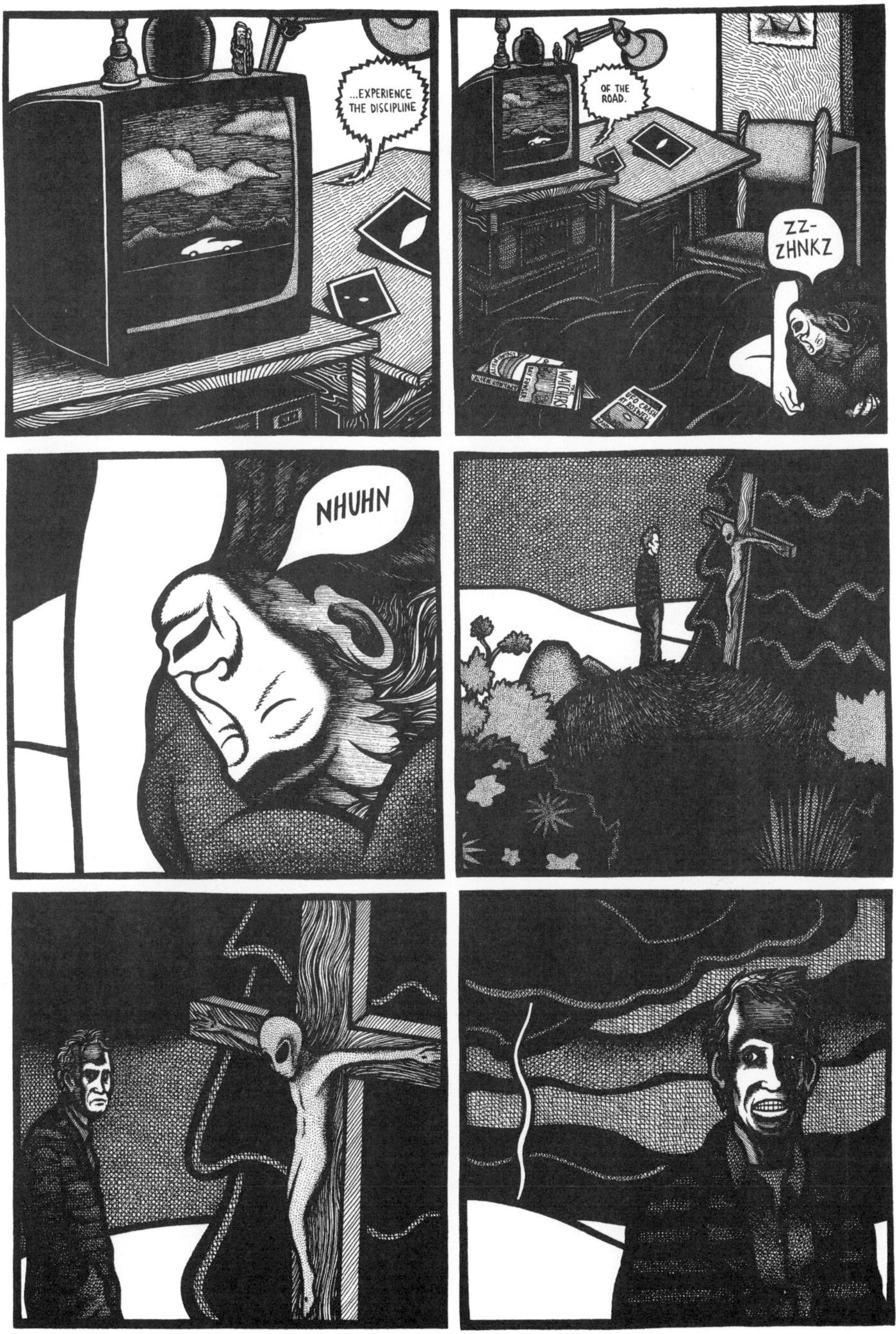
...EXPERIENCE THE DISCIPLINE
OF THE ROAD.
ZZ-ZHNKZ
NHUHN

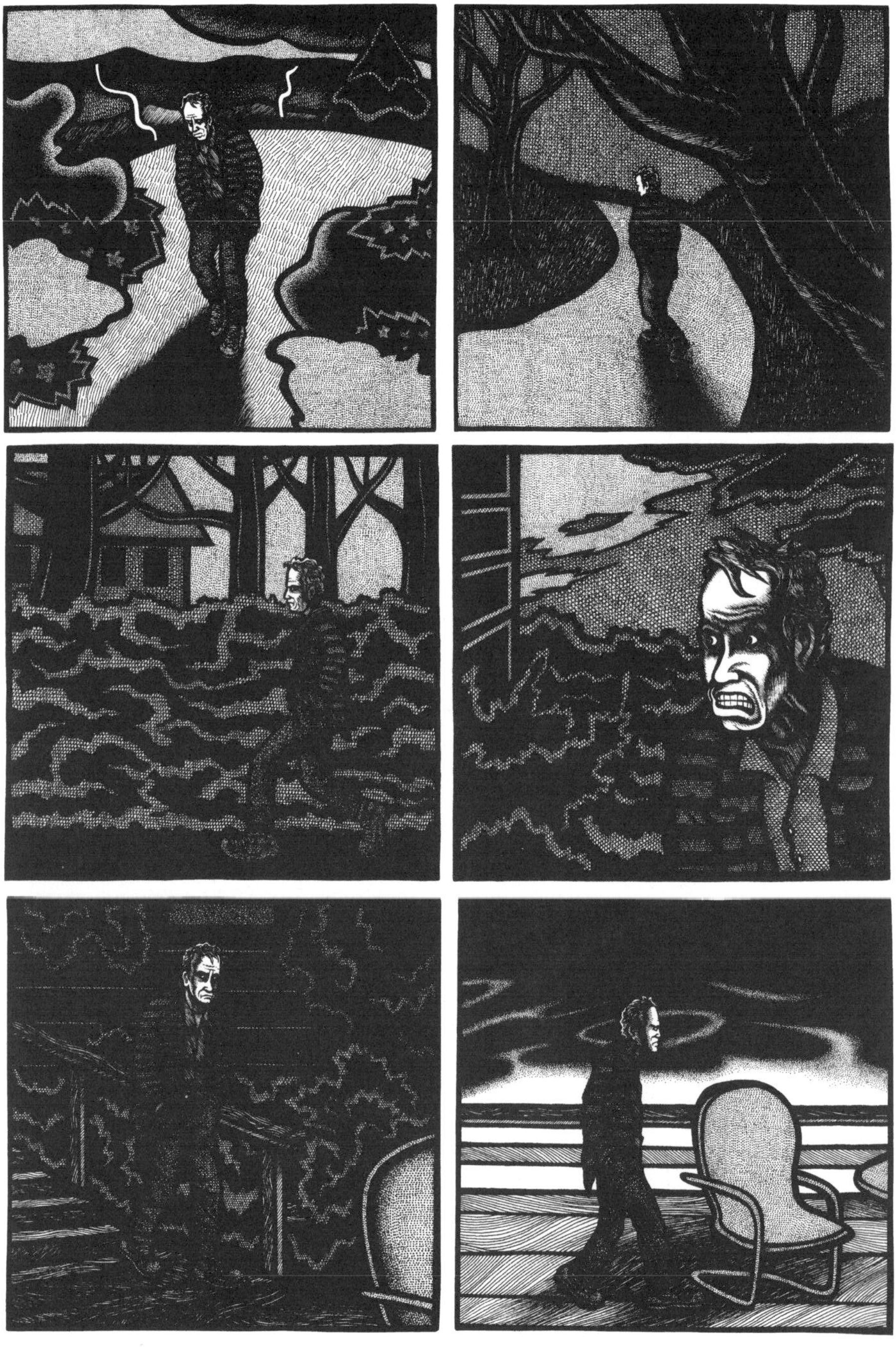

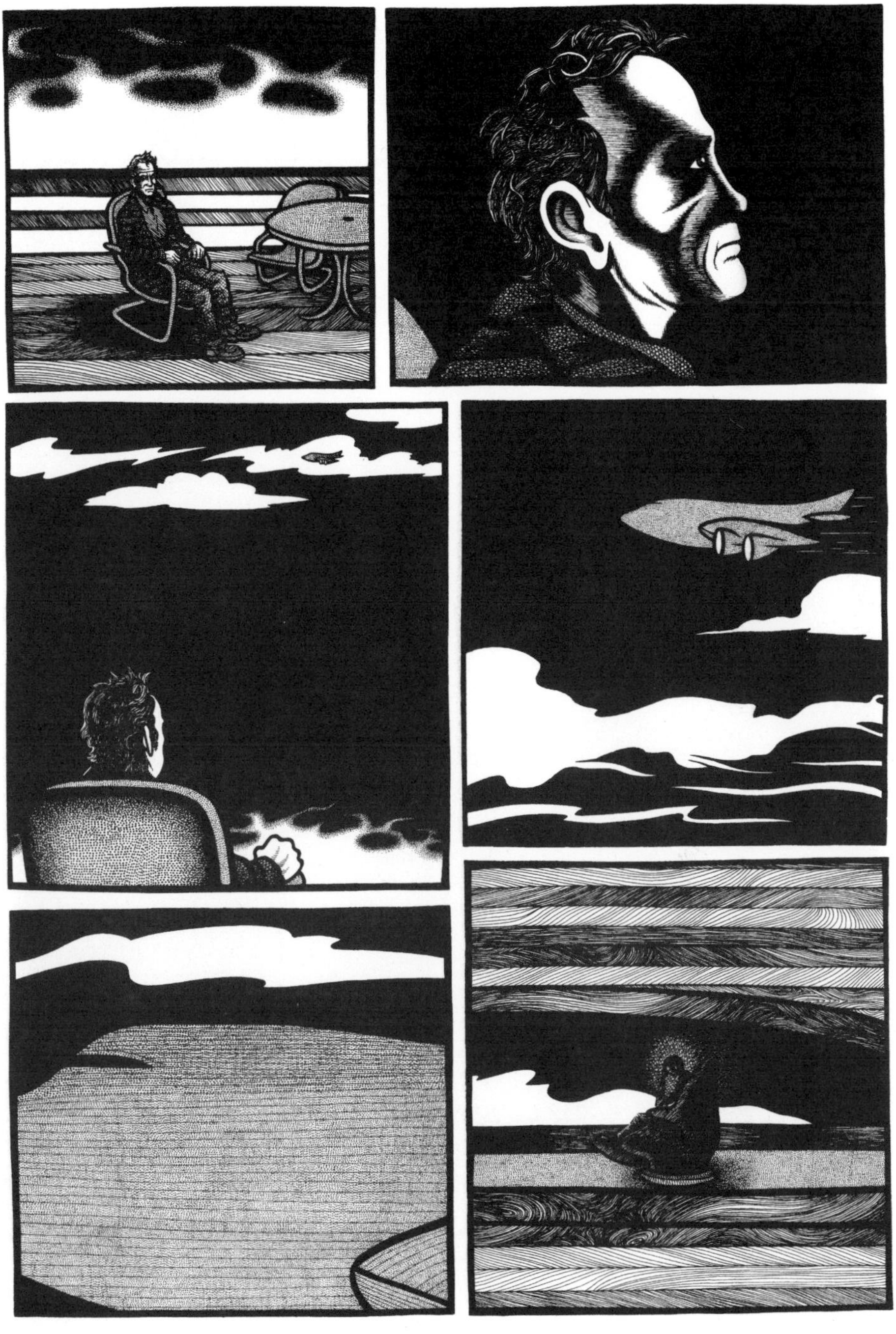

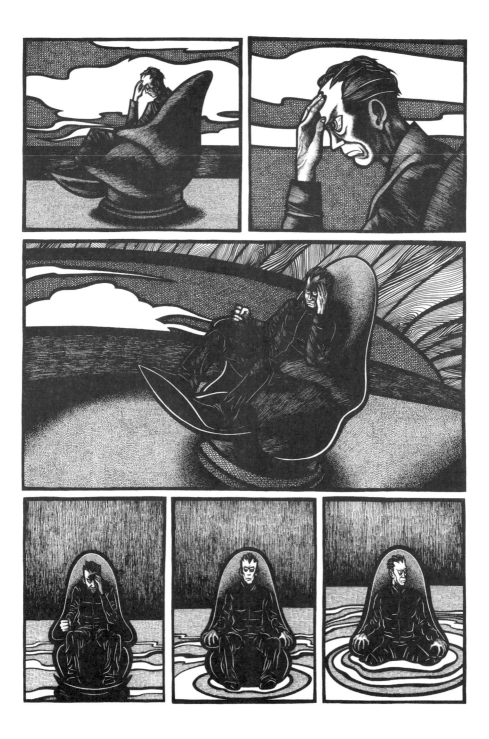

COMPULSIVE

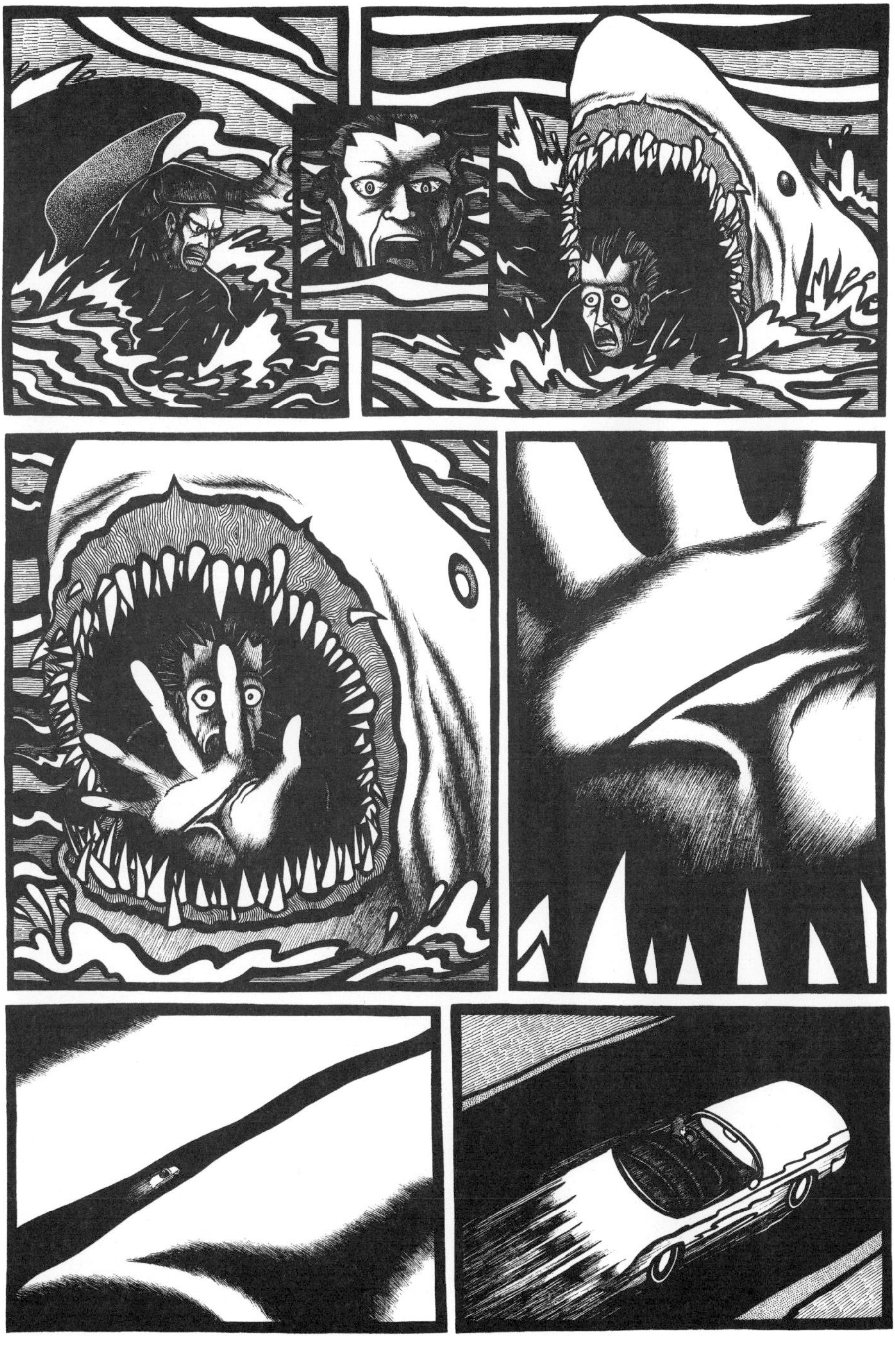

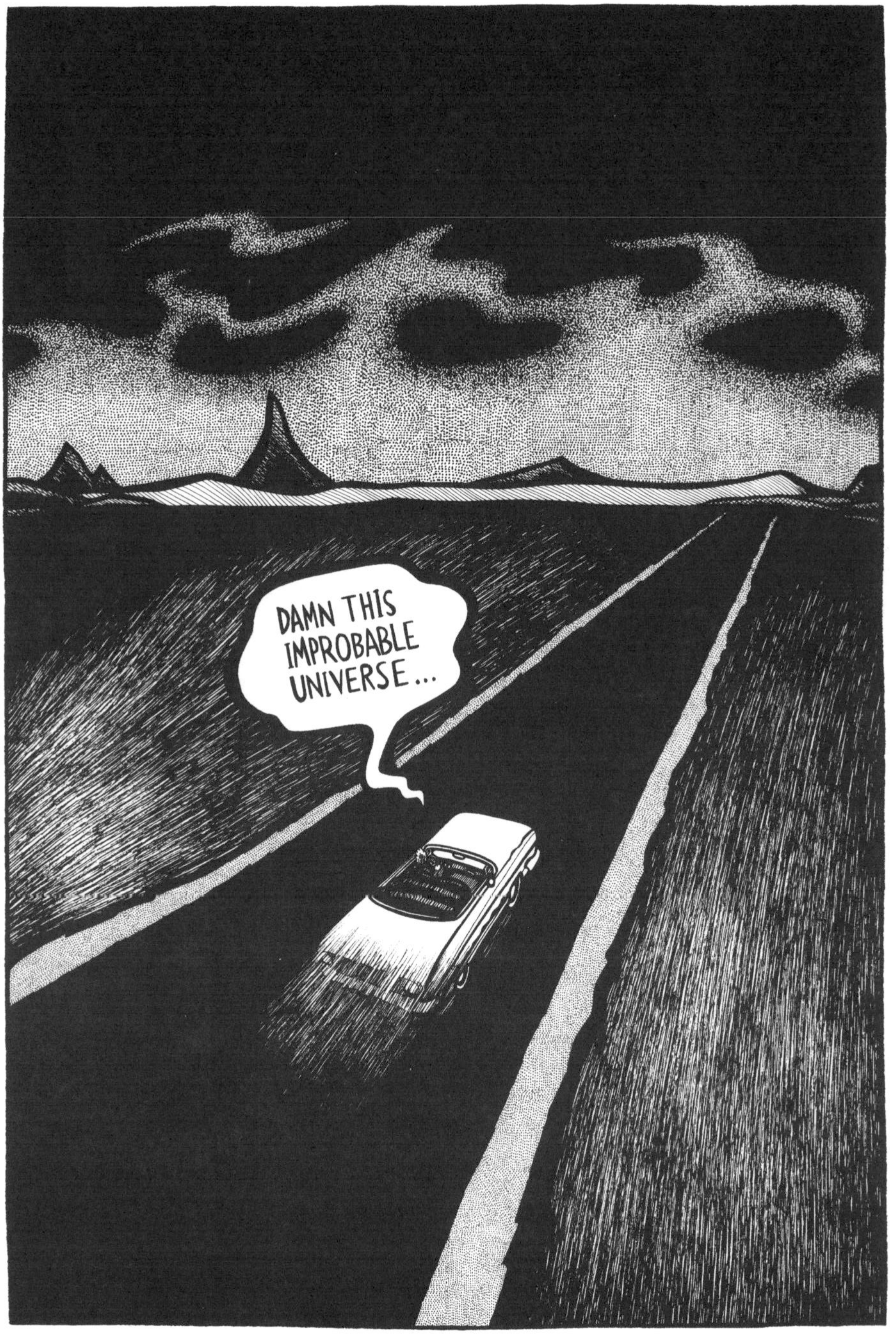
DAMN THIS IMPROBABLE UNIVERSE...

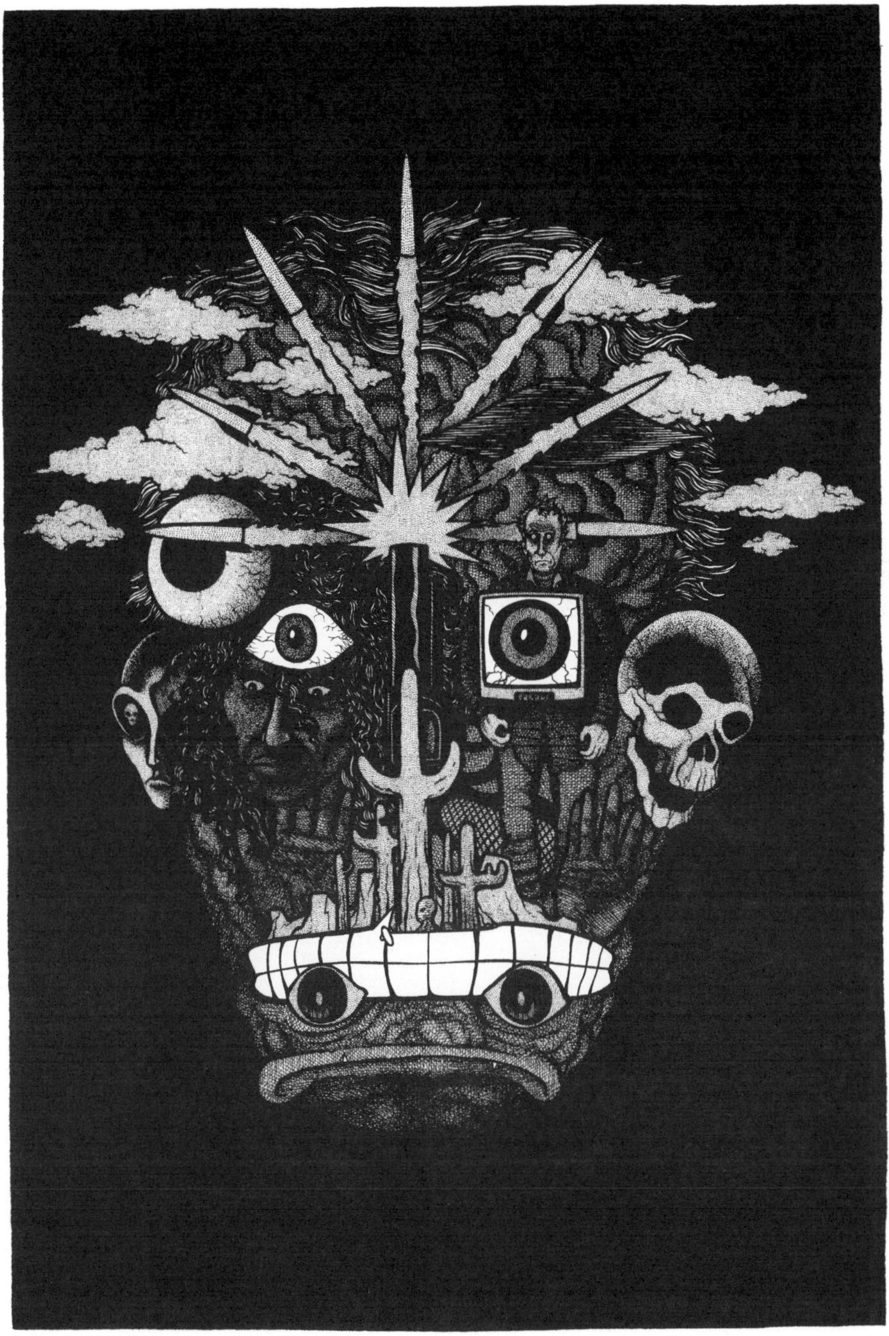

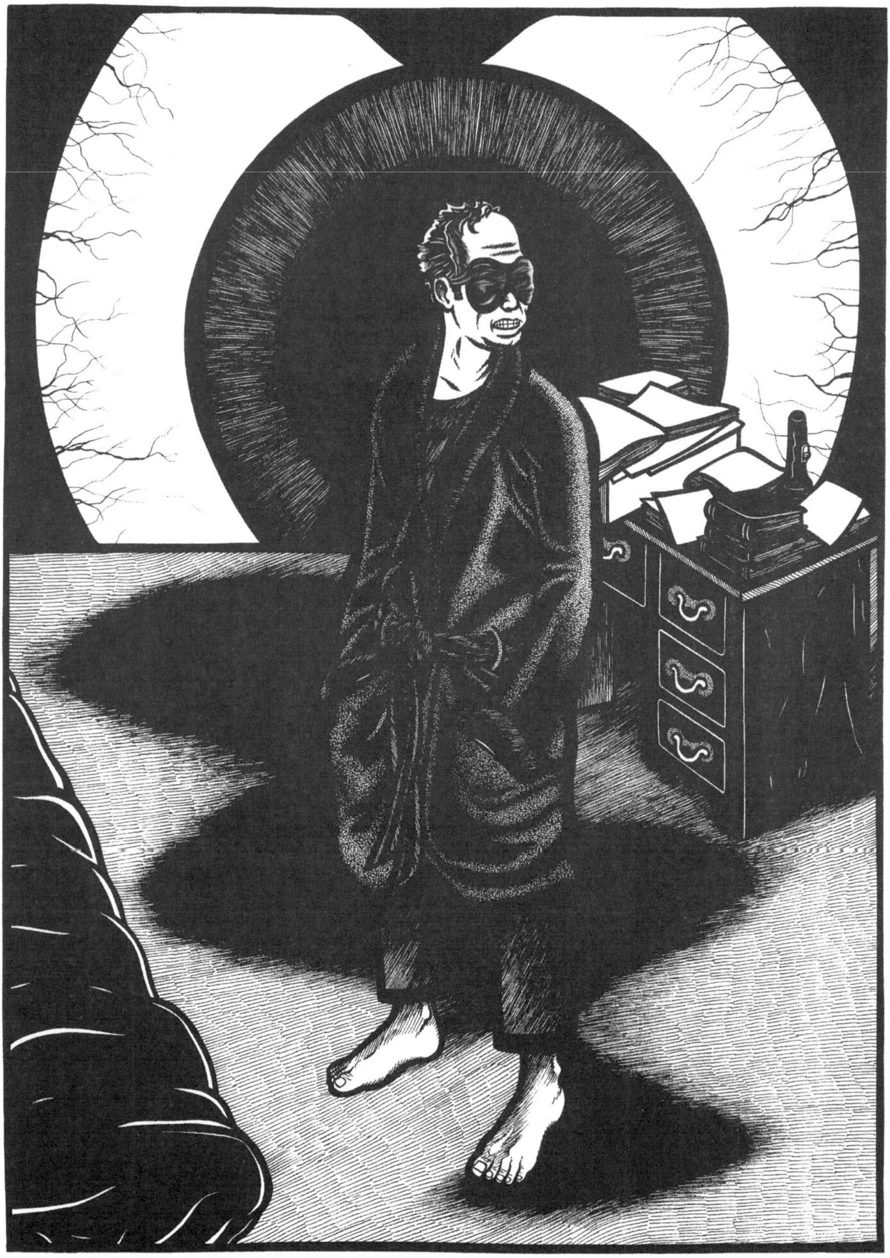

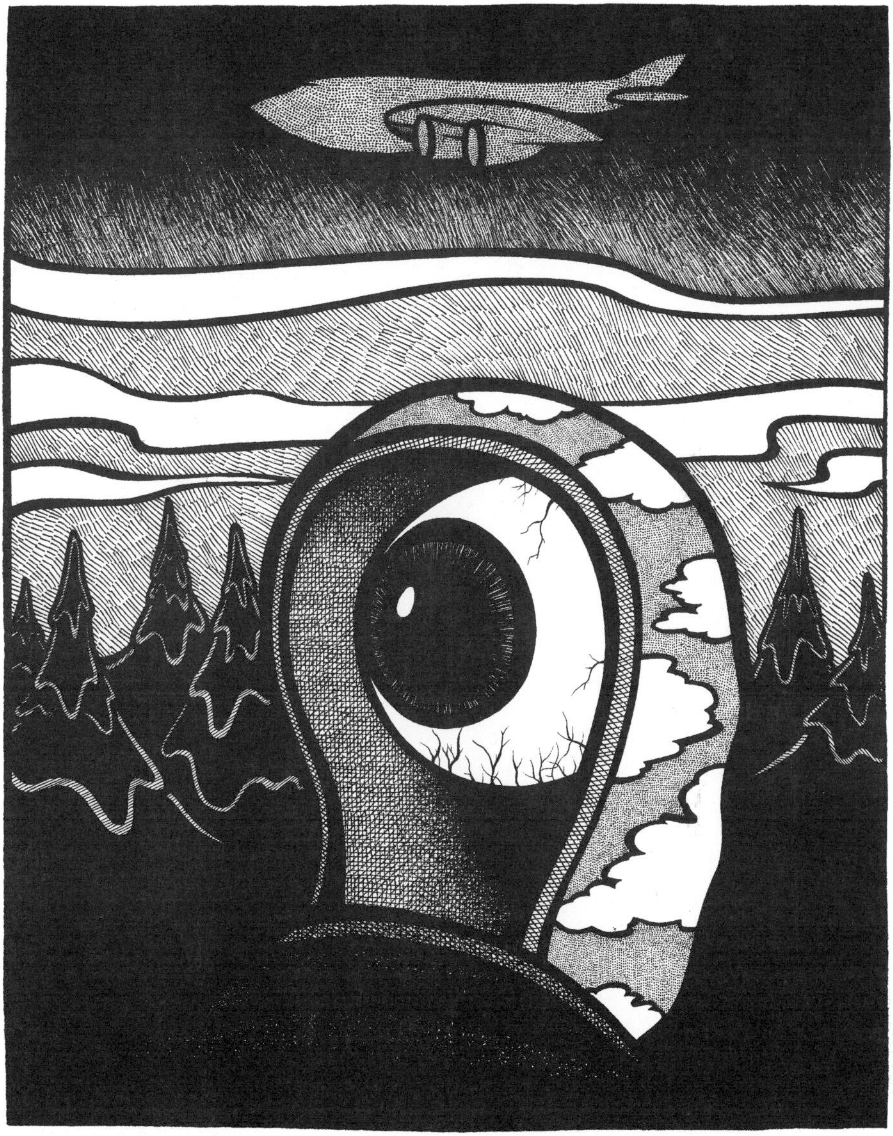

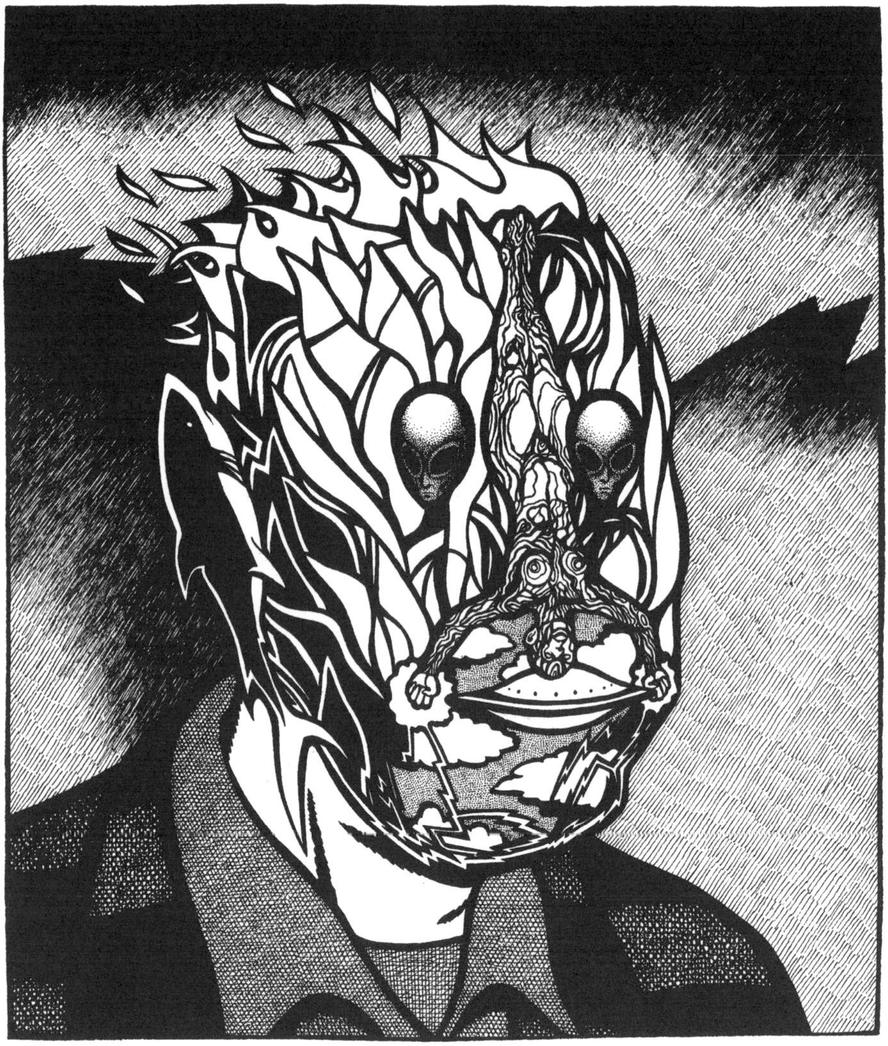

AUTHOR'S NOTES

THE STORIES *THE GLACIER, I KILLED DAN CLOWES, MAMMALOGY,* & *THE GUNSLINGER* ALL ORIGINALLY APPEARED IN ISSUES 1-3 OF **TALES TO DEMOLISH**, PUBLISHED BY SPARKPLUG COMIC BOOKS (2003, 2006).

THE STORIES *A DAY AT THE ZOO, PROTONA, IT'S OK... I'M WEARING A TIE, CONFLUENCE,* & *SECRET ORIGINS* ALL ORIGINALLY APPEARED IN **THE AVIATRIX**, PUBLISHED BY BUENAVENTURA PRESS (2009).

THE ACCUSER WAS TO BE THE LAST CHAPTER OF A WORK INTENDED TO BE PUBLISHED BY SPARKPLUG COMIC BOOKS IN 2005. EACH CHAPTER WAS DRAWN BY A DIFFERENT ARTIST. THE PROJECT WAS COMPLETED BUT NEVER PRINTED.

THE HIGHWAY FIRST APPEARED IN THE SELF-PUBLISHED MINI-COMIC **ULTRALONE** (1996).

THANKS

ERIC REYNOLDS, PAUL BARESH, DAN CLOWES, ADRIAN TOMINE, CYBELE KNOWLES, DYLAN WILLIAMS, ALVIN BUENAVENTURA, AND, AS ALWAYS, DIANA.

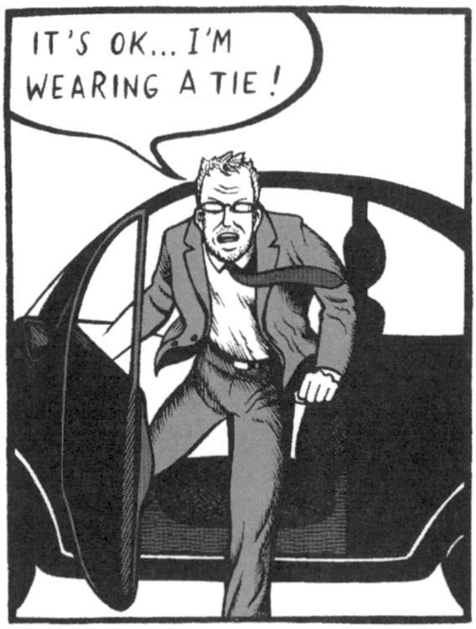
IT'S OK... I'M WEARING A TIE!

THE COMIC ART OF ERIC HAVEN WAS FORGED IN THE ICY WASTES OF SYRACUSE, NY, AND RECONSTITUTED IN THE FECUND MENTAL LOAM OF THE SAN FRANCISCO BAY AREA. HIS COMICS HAVE APPEARED IN THE L.A. WEEKLY, THE BELIEVER, MAD MAGAZINE, AND ON THE TV SHOW MYTHBUSTERS, WHERE HE WORKED AS A THREE-TIME EMMY NOMINATED PRODUCER. HE LIVES IN OAKLAND, CA, WITH HIS WIFE DIANA AND TWO STRANGE, MYSTERIOUS HOUSE CATS.